Christmas 1984

love from
Richard x

WORLDS APART

WORLDS APART

An Explorer's Life

ROBIN HANBURY-TENISON

GRANADA
London Toronto Sydney New York

Granada Publishing Limited
8 Grafton Street, London W1X 3LA

Published by Granada Publishing 1984

Copyright © Editions Robert Laffont S.A. Paris 1984

British Library Cataloguing in Publication Data

Hanbury-Tenison, Robin
    Worlds apart.
    1. Voyages and travels——1951–
    I. Title
    910.4   G465

ISBN 0–246–12382–6

Phototypeset by
Wyvern Typesetting Ltd, Bristol

Printed in Great Britain by
William Clowes Limited,
Beccles and London

The quotation from *The Fox* by D. H. Lawrence is by permission
of Laurence Pollinger Ltd and the Estate of Mrs Frieda Lawrence Ravagli.

For Marika and Louella
Lucy and Rupert

Contents

Note on Illustrations

Map of tribes visited in South America and the routes of the author's journeys by jeep, rubber boat and Hovercraft

CARIBBEAN SEA

ATLANTIC OCEAN

TRINIDAD AND TOBAGO

Caracas
Cuidad Bolivar
Orinoco

VENEZUELA
GUYANA
FRENCH GUIANA
SURINAM

Panamá
CUNA
CHOCO
GUAYMI
PANAMA

CHOCO

PIAROA
MAKIRITARE

Quibdó

COLOMBIA

Casiquiare Canal
Boa Vista

SANEMA
YANOMAMI
Toototobi

TIRIO

Belém

Uaupés
MAKÚ

Negro

WAIMIRI
ATROARI

Amazonas

Santarem

Quito

ECUADOR

Amazon
Solimoes
Manaus

Altamira

Maraba

GAVIÃO

BRAZIL

KUBEN-KRAN-KEGN
GOROTIRE
KARAJA
TAPIRAPÉ

KRAHO
XERENTE

Madeira

Tapajos

Kingu

Tocantins

Island of Bananal

Recife

Pôrto Velho

PERU

PAKANOVA
SURUI
TAUANDÉ

CINTA
LARGA

PARESI
MAMAINDÉ

XINGU NATIONAL PARK

XAVANTE

Lima
Cuzco

Guaporé

BOLIVIA

Mato Grosso

Rio das Mortes

Cuiabá
Caceres

Araguaia

Brazilia

Anápolis
Goiâna

QUECHA

La Paz
Cochabamba

Santa Cruz

BORORO

BRAZIL

Corumbá
Porto Esperança

TERENA
KADIWEU

KAIWA

Rio de Janeiro

São Paulo

PARAGUAY

Asunción

GUARANI

C
H
I
L
E

PACIFIC OCEAN

URUGUAY

Buenos Aires
Montevideo

SOUTH ATLANTIC OCEAN

ARGENTINA

INGARICO
PAIMERU
MACUSHI

YAWALAPITI
WAURA
KUIKURO
KAMAYURA
TXIKAO
TRUMAI
KAYABI
SUYA
JURUNA
TXUKARRAMAI

NAMBIQUARA

Map of author's desert journeys in the Sahara and Kalahari with the route of the Hovercraft expedition

MEDITERRANEAN SEA

Algiers

TUNISIA
Tripoli

MOROCCO

ALGERIA

LIBYA

EGYPT

Tassili N'Ajjer

SPANISH SAHARA

Djanet

Sabhah

Marzûq

MALI

TUAREG

TOUBOU

Tassili Du Ahaggar

TUAREG

Bardai

MAURITANIA

Timbuktu

Ifêrouane

Zouar

TIBESTI

Dakar

SENEGAL

Niger

Air

Agadez

CHAD

SUDAN

Niger

Niamey

NIGER

Lake Chad

UPPER VOLTA

Fort-Lamy

GUINEA

Niger

NIGERIA

Benue

Chari

ETHIOPIA

SIERRA LEONE

IVORY COAST

GHANA

TOGO

DAHOMEY

CENTRAL AFRICAN REPUBLIC

SOMALIA

LIBERIA

CAMEROON

PYGMIES

Kisangani

UGANDA

KENYA

GABON

CONGO

RWANDA

Brazzaville

BURUNDI

Kinshasa

ZAIRE

TANZANIA

INDIAN OCEAN

ATLANTIC OCEAN

ANGOLA

ZAMBIA

MALAWI

Lusaka

Okavango Swamp

ZIMBABWE

MOZAMBIQUE

NAMIBIA

SAN (BUSHMEN)

KALAHARI DESERT

TRANSVAAL

Gaborone

Pretoria

SOUTH AFRICA

Map of tribes visited in Indonesia and Malaysia

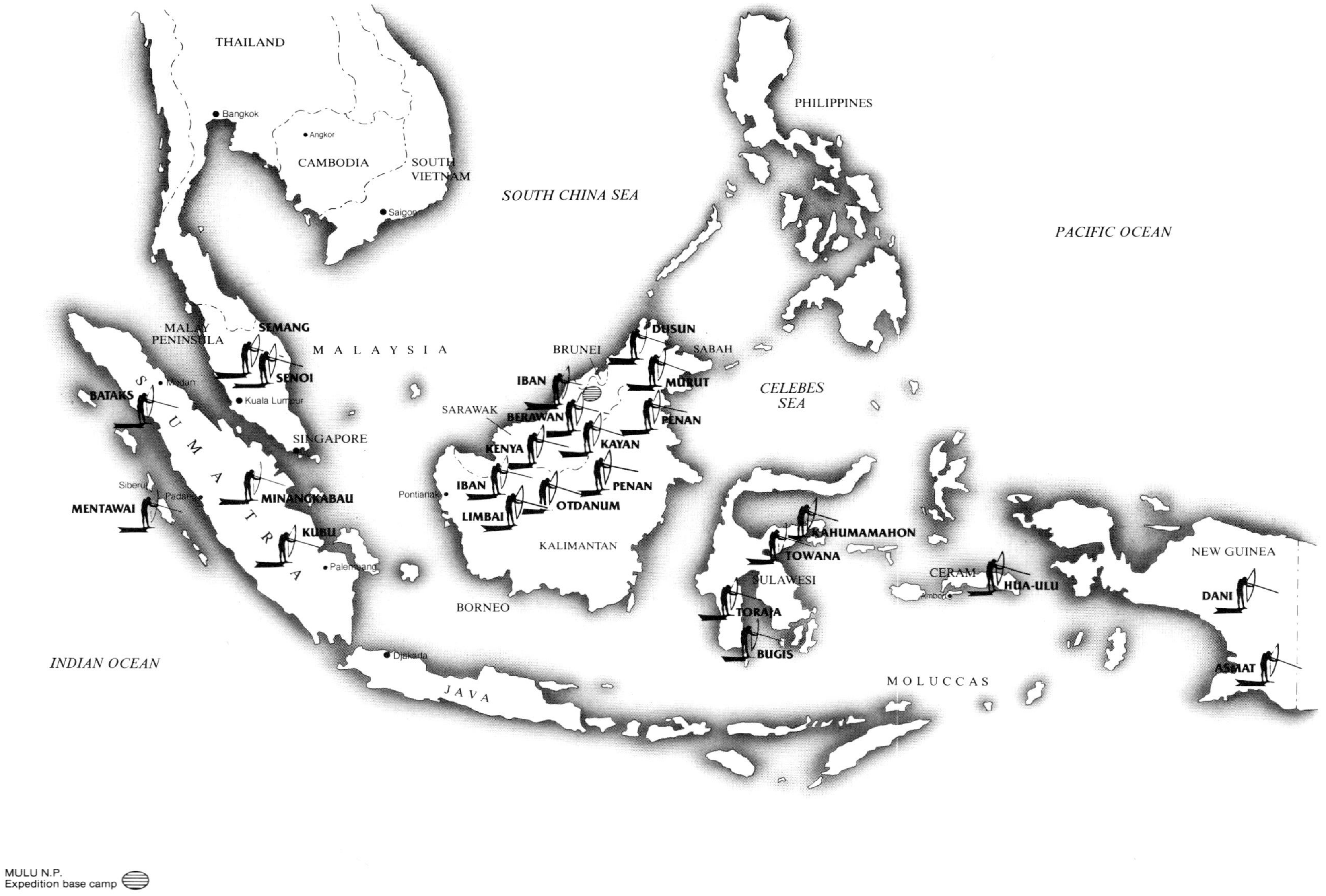

PACIFIC OCEAN

NEW GUINEA

DANI

ASMAT

HUA-ULU

CERAM

MOLUCCAS

PHILIPPINES

CELEBES SEA

SAHUMAMAHON

TOWANA

SULAWESI

BUGIS

TORAJA

SOUTH CHINA SEA

SABAH

DUSUN

MURUT

PENAN

BRUNEI

KAYAN

PENAN

SARAWAK

IBAN

BERAWAN

OTDANUM

KALIMANTAN

KENYA

IBAN

LIMBAI

BORNEO

Pontianak

JAVA

Djakarta

THAILAND

Bangkok

SOUTH VIETNAM

CAMBODIA

Angkor

Saigon

MALAYSIA

SEMANG

SENOI

Kuala Lumpur

SINGAPORE

MINANGKABAU

KUBU

Palembang

MALAY PENINSULA

Medan

S U M A T R A

Padang

Siberut

BATAKS

MENTAWAI

INDIAN OCEAN

MULU N.P.
Expedition base camp

Introduction

All men dream: but not equally. Those who dream by night in the dusty recesses
of their minds wake in the day to find that it was vanity: but the dreamers of the
day are dangerous men, for they may act their dream with open eyes, to make it
possible. . .

T. E. Lawrence, *The Seven Pillars of Wisdom*

To have followed a dream and seen it become reality, to have achieved
more than I knew I had in me has meant more to me than the comfort and
security of a conventional life.

As a traveller, my fascination with deserts and jungles has taken me all
over the world so that my love of adventure has been fulfilled.

On the way I have seen what 'progress' is doing to the world, destroying
not just the beauty but the very fabric of this extraordinary planet. And I
have lived with many peoples whose view of life is still different, who do
not destroy but respect, who are not greedy but live in harmony with the
rest of life.

My quest for adventure became a dream to help such people to survive.
The creation of a completely new international organization which set out
to change the world's prejudiced view of minorities was a daunting task.
Why not leave them alone? If only we could, but, already besieged by
bureaucrats and missionaries, greedy developers and settlers hungry for
their land, while they themselves are often unaware of our existence, they
desperately need sympathetic allies if they are to survive.

My own life has been one of extremes, which is exactly how I would
wish it. From the comfort and security of my country life as a farmer in
Cornwall I have been able to explore, in conditions of extreme discomfort
and occasional danger, some of the remotest regions left on earth.

Like Lesley Blanch's Balkan peasant who longs for faraway countries and leaves his own land and home to find them, I must have been born under a Lilac Bleeding Star. But while travel has always been compulsive for me, I have never felt myself compelled to wander the world for ever. Instead the strong tap root of my home and family has kept me sane and happy when I was lonely and far away.

Marika and I married when barely out of school, yet our love and friendship grew stronger than either of us knew was possible at the beginning. While I travelled, she became one of the most successful and prolific food writers in Britain. Our children, Lucy and Rupert, gave us great joy and happiness and our cup overflowed. It must have been more than the gods could allow. At the height of her energy and ambition, just when it seemed that even her impeccable ideals of achievement in career combined with loving domesticity and shared happiness were secure, we discovered she had cancer. She was told she had only a short time to live. We fought it together and tried every available conventional and unconventional cure, but I think Marika always privately knew that this was not her way and so she set out to beat it by herself. She made the subject of cancer her own for a time, talked wittily and movingly on radio and television about what it felt like, and received numerous letters telling her how much her strength and bravery were helping others. When the brain tumours came and the end was inevitable, with a courage and concern for others which will always amaze me, she calmly saw to it that her departure was as well orchestrated and painless for those left as it could be. She was so cheerful and unafraid, she rejoiced so lustily and with such wit in the affection of her friends as they came to say goodbye, that to her own surprise she found herself admitting to me a few days before she died that she felt near to a state of grace.

I owe it to her not to be afraid to carry on living life to the full and sharing everything with others through writing, as she did so splendidly in more than thirty books.

I have been asked to try and put into this book the story of how I have changed and developed over the years to come to the beliefs I now hold; how I changed through experience from a traveller to an idealist. I suspect that I am much more a product of the subtle influences others have had upon me than of the direct and vivid experiences of a life of travel and adventure, but I can only tell it as it happened. Doubtless the audience will see more in the play than the actor.

1

What I Owe to Oxford

I had no logical faculty: or rather, it was never aroused at school; all that came later with maturity and the endless discussions of undergraduate life at Oxford. It comes under the heading of 'What I owe to Oxford'.

A. L. Rowse, *A Cornish Childhood*

My mother had an extraordinary solitary childhood. Having lost their only other child, a son, her parents retired from the world to a Scottish castle on the wild and windswept coast of Morayshire. Gordonstoun, now a well-known school, was rented by them for some 25 years in preference to their estate in Monmouthshire, which was already in 1900 regarded as too smoky for my grandfather's health. Alone, save for a series of foreign governesses, with whom she spoke German in the morning and French in the afternoon, she suffered unimaginable loneliness while at the same time developing an iron inner strength. She must have longed to run wild and fly away from button-booted spinsters across the cliffs to the thrilling world of rocky seashore and the birds and flowers she learned to draw so well. This craving for freedom gave her the philosophy, when she had children of her own, to wish them to 'do dangerous things sensibly'.

By the time I was born, by far the youngest of her five children, she had moved to yet another large and lonely house. This one lay deep among the bogs and woods of central Ireland, the family home of the British cavalry officer just back from serving in India, whom she had married at the age of 21. I hardly remember him, as he was absent in England in the war years and left home when it was over to live in the Bahamas. He died in 1953.

It is easy to glamorize one's childhood with idyllic memories of sunshine and flowers. I know I was lonely, frightened and frustrated by life's pointlessness, while the schools in England to which I was sent seemed to me at the time, and in retrospect, mediaeval torture chambers where my fear of the cruel tongues of my contemporaries was only exceeded by the dread of the agonizing beatings inflicted on those who stepped out of line.

My visual memories are all of being intensely aware of the trees and water which surrounded my home. The deep lakes were almost everywhere fringed with hanging woods of beech and oak, except where a rushy park meadow allowed the cattle to reach the water and stand hock deep to drink and scatter their reflections. Bare open-leaf mould and moss-covered carpets, where we gathered toadstools from which my mother brewed memorable stews, were surrounded by dense entanglements of impenetrable brambles, and wonderful jungles of head-high bracken for a small boy to explore.

There was an island, too, which became very important to me. It lay some 500 yards out from the shore and boathouse, a dense mass of vegetation crowned by a great spreading beech tree. One day in the summer of 1942, when I was six, I left others eating their picnic on the rocks where the boat was tied up, and crawled through to the centre. There I found a tiny magic open glade which remains to this day for me the archetypal camp site. My mother joined me and we camped there for the first time that night under the stars, while the pipistrelle bats swooped around our heads. Soon I was allowed to stay alone and, after an older friend, an evacuee from the Blitz, had built me a thatched, timbered, dry and secure tree house 30 feet up the beech tree, I slept there whenever I could. It seems to me now, looking back, that I spent all my holidays there until I was an adult, rowing home across the glassy lake at dawn followed by the rippling vees made by an otter and her young. I would catch a few fat perch from the jetty by the boathouse and carry them proudly up to the house to be cooked for my breakfast. It can't have been like that often and I know that there were many more nights when I slept in the big house. I used to walk the passages at night, consumed by an exquisite terror which I can recall today as the match of any I have since experienced. I sat for hours at the top of the main staircase under the stern gaze of expression-less ancestors and the glassy eyes of antelopes and buffaloes, mounted and mouldering in the Monaghan damp. I knew where the ghosts were, having seen a glimpse or two in passing. To those parts of the house I dared not go by night, and even by day ran through them quickly.

I had a dachshund and later a labrador for company; I was shy and spoilt and seldom gainsaid, and my mother was the centre of my universe. Until I was eight she taught me Latin, history, French, English, mathematics and geography in a fascinating blend of erudition and eccentricity. Looking back through one of our old exercise books I find it lavishly

My mother on the lawn at home in Ireland with the lake and
the island in the background.

illustrated with exotic thumbnail sketches of animals (always accurate), people (often nude) and volcanoes (never dormant). Like a Jesuit she imprinted her beliefs and vision on me so strongly that I could never lose them. I find the words and phrases as alive today as they were when I first learnt them. In geography America was full of Indians, log cabins and buffaloes. My dictation was 'A journey across the world'. There is a reference to the first balloon flight over Paris, Halley's Comet, vegetation belts and equatorial forests – all in one week. I suddenly realize that those pre-school influences were much stronger than those of all my later years of professionally moulded education, from which I seem to remember very little.

All my first and most lasting impressions came from my mother, and hers is still the standard by which I measure my morality. She is my sense of right and wrong. Some find this through a priest in religion or through a teacher in school. Perhaps some are born with it or may even be strong enough to find it for themselves. Those with a parent in the role are, I believe, exceptionally fortunate.

She drew wonderful pictures in which a whole mysterious, magic natural world is blended in flowing lines like an Arthur Rackham under-water dream of fairyland. Birds with outrageous tail feathers, sharp furry animals, snakes, reptiles swirl in and out of convoluted vegetation to create her individual view of a devious, painful, sinister but ultimately benign and always beautiful cosmos.

The interior life which I, like all lonely children, lived in secret was peopled with half-heard voices from exotic, distant lands. I can remember sitting in the fork of an old oak tree on the edge of the lake and being filled with such an urge to do something positive that the frustration was almost unbearable. What it was I could not begin to imagine, but travel was an integral part and might even, I felt, be an end in itself. Anything to get away. And yet my surroundings were idyllic for a small boy. From an appallingly early age I carried a gun and I used to drag as many as a dozen fat rabbits back to the house before breakfast in the spring. I learnt to paunch them as well as to clean fish so that blood and guts became familiar companions. The instantly alerting tannin smell of oak rot, leaf mould, honeysuckle and hay all belong there as does the peculiar stink of worms sweating as they are threaded on a hook. So does the feel of fresh wet fur, brambles which catch and tear, soft mud between the toes and fish slime on my hands, recalling the many large and ugly pike I dragged up from the muddy bottom of the lake; the sound of wood-pigeons cooing at dawn, and rabbits thumping in alarm, all have their origin for me in Lough Bawn.

The horrors of childhood, the first-hand experience of the redness of nature's tooth and claw were all tempered by my mother's gentle and

An early catch of trout.

compassionate understanding of the intrinsic beauty and wholeness of all life, but still I wanted to escape. The cruelty I saw around me in a country upbringing taught me that the gentlest of people, and there are none softer than the sons of County Monaghan, daily perform acts which are intellectually abhorrent yet, because done with neither guilt nor glee, leave the perpetrator innocent. Rats were caught in cage traps, where they ran around before being drowned in the horse trough in the yard. The memory of their despairing struggles still sickens me, but it was then the accepted method of disposal and certainly quick and effective. Perhaps being so close to the savage underside of nature as a child taught me not to condemn the different attitudes to life and death, kindness and cruelty exhibited by cultures other than our own.

If I had had a friend and companion as a child, I might have come to terms with the inevitability of conforming to a set pattern of ideals and aspirations, but my brothers and sisters were all much older and, though kind, were distant, while my contemporaries at school filled me, almost without exception, with a kind of dread of life. I could not feel easy with their daily preoccupation with status, sport and the system.

Although I never found academic work very taxing, arrogantly assuming privately that my innate intelligence would see me through, I never fully discovered the excitement of an intellectual awakening under a great teacher. Instead I learnt through the idleness engendered by neither needing nor wanting to work hard, a new sort of boredom. Unlike the frustrations of the country which only made me long to see and to do other more stimulating things, this was a much more dangerous and nihilistic feeling of despair. The future seemed to hold nothing for me and I longed for a peg to hang my life on.

As the youngest son of a landed family quite properly preoccupied with preserving the estates intact and therefore practising primogeniture, I was encouraged to go into the Army. My eldest brother, who had served with distinction in the Irish Guards at the end of the war, arranged a commission for me in his old regiment. As a resident of Ireland, I was not eligible for National Service, which was coming to an end anyway, but I should volunteer as a regular officer. Already at Eton I was beginning to doubt if I would find fulfilment as a soldier. In one way it all seemed too easy, while the prospect of committing myself to being so completely part of a disciplined system appalled me. Prevaricating with the excuse that I wanted to go to university first, I gained a place in the same long-suffering brother's old college, Magdalen, at Oxford, largely, it seemed at the time, on the grounds that most of my Hanbury ancestors back to the 16th century had been there too. We settled on late Army entry, with my degree replacing the first three years' service. I did in fact spend some time during my first long vacation with a squad of new recruits undergoing basic training, the interesting process by which a man is turned into not just a soldier but a guardsman, and I hugely enjoyed it. It was perfectly designed as a sublimation of all the masochism beaten into every public schoolboy, especially the small and pretty ones such as I was in those post-war years. Life was organized so that one should live in a state of perpetual terror with no time to think or argue. Conformity was everything and I and the other wretch from Oxford were in trouble from the start, simply because we looked different, wearing floppy berets instead of the peaked caps of the National Service entrants.

On the other hand, I found that the emancipation of a whole year at university had begun to open my eyes to the cracks in authority and the fallibility of those in command as well as allowing me to enjoy life much too much to be frightened for long, while almost welcoming fear as a diversion. As a result I was both intrinsically unsuited to a military career and at the same time rather good at beating the system and so was thought by everyone to be doing well. Occasionally I went too far, as when a friend was reprimanded in the wash-house for doing his ablutions in the wrong order and I sprang to his defence, explaining to the 'trained soldier' in charge, in a superior tone of voice, that 'That was how we all did it at Eton.'

That earned me three nights of standing to attention beside my bed during the brief lull between cleaning our kit and reveille when we were normally allowed to sleep.

I found I revelled in the discomfort and strict regime, a lesson most usefully learnt for later bad moments on expeditions when I could always tell myself that I had survived worse. I left with genuine regret and the friendly backslaps of the sergeants telling me that I would make a fine soldier and they looked forward to seeing me back next year. They never did.

Before going up to Oxford in 1954 I spent a summer term at Innsbruck University to polish up my German and study art. A couple of life classes convinced me that I was not destined to be a professional painter and my largely *Lederhosen*ed fellows had an all-too-familiar smell of school about them. Since no one seemed to mind whether I attended lectures or not as long as the small fees were paid, I spent most of my time seeing Europe. Innsbruck was a marvellous centre for a penniless student in those days, when hitch-hiking was a new phenomenon, and on a good day I could count on one in three cars stopping. I had a small collection of national flags one of which I would display once I had established the origin of the approaching vehicle. The Americans would always pick up the poor British, while the local Austrians tended to stop in surprise at the unusual sight of an American hitching, and the French usually stopped for their own. This last combination had the added attraction of testing my French to its limits and providing a small spice of danger.

Starting from Europe's most central crossroads I could choose to explore Austria, Italy, Switzerland or Bavaria. Had I wished to do so I could easily have gone as far as Rome or Paris, but sheer distance was not my object. It was the freedom of the road which thrilled me. After a lifetime in the security of home and boarding school I found it almost unbearably exciting not to know where I would be spending the night. As often as not this was a hedge or farmer's barn, but I was well used to nights under the stars, solitude held no more fears after the island and ancestors by night, and people were universally kind – another invaluable lesson learned. If you are alone, polite and, if possible, funny almost any other human being almost anywhere in the world will help you.

At this time I was in a kind of emotional limbo. Released from school at last, I had not yet begun to identify my real interests and I was not even able to grasp and enjoy my freedom fully. I therefore spent much of my time looking, wondering and longing. I was based on a family living in a chalet high above the valley in a village which in winter was a ski resort. In spring, when I arrived, the gentians and irises spread dazzlingly across the Alpine meadows, inviting exercise. To everyone's surprise, including my own, I kept on walking from a short stroll on my first day, reached the top of a small mountain, still under snow for the last mile or so, and missed lunch.

The family I was staying with were aristocrats fallen, like most Austrians after the war, on hard times and living very simply. But intellectually they intimidated me. The children, with whom I played violent outdoor games, were all working furiously for scholarships; the father was a brilliant philosopher who terrified me both by his size and his intellect; it was the mother with whom I immediately fell in love. She talked to me, treating me like an adult for the first time and I felt that she knew everything, could answer any questions about life if I only dared to ask. Instead we discussed literature and I still have the list I made her write for me of the books I should read in order to improve myself. We also played a lot of very high-powered bridge when, partnered by Mephistopheles and secretly worshipping his wife, I learned to survive even the terrifying humiliation which only a poor bridge player knows.

It was from this highly charged atmosphere that I fled and hitched. While travelling I pursued culture avidly both from habit, it being the sort of thing expected of a young man of my background, and also to impress my idol.

The baroque churches and palaces of Bavaria and Vienna suited my mood perfectly. For a romantic late adolescent the fantasy of Neuschwanstein, where I slept out in the woods above and awoke to look down on Mad King Ludwig's towers and pinnacles catching the dawn light, implied all I sought in life. The sugar-icing clouds of rococo extravaganza achieved by the most pretty of all churches at Wies gave me intimations of immortality. In Vienna there were galleries and museums, especially the Kunsthistorisches Museum with its superb collection of Breughels, and the Imperial Summer Palace of Schönbrunn with more cheering rococo, where I could sit and look and learn.

Best of all there was opera, not yet in the soon-to-be-restored State Opera House where a few years later my brother as a young diplomat and his wife were to waltz at the Inaugural Ball, but in a rather shabby theatre where I sat night after night feeling the first stirrings of a love of music and great singing. It was to be a love and understanding that never developed far, but in Vienna just then the romance and pathos were irresistible. The city was still occupied by the troops of four nations and it had suffered more than most from poverty and degradation during the war, so that they seemed to be singing their hearts out in the hope that life would improve again and their fragile spring would blossom into glorious summer – a mood with which I felt in harmony.

There were also cafés with amazing sticky cakes and plump matrons in shabby furs and, late at night, low bars where rich soldiers, poor refugees and survivors of the wreckage and austerity produced an atmosphere of sophisticated gaiety which I found intoxicating. Seeking romance, about which I was still profoundly naive (I would not have had much idea what to do with it if it had been offered), I sat drinking and talking through the night to world-weary ladies. Sometimes I was allowed to stay on after everyone else had left and sleep stretched out on one of the overstuffed plush banquettes. All excellent practice for my German, but never the great introduction to romantic love affairs for which I longed.

Instead I kept moving, exploring the Harry Lime country of the Russian quarter with its fairground and giant Ferris wheel and Russian soldiers who gave me bad frights more than once by arresting me when I photographed them, only to let me go once the film had been confiscated.

South to Italy, where the austere lines of Roman temples and Palladian villas in the Veneto began to bring me down to earth. Then, for the very first time, Venice and the promise of endless return visits to the most beautiful city in the world, where I have been happier than in any other. In fact I can hardly think of another city, except for London sometimes, where I have ever felt at home. There I met an old childhood friend from Ireland who over the years of my youth constantly strove to give me a veneer of culture. It is to Speer Ogle that I owe the pleasure that comes from looking at pictures and buildings. He taught me to appreciate, to respect, even perhaps to revere, a work of art and I will always be grateful. He was the perfect companion with whom to undertake a Grand Tour before going up to university.

We steamed down the Dalmatian coast, seeking culture, to Dubrovnik, where I had a small commission to perform. Shortly after World War I my youngest Tenison uncle, Michael, on his Grand Tour fell ill in Dubrovnik and died. His companion was sent a large sum of money by the family to pay for proper burial and perhaps a memorial, but instead he absconded and was never heard of again. Eventually, through the intercession of our ambassador, Uncle Michael was removed from the paupers' grave and re-interred in the small Anglican cemetery. No member of the family had ever visited his grave and my Aunt Marguerite, his sister, wanted me to take a photograph of it for her. A simple task, except that no sooner had I stepped ashore at Dubrovnik than I too fell ill of a strange fever and, for about the only time in my life before or since, was totally incapable of getting out of bed for three days. Speer's assurances that if history repeated itself he would not run off with the money for my grave were small comfort, until at last he supported me down a long dusty lane where I finally photographed a simple white marble cross under the cypresses.

We travelled on by bus through Montenegro, along the Albanian border

through Macedonia to Mount Athos, the amazing monastic community
on the easternmost of the Chalcidice peninsulas. There we stayed and
were entertained by eccentric monks in lavishly beautiful surroundings,
walking between monasteries often built on the edge of high cliffs falling
into the sea.

The sea was tempting in the heat of the day and, although swimming
was strictly forbidden to monks and visitors alike, we decided to risk it
once when we were walking far from any habitation along a narrow track
high above a secluded sandy cove. The decision took some time to arrive
at. Speer was an essentially law-abiding person and passionately dedicated to avoiding causing offence. He was afraid that we might be seen
and upset the holy men. He was also afraid of snakes, and to reach the
cove necessitated a long scramble through thick undergrowth. However, I
was hot, and insisted. We arrived safely and the sea was warm and clear.
Speer thought he saw a shark so we lay on shallow rocks where the water
lapped over us, and sunbathed. Once, when I opened my eyes, I thought I
saw a bearded face crowned by a black hat peering at us over the cliff, but
when I looked again it had vanished.

That evening at Gregoriou, we were with a group of monks when an
excited lay brother returned from the olive grove to say he had met a
hermit who had seen a vision. Looking out to sea from his lonely shelter he
had seen water sprites disporting themselves among the waves. He had
run all the way to tell his nearest neighbour of this marvel but when they
had returned to the scene the sprites had vanished. Sometimes after that
we washed our tired feet in cool mountain springs, but we never risked
bathing again.

Speer and I continued by train and bus through eastern Turkey visiting
mosques and ruined temples from Istanbul to Izmir. Then back again to
mainland Greece and the Peloponnese where we over-indulged ourselves
in mental feasts of marble ruins among the olive groves at Epidaurus,
Delphi and Olympia. It was all great fun and highly edifying; we were
good companions and I learned the lifelong habit of keeping a journal
faithfully and daily when travelling, but I still fretted for something more,
and was not convinced that life had much to offer.

All that changed the day I arrived at Oxford. To my complete surprise,
as I settled once more into the institutional surroundings of a quadrangle
and staircase with names on the doors, I found I liked my immediate
neighbours and contemporaries. At first I think it was simply that they did
not appear preoccupied with the petty run of school life but instead treated
me as an equal. And they talked! All night we talked, not just about plans
for exploits and adventures but about ideas. For me it was an overnight
awakening and I must have blossomed through it, as I suddenly found it

easy to make friends. The joy of those first days has never left me. Even today if I feel depressed I remind myself how hollow life seemed before and what fun it has all been since.

I loved Oxford. It was a golden era and not just for me. The pressures of work and the ruthless competition for jobs which was to follow had barely begun so that there was a sense of leisure and intellectual freedom to pursue learning for its own sake rather than as a means to a career. I was offically studying Politics, Philosophy and Economics, but as I was undistinguished and unambitious academically and, to be honest, uninterested in politics, bored stiff by economics and only occasionally stirred by philosophy, I went to more lectures on subjects unrelated to my degree than to relevant ones and nobody thought it odd. With lecturers like A. J. P. Taylor on history, Maurice Bowra on philosophy and Kenneth Clark on art, it was a treasure chest into which I barely dipped.

One of my first and most enduring friends was Anthony Page, destined it seemed from birth to be a director of plays and films. He introduced me to the theatre, even getting me to play the part of Froth, A Foolish Gentleman, in *Measure for Measure* in the open air in Magdalen Deer Park, a part I was well suited to: it demanded little more than poncing about in a pair of pink tights and bowing with a huge ostrich-feathered hat to the ladies in a foppish way. It did, however, prove to me that I was not cut out to be an actor. We went on tour to Abingdon where before the matinee performance, I went down the river in a punt with a friend. We enjoyed the admiration of American tourists ravished by our brilliant costumes. Suddenly we noticed the time and realized that I had missed my cue. Furiously punting back upstream, I dashed red-faced on to the stage five minutes late to find Bobby Moore, now a deservedly successful television actor, playing Pompey, desperately improvising more and more outrageous descriptions of 'that foolish gentleman' due to appear at any moment. My long-awaited headlong entrance marked the end of my career on the boards.

Anthony and I used to indulge ourselves occasionally in orgies of both the theatre and cinema in London. By a judicious juggling of performance times we once saw five plays in two days and, because film programmes allow more flexibility if one is prepared to see only the main feature, nine films in a similar period. Life as an undergraduate was so full of interest and excitement that such vulgar ruses were necessary if everything was to be packed into the available hours. Essays were nearly always written through the night to an accompaniment of black coffee and loud Beethoven. They were finished at dawn, an hour or so before delivery. If unfinished or unwritten, I substituted a brace of pheasant and was forgiven, something which I suspect would not be looked on so kindly today. Then there were the parties. When I was a child in Ireland there were virtually no parties. Distances were too great to travel by pony and trap during the war and afterwards there was petrol rationing, which had the same effect. It was therefore with the dazed sensation of a child let loose in a sweetshop that I discovered that in Oxford there were parties of one sort or another almost every night; and London was only an hour away with an apparently unlimited further supply. At these parties were girls who raised all sorts of interesting possibilities in the mind of a late-developing 18-year-old. They even seemed to enjoy his company, a completely new and heady sensation. Perhaps the fact that I was so patently enjoying myself made people more tolerant.

With Anthony and my closest, long-lasting friend John Hemming, now a D.Litt. of Oxford and Director of the Royal Geographical Society, I shared for my second year an old detached towerlike building at Magdalen called the Grammar Hall. This was an excellent venue for parties since we had no neighbours to disturb. At one, which we gave for the black film star Dorothy Dandridge who had just played the lead in *Carmen Jones*, a young photographer called Tony Armstrong-Jones recorded the decadent scene as we saw in May morning and I fed the star scrambled eggs. In the basement lived a charming, short organ scholar who played the piano exquisitely and was an invaluable asset at parties. Today he is an inter-national star: Dudley Moore.

Later, with Richard Mason, a medical student and charismatic original whom many loved, John and I managed to acquire the lease of a house in Museum Road which had the unique attraction in those unliberated days of having no landlady. This became the recognized base and overnight accommodation for the girlfriends of all our friends when they came down from London. As a result life there was one continuous party. Both John and Richard were working extremely hard for their finals and occasionally complained about the noise. I was an unashamed sybarite and dilettante who continued to enjoy every moment with no thought to the future.

But we did plan expeditions together, and even then all three seriously intended to be explorers. Atlases were studied and the achievements of the great travellers of the past were compared. It seemed impossible that we would ever achieve anything, and yet we were determined. John and Richard made an epic journey by Land-Rover through the Middle East during one long vacation, but I was too frivolous, and busy enjoying myself, to do anything more serious than return to Italy and live at San Gimignano for a time, painting, for the sheer pleasure of it.

2

Abroad

To travel in Europe is to assume a foreseen inheritance; to Islam, to inspect that of a close and familiar cousin. But to travel in farther Asia is to discover a novelty previously unsuspected and unimaginable. It is not a question of probing this novelty, of analysing its sociological, artistic, or religious origins, but of learning, simply, that it exists. Suddenly, as it were in the opening of an eye, the potential world – the field of man and his environment – is doubly extended. The stimulus is inconceivable to those who have not experienced it.

Robert Byron, *First Russia, Then Tibet*

On leaving Oxford I set out to see the world and part of me never expected to return. I had no thought of a conventional career or life in Britain. Instead I set off on an expedition with another friend from Ireland, but a greater contrast with Speer Ogle would be hard to find. Johnny Clements, the lanky, amiable son of a neighbouring landowner, had only two pretensions to expertise, but in each of those he was a wizard. He knew about horses and about the internal combustion engine. Both talents were to prove invaluable.

The year before, Adrian Cowell had led a university expedition of three new Land-Rovers to make the first overland journey to Singapore. I planned to emulate this feat but in a World War II battle-scarred Willis jeep which cost us £100, and we intended to go to Ceylon instead. Ceylon was chosen because it was one of the very few places where the AA told me a vehicle could be disposed of after leaving Britain without enormous penalties, so we had to get there. I would then continue to seek my fortune while Johnny returned to Ireland.

We drove across midsummer Europe, sleeping in pine forests and starting the first of a series of major repairs to our little jeep which were to

With Johnny Clements (right), setting out from London in
1957 to drive to Ceylon.

keep Johnny fully engrossed for the next three months. So intense was his
preoccupation with the health of our vehicle that he became quite
oblivious to his surroundings, caring neither about the scorching heat of
the sun by day in deserts nor the cold of nights in high mountains. Food,
money, language were all but means to the end of his obsession, to nurse
our jeep through to India. Ancient cities, temples, scenery were welcome
only in so far as they caused me to stop and leave him to get on with the
important maintenance and repair jobs which were due. The perfect
travelling companion, he convinced me that he positively enjoyed his role,
thus leaving me guilt-free to pursue my fantasies at leisure.

After a brief and refreshing weekend fishing in Styria with my brother
Richard, now *en poste* in Vienna, where Speer joined us to speed us on our
way, we bumped off south and east.

Through Yugoslavia and Greece again, this time with barely a pause, to
Istanbul and Asia Minor. We both liked Turkey a lot. Johnny was treated
with proper respect due to his size and knowledge of engines, while I
responded to the Turkish humour and outgoing generosity. Our major
and continuing problem was the regularity with which something on the
jeep broke or fell off. We had hardly left Istanbul when the clutch gave out.
As a result we spent two happy days with a ruffianly road gang who

became friends unto death as they helped Johnny dismantle the transmission, provided welding gear and shared their food and hut with us.

One of the reasons why everyone who possibly can should travel, and not as a tourist, is that direct experience of the friendship of people of other races, creeds and cultures is the best way to overcome prejudice and even perhaps develop a love of all humanity. Suspicion of the national characteristics of others is deeply ingrained in us all, however liberal we may think we are, and it lies at the heart of many of the world's problems. English literature is full of derogatory references to Turks. They are branded as 'unspeakable' by Carlyle, 'wicked' by Dickens and bracketed as 'jews, Turks, Infidels and Hereticks' in the Prayer Book, so that the idea is implanted from earliest youth that they are not only different but inferior and evil. . . I think I had by then sloughed off most traces of insular suspicion of other Europeans, but I do remember being surprised at how extraordinarily charming those Turkish roadworkers were. As we all strolled at night along a beach under the stars, our arms around one another's shoulders in the Turkish way, we felt as close and trusting as old friends, yet we had almost no common language. Since then I have learned more and more to look beyond the outward appearance of people to the character of the individual, and I have lived with and grown to love members of some of the most 'different' societies on earth. But no one should be fooled into thinking this is easy.

People of different appearance, colour, behaviour, manners and with their own peculiar prejudices are difficult to accept as equals at first. The young today are vastly more liberated in their approach to these matters than we were 25 years ago, but even that has its pitfalls. If you are a passionate worker for women's liberation how do you make friends with someone whose whole culture appears to place women in an inferior role? But there is little hope of peace in the world without understanding across such wide cultural gulfs as these. Those Turks were not, of course, all that different anyway. They just helped me along the road to liking the human race a bit more.

In Ankara we did meet someone truly different. Exhibited in the fun fair was a sad colossus; a man of 24 who, his promoters claimed, was 2.4 metres (8½ feet) tall. I found meeting him like an experience in a nightmare. Johnny and I paid the small fee for a private audience and were shown into his caravan. He towered over us, his well-proportioned sheer bulk making us feel that we were looking through a telescope. I shook his gentle vast hand which enveloped mine totally as though my whole palm were no more than a little finger. Johnny, being much larger than the average Turk and having hands of no mean size and hardness himself, posed a challenge. When his hand was taken he was kindly but firmly lowered to his knees and made, though resisting with all his considerable strength, to bow before 'the biggest man in the world'. The awful pathos of being a freak so gigantic as to be good for nothing but such tricks affected me deeply. I saw the hopeless misery of a parody of Prometheus in his sad, caged eyes and I was glad for him when I learned years later that he had died soon after.

Our journey was not a race against the clock nor were we trying to prove anything. Instead we were free to wander at will, go and see whatever took our fancy – or rather mine, since Johnny was willing to go anywhere. Thanks to advice from the British Archaeological Institute representative in Ankara we went to Ürgüp where in the Middle Ages Christian monks had carved cells inside fantastic rock pinnacles, to find they were still inhabited and formed part of the town. Lost in the barren Turkish countryside we stumbled on the Hittite settlement at Bogazköy and camped late at night among the ruins, to awake at dawn and see a huge temple and 4,000-year-old rock carvings in bas-relief of marching men on a cliff face towering over us. Great carved Sphinx gates, tombs of princesses, remains of Hittites, Phrygians, Greeks, Romans, Byzantines, mostly still awaiting excavation, we enjoyed and wandered on. The Black Sea coast was a relief from the heat and dust of the interior. We found an idyllic sandy beach with deep rock pools where we camped, fished and swam while flights of oystercatchers whistled past and tree frogs sang all night in the bushes behind us.

A kind peasant, when a storm nearly washed our camp away, insisted on leading us up through his maize fields and hazelnut groves to his tiny cottage where the cattle occupied the ground floor. Several heavily veiled ladies, wives perhaps, were shooed out of the only bedroom and our hands and feet were ceremoniously washed in a beaten copper bowl before we were given delicious yogurt to eat and put to bed on mattresses covered with thick multi-coloured quilts. Such spontaneous hospitality to complete strangers is one of the most inspiring things about real travel; also it is one of the few things which constantly restores my faith in human nature, though there is usually a marked inverse relationship between the stage of economic development of the host and the quality of the hospitality given.

From Trebizond, where I walked the walls alone before dawn and we drank tea in piratical old Venetian warehouses on the front with a young English archaeologist, we drove over the Zigan Pass (made famous by Xenophon and the ten thousand) and, camping by the roadside as we stopped to repair the jeep, passed snow-covered Ararat and so into Persia.

Tehran, the blue domes of Isfahan, the columns and carvings of Persepolis, the wild hills behind Shiraz where we rode on borrowed horses, all were admired and enjoyed before we decided to do something a little more adventurous. This was to try and drive across the middle of the Persian desert from Yazd to Tabas, a route seldom attempted. Between the great salt deserts, the Dasht-e-Kavir and the Dasht-e-Lut, which sweep right across central and southern Persia, there was said to be a narrow neck of hard ground. Over the worst stretch Shah Abbas had built a causeway some 350 years before, called the Carpet of Stone which, though bumpy, should carry a vehicle. Beyond was the Sand of the Camels where the jeep would be tested to the limit in the dunes. On either side, the flat white treacherous salt swamps stretched to the furthest horizons, bottomless beneath the tempting crust. The whole distance was some 400 km with only a string of abandoned ghostly caravanserai to mark the route and tell us of the days when this was part of one of the great silk trade routes between China and Constantinople.

A breakdown camp somewhere in the Persian deserts.

For once the jeep behaved – it always did when our lives quite literally depended on it. We set off on a glimmering white afternoon to drive for a night and a day through a ruthlessly barren landscape. Somehow ibex and the wild ass or onager lived there as well as gazelles which bounded out of our way. Ubiquitous ravens croaked deeply overhead when we stopped and once we saw a hoopoe flopping past like a brightly coloured butterfly in the middle of an ocean. Utterly convincing mirages teased us towards cool lakes with green palms and non-existent hills reflected in them. At last far away we saw a solid speck which as we neared it grew into a fine gateway with a massive ochre castle behind it, alone in the flat plain.

We had been told at the British Embassy in Tehran before leaving that, as far as was known, only three Europeans had been to Tabas in the last 200 years; the name means 'the end of the world'. As we drove through the walls, dusty and bleary-eyed, people turned to stare at us in amazement and we saw no other vehicles in the wide tree-lined streets ahead of us. At the end was a large two-storey building flying the Persian flag, which we took to be the Governor's palace. Most of the other residents of Tabas, except for the police, wore turbans and baggy trousers, but by contrast the Governor was in a dark suit. Lonely in his remote outpost he expressed delight at being able to welcome people he clearly regarded as intellectual equals in spite of our outward appearance. Thanks to our very limited common languages – a little French on his part and much less Persian on mine – we were able to preserve the illusion that if only we could communicate there would have been no limit to the metaphysical depths we might not plumb. Instead we smacked our lips appreciatively over the strong coffee and muscat grapes he gave us before we were led to our accommodation. As we had not been expected and there was no hotel, this was, to our surprise and delight, the gatehouse to the public gardens. Inside a domed building covered in blue and white tiles was a spacious bare room from which we looked down on a patchwork of brightly coloured flowerbeds, trees and streams. Date palms and apples grew side by side, the only place in the world where this happens, our host told us proudly. Walnuts, gums, maple and pine, mulberry and roses, tobacco, liquorice, figs, oranges, scarlet pomegranates and little white autumn jonquils all grew together in a rich profusion. Outside the town the arid, featureless desert scratched with dry fingers at the garden walls.

All this was made possible by the continued existence of one of the underground watercourses built centuries before and leading from the far distant hills on the Afghan border. A deep, clear pool of fresh water bubbled invitingly and there we were given soap and told we could swim and wash our grimy bodies. Next day, after being fed on tea, unleavened bread, dates and water melon, we were shown the 14th-century school and mosque with its two charming tiled minarets. On the pool in the courtyard a little migratory phalarope swam quite unafraid of the people. Unlike everywhere else we had been, no one stared or pointed at us after the first surprise, nor were we pursued by hordes of children. Instead, as I have since noticed is often the case in truly remote and unspoilt places, we were treated with a perfect dignity and politeness, neither ignored nor harassed.

Sadly Tabas, which for long had delicately preserved the civilized detachment of another age, was devastated with much loss of life in 1978 when an earthquake levelled most of the houses, burying the population under the rubble. Shortly after that it was the scene of the abortive American airborne attempt to rescue their imprisoned hostages.

In Meshed we camped in the overgrown garden of the virtually abandoned British Consulate, where a handful of lonely, elderly Pakistani guards watched over us. I bought a yellow sheepskin Afghan coat in the market, thereby anticipating a fashion which was to sweep Europe in the 1960s and ensuring my survival during many icy nights to come.

In Herat I rashly climbed one of the immensely tall and crumbling minarets at the tomb of Tamerlane's daughter-in-law, urged on by the cheers of Afghans below and attacked by panicking pigeons crashing out of the dark near the top. My reward was a stupendous view and a solemn handshake from the old mullah who said no one had been up there during his lifetime.

In both places, as everywhere, Johnny spent his time with blacksmiths, conscientiously rebuilding bits of the jeep out of scrap metal.

We had been warned that there would be danger from bandits in Afghanistan. A month before, an American boy, the son of an ambassador, and his Swedish girlfriend had disappeared. It was certain that he had been killed and she was unlikely to be seen again. Indeed for years afterwards I heard rumours that she was alive and longed for someone to rescue her.

Wandering along precipitous camel trails through the wild heartland of the country we nursed the jeep over narrow ridges, winding down impossible slopes to camp in little green strips of valleys where poplars grew, their autumn leaves yellow and bright beside the icy water. We slept in crumbling deserted forts and in the open, huddled against the bitter cold at night which froze the puddles. The air was clear, the landscape Tibetan and we saw no other vehicles, only distant camel trains. In the highlands between the cobalt blue Band-e-Amir lakes and the Koh-e-Baba mountains we stopped for Johnny to undertake some complicated mechanical manoeuvre.

I strolled off with my fishing rod to catch some trout for lunch. The stream had pools in which I could see fat fish but they ignored my European flies and so I went on up the valley until I came to an open meadow where the silence was absolute. I became absorbed and oblivious of my surroundings.

A sound like distant thunder made me look up at the rich blue cloudless sky before I turned to see twenty wild horsemen in turbans and flowing robes bearing down on me. They carried long-barrelled rifles and bandoliers of bullets. With Genghis Khan moustaches and fine, dark, hawk-nosed features, they had to be bandits. Beside their spirited horses loped large, hairy hounds. I felt I should be frightened but all I could think of was that if I had to go I could have hardly found myself a more romantic end.

Forming a perfect half-circle between me and escape, they made their horses rear as they came to a halt and then stand motionless with heaving sides as they watched me reel in my line. With my very few words of Persian I greeted them while they stared at me in stony silence, then bowing towards the water I indicated that their horses might like to drink and said that there were no fish today anyway. Still failing to break the ice, I dismantled the rod and walked along the line, patting the horses' necks and expressing as best I could admiration for them. Suddenly the tension broke and hands were extended for me to shake, broad grins creased every face and loud guffaws shattered the silence. I was beset with questions I could neither understand nor answer, but did my best to indicate that down the valley were my jeep and a friend. My antics entertained them, they roared louder, slapping their sides and each other, and their horses reared and bucked entering into the spirit of the afternoon. The undoubted chief, so swathed in belts of ammunition that bullets fired at him would have bounced off, leant down and grabbed my hand. Thinking innocently that he wanted to shake it again, I gave it to him freely. Instead he clamped it between the stirrup and his foot and spurred his horse into a gallop. I flew beside him taking giant strides so as not to fall and be dragged.

Within minutes we had all reached the jeep to see only Johnny's feet poking out from underneath – fresh cause for merriment and speculation. He is fairly long and thin by any standards, but for an Afghan excessively so, and as he inched his way out feet first their laughter became more respectful, only to break out anew when at last his face, black with oil from the sump, finally emerged. Nothing ever surprised Johnny and the possible danger of the situation never occurred to him. But he knew a good horse when he saw one and going straight up to the chief's magnificent stallion he began to admire its finer points. Horse language is universal and Johnny was immediately recognized as a connoisseur and therefore a man to be reckoned with. My hand, only slightly squashed, was released from its clamp and Johnny's was shaken all round. He suggested that we might be allowed to take photographs and at once they formed two battle lines and charged each other at full gallop passing with only inches to spare, yelling and whooping wildly as they waved their rifles over their heads. I longed for a cine camera and colour film.

One by one they rode up to us, leaning far out of the saddle to pick

Johnny with Afghans in the Koh-i-Baba Mountains.

things up from the ground and pulling their horses right up on their hind legs like circus animals. They let us ride too and we sank into surprisingly comfortable, deep saddles, padded fore and aft with coloured striped blankets and sheepskin mats; each one had a leather water-bottle hanging from it as well as a long holster for the rifle. These last varied from ancient 19th-century muzzle-loaders to modern Russian-made guns modelled on the bolt-action .303. Some of them were clearly brand-new. We tried to find out where they came from and they pointed to the north where the Russian border, marked by the Oxus river, was about a hundred miles away with little but wild mountainous country in between. At the mention of Samarkand they nodded vigorously and we gathered that they had just ridden down from there. They recognized no frontiers and no governments, their lives being ruled more by the seasons than by politics. As outriders and guardians of a large camel train, they were the descendants of a long nomadic tradition in a region where travel has almost always been hazardous, and safety has lain in independence and self-sufficiency.

Now roads have crossed the mountains, frontiers are guarded everywhere, Afghanistan is occupied by Russia and nomads have doubtless become rebels. I cannot believe that our friends would ever acknowledge any other authority than their own. Nomadism is frowned on everywhere in the world today, governments favouring settled agriculture as being more 'modern' as well as easier to tax and administer. Heavy truck routes have eroded the trade fringe benefits of their way of life which becomes harder to justify and support, making their survival precarious.

The group we met in 1957 were proud and free, bursting with vitality and a joy in living seldom felt and even less often expressed by settled peoples such as we have almost all now become.

In Pakistan and India we had many adventures, seeing tigers from the lawn of a deserted Maharaja's palace where we camped, and Everest in the distance from a very small mountain which I climbed on a side trip to Nepal. But it was Kashmir that I most wanted to visit and I had great difficulty getting there in October.

Marooned by landslides on the approach to the Banihal Pass, I abandoned the bus in which I was travelling, having left Johnny to see to the jeep and join me later, and walked through snowstorms and blizzards for a week, covering as much as 40 km in a day. The roadside was littered with abandoned vehicles from which frostbitten Indian students and children greeted me cheerfully. Full of British phlegm I strode on past them, warming myself at occasional *chaikhanas* where I drank tea from large copper urns.

Some German contractors digging a new tunnel under the mountains guarding Kashmir had just broken through a few days before. Everyone believed that this was what had angered the god of the mountain and caused him to bring down the worst storm in history. It took me a whole day to struggle through the snow up to the German camp. By the time I arrived it was pitch dark and a blizzard was driving the snow horizontally across the small collection of low wooden huts. I burst into the Kommandant's office to be greeted by a positive caricature of a Tyrolean with little green hat and shaving brush, *Loden* cloak, *Lederhosen* breeches and a big, bushy red beard. He was delighted to see me and we sat up half the night reminiscing about his hometown, Innsbruck. The rest of the Germans all seemed to be stolid and monosyllabic, and would, I think, have thrown me out, as my presence was totally unauthorized. But my Austrian friend and the fact that I spoke German persuaded them to let me walk and crawl through the tunnel, thus becoming the first person to enter Kashmir by any route for a week. The air was sharp, almost harsh, and very clear, so that I was exhilarated and light-hearted, a feeling that was to stay with me until I left.

At first, as I emerged from the tunnel the scenery was Alpine, with firs sagging under great dollops of snow after the blizzard and the sun beginning to struggle with the morning mist.

Below the pinewoods were poplars, rising up tall and fragile in the sheltered valley. Along a freezing stream, where icicles hung from the snow-capped rocks, grey willows were pollarded in places like a Wiltshire riverbank. An endless flock of chilly sheep and goats streamed down the far slope controlled by a harassed shepherd whose strange cries and whistles echoed clearly across the valley.

And so at last I reached Dal Lake, a lotus land where time slips away across the still waters and the sheer beauty seems a justification for living. On the lake were houseboats, ornate relics of the days when the British Raj escaped to the hills in the hot season. Spacious and comfortable with wide windows, verandahs and even roof gardens, they reminded me of the Oxford barges on the Isis below Folly Bridge. Gondolas with thatched canopies plied between the boats and the shore, paddled by a seated oarsman in the stern. Brightly coloured notices in English advertised the names and special features of the houseboats, such as 'Shangri-La. Fully sprung mattresses.' I was persuaded by Mr Ramzan Dongola that his houseboat was not only the finest but also the cheapest on the lake and there Johnny joined me, having flown in on the first plane after the storm.

Ramzan was, like most Kashmiris, an enthusiastic salesman, with relations everywhere who 'make the finest goods and because you are on my houseboat will sell to you extra cheap'. With him we visited a succession of dark little rooms throughout the four old cities of Srinagar where old men and very small boys worked day and night producing papier-mâché and carved walnut wood boxes on which they painted minute designs and pictures. We saw glittering displays of brightly coloured objects, tables and chairs, trays, ornaments and jewellery. We were shown in detail each stage of their construction, from the shaping of the raw materials to the moment when strips of gold leaf were lovingly applied to the finished product.

We drank endless cups of Persian tea seated crosslegged on a pile of carpets while a succession of rugs, shawls, carpets and tablecloths was reverentially spread out before us. We must have been a disappointment to Ramzan who suddenly decided we should go big-game hunting. Since we wanted to see more of the country and he assured us that it would cost us almost nothing, we agreed to go. With many whispers and oaths of secrecy he told us that he knew a place where no one else could go but where the villagers were plagued by giant black bears and would welcome us and help us for nothing if we would shoot them for them. We were intrigued. Ramzan provided everything including the guns and a vehicle but as we had no permits of any sort we had to pretend that we were off on an elaborate picnic. In the early hours we drove hooting through the streets, waking up and collecting half a dozen cronies of Ramzan's who were to help on the expedition. Several had their own guns. All day we headed north over progressively rougher roads until we reached a village where the headman and about fifty villagers were assembled to discuss tactics. It was decided that the next day they would beat the mountainside to drive *chukor*, the Himalayan rock partridge, for us to shoot before the serious business that night when we would sit up among the crops and wait for bears. Johnny and I had both grown up in Ireland with guns in our hands and so we were confident that we would acquit ourselves with honour in the villagers' eyes. By the time this was decided, it was dark and we were disappointed to learn that the house we were staying in was, for some reason best known to Ramzan, 'a short walk away up the hill'. An hour's trudge uphill brought us to the hut where we were to sleep and which we entered through a hatch in the roof. Inside, the smoke was dense and the only light came from the fire. A donkey was tied in the doorway and a monstrous goat trotted around gurgling and making mad little rushes. An old crone was bent over a pot on the fire while a flock of children played around it.

After a day spent ineffectually chasing *chukor* along vertical mountain slopes we returned in the dark to a small field near the village. Each of us had a companion, calling himself rather optimistically a *shikari*, defined by the dictionary as a professional big-game hunter or guide. Mine built me a rough shelter in a maize field where I was able to lie down and go to sleep for a few hours. About midnight, he woke me up to say that he could hear something. We squatted side by side, me with Ramzan's old and very pitted hammer-gun across my knees. There was almost no moon and clouds drifted across what there was of it. I realized I could not see the end of the gun, and the fields below were a mass of moving shadows. Suddenly the *shikari* became excited, leapt to his feet and began to exclaim 'Tsut' loudly, pointing down below. I looked and saw what looked like a small grey cat passing flat out from left to right. It wasn't until it was well past that I realized that my companion considered this to be a bear and had been trying to say 'Shoot'. I still thought it had been a cat. We sat still and frozen for two hours during which nothing happened except two promising bangs from Johnny's direction. Making a tremendous amount of noise one of the villagers came scrambling up to tell us that there was a bear in his field. Urging each other to be quiet, we set off to stalk it. Crouching double and trying to run on tiptoe, we tripped across the stony fields like three sugar plum fairies, stopping to peer over the stone walls and identify each dark patch. To my surprise, one of them was suddenly unmistakably a bear. It stood on its hind legs about thirty paces away and seemed to be looking in our direction. I shot it.

Johnny, it turned out, had also been successful and not only was his larger than mine, a positive giant measuring over seven feet from head to tail, but he claimed that it had been a moving shot and was therefore more sporting. Ramzan promised to arrange for both the skins to be cured and shipped back to England for us, and I believe Johnny still has his. But mine when I eventually returned home a year later, although it had arrived safely, had been badly cured and stank so much that I was persuaded to have it destroyed. That had, after all, been the original object of the exercise and all the pretence of big-game hunting little more than a clever dodge of Ramzan's to entertain us and take a little of our money. However, the villagers' gratitude at ridding them of two such mighty crop despoilers made us feel for a time as though we had each killed a man-eating tiger . . . until we discovered on our return to Srinagar that the area where we had been shooting was a strictly protected government game reserve which we had only been able to visit because of Ramzan's inside information that the head warden was away. This made us see our achievement in a slightly different light.

So much of life is not memorable and fades away. Sometimes, even when I re-read descriptions in my old notebooks and diaries, nothing comes back to me. But some golden moments remain for ever. They can be recaptured just by the mention of a place's name. For me this is true of Srinagar and Kashmir. When I read what I wrote at the time, I can feel the clear cold, see the azure blue, smell the flowers and hillsides, hear the voices across the water. The poplars reflected in the lake, the painted houseboats and the little charcoal stoves for warmth. The importunate vendors and the energetic hospitality which we knew was intended to make us buy and made no pretence of being for any other reason. The warm sunshine and always the cloudy, snowy, formidable mountains on every horizon. A boat making a long, wide vee across the incredibly still surface of the lake in which the mountains are reflected like a watercolour in the rain.

Johnny and I parted amicably, he to return by ship to Ireland, I to dispose of the old jeep as planned for exactly the cost of bringing it into Ceylon and then continue east on my own.

Irrawaddy, Mandalay – the names themselves conjure up a picture of exotic eastern lands, remote, inaccessible places where great happenings have occurred and great beauty remains. The idea of visiting the river and the city in the heart of Burma had stolen my heart and was part of the romantic notion I had as a young man that travel was in itself an end to be pursued. Contentment would, I felt, flow from visiting such places and, having done so, I would be fulfilled and satisfied.

Of course, it never happens quite like that. Travel for its own sake must pall in time; the mere collection of experiences, let alone the simple acquisition of a list of countries and sites to which one can say one has been, is a pointless and rather selfish exercise which has no value unless it is put to some use. It may, if one is lucky, get certain adolescent longings, including *Wanderlust*, out of one's system. It may lead to a realization of some of the things that are wrong with the world and a desire to harness what has been learnt to some useful purpose. But the search is often full of disappointments and disillusionments from which the most useful lesson to be learnt is that for all the exotic overtones, man the observed and man the observer is much the same in Bangkok, Bamako and Birmingham.

In spite of all this, Mandalay on the Irrawaddy was all I could have hoped for when I arrived there. The air was cool and sweet after the heat and smells of the coast. The centre of the town, laid out by a French architect in the 19th century, was pleasantly dilapidated with wide, tree-lined streets. Along the western flank ran the wide, muddy Irrawaddy, while to the north the streets ended at the splendid moat of the old palace. Attractive, crumbling red walls were almost all that remained standing after the ravages of the war. Opinions were sharply divided as to whether it was a British or a Japanese bomb which had finally destroyed the entirely wooden palace. I cooled my feet in the moat among the lotuses, sitting under a flowering tree which cast its blossoms and reflections in the water.

As I strolled the streets, wondering idly where to stay, I met – to our mutual surprise – a young Englishman who was living there for a few months on his own to learn Burmese before taking up his post as Third Secretary at the British Embassy in Rangoon. Even more surprisingly we knew each other, having met at a Cambridge May Ball. Several years later he was to marry my cousin Jenny. Martin lodged with a kind and hospitable Burmese family and there I was able to sleep too. His enthusiasm for all things Burmese, from the elegant ladies in tight brocade skirts who mothered him to the language and history of the country, gave me an inkling of the richness of the East. While he envied my freedom to travel wherever the spirit moved me, I admired his knowledge and we have remained friends over the years. In the evening we climbed the hill which dominates the town by one of the snake-like, stone-covered stairways which ascend on every side of it to the cluster of pagodas perched on the top. High on one of these we sat and talked, looking far across the river to the hills beyond. The valley, dotted with small ridges like a Tuscan landscape, was a panorama of pagodas. Wherever we looked, white, gold, red and brown temples caught the evening light. Some onion-domed, some tiered, tiled and painted, they date from every century from the 8th to the 20th. No matter how far one travelled into the countryside around, some king or prince or holy monk had stopped there and commanded that a shrine be built to commemorate the event. Most were in ruins though many still contained gigantic smiling Buddhas, some glowingly covered in shining gold. Over the centuries, the righteous had come and stuck a postage-stamp-sized patch of gold leaf until it had built up occasionally to a substantial thickness. A few of the pagodas themselves had gold on their roofs and these glinted in the setting sun. After the crowds of India, central Burma seemed pleasantly underpopulated with so many beautiful buildings and so few people. Although at that time racked with unrest and teeming with rebellious groups, it appeared outwardly calm and tranquil, with a population of smiling, friendly people interspersed with shaven-headed, yellow-robed, meditating monks.

Martin arranged a duck shoot some thirty miles away at a lake. When we arrived, after driving out of Mandalay before dawn in his Ford Popular, the headman of the lakeside village warned us that a large party of insurgents had just settled nearby and that if they heard us shooting they would certainly kill us for our guns. Most of the countryside away from the main towns was at that time in the hands of a wide assortment of armed bands, ranging from Chinese Communists to Dacoit robbers, more interested in stealing than killing. This particular group was said to consist of political insurgents in opposition to and fighting against the government. They were the most dangerous to run into, especially for a young diplomat. It turned out, however, that there was another good lake not far away and, after bumping there along a rough track, we established friendly relations with the headman. He decided to come with us, bringing his formidable, rusty, single-barrelled blunderbuss.

It was a most beautiful lake, bordered with dense clumps of rushes through which open stretches of water wound in and out. The most vivid water-lilies grew there, blue and red and yellow, as well as lotuses, bright waterweeds and flowering bushes and trees. Tropical jungle is usually a blend of shades of green, relieved by a very occasional flash of colour, but this was like a botanical garden, the most colourful wilderness I had seen. The lake itself often seemed little more than a flooded marsh, being so thickly overgrown in places that the water disappeared. Here spinneys of trees grew on floating islands where banks of vegetation hung out over deep pools.

We squatted in the bows of unstable, narrow, flat-bottomed dugout canoes, each one propelled by a lean, dark villager with a loin-cloth and long bamboo pole. Within seconds we were out of sight of each other, skimming fast along narrow channels and nosing through weed-beds. I was so absorbed by my surroundings that I forgot the purpose of our being there and, left alone, would probably not have remembered to shoot anything.

In almost every tree, if I looked closely, I could see birds, ranging in size from large storks to small, clean, white egrets perched at the extreme edge of branches, but to the evident disgust of my punter I refused to shoot these stationary targets. With the sound of the shots from around the lake, the air was soon full of all manner of other birds. Delicate hovering terns which whirred like humming-birds before diving into the water; gauche, black cormorants which ejected a dirty white stream behind them before taking off; several different sorts of kingfisher, one as big as a pigeon and with a bright orange breast and blue wings; swarms of gentle doves and noisy jays. Clearly the inhabitants of the lake were quite unused to such disturbance and had no idea what was happening as they hurried past in all directions like confused, rush-hour traffic. Then came the duck, flying fast and clearly edible. They came in such numbers that I could select the largest and spare the attractive little whistling teal who, with their short wings, seemed to be trying so much harder to escape. Once he had come to terms with my strange desire to stay in one place and let the birds fly over me rather than hurry towards each flock that landed on the surface, my boatman became quite appreciative and I even understood him to congratulate me on some of my more spectacular shots. With a full canoe we made our way back to the shore.

An old man with two enormous elephants offered to give us a lift to the village. On the way we stopped for a swim in the river, an amazing sensation floating on a bungy raft, with a mobile and most accommodating

After the Burmese duck shoot.

built-in shower. After we had dried, dressed and mounted again, my elephant who had a delightful, gentle nature, kept probing me over the top of his head with his inquisitive trunk, clearly expecting a reward. Fortunately, I had with me an old packet of rather stale Smarties which I dropped into the open end, one at a time. He then conveyed it to his mouth, breathing in hard so as not to lose it on the way and chewed respectfully and rather noisily until he considered it polite to ask for another one. In this way, we reached the village where we were feasted and our exploits recounted until far into the night.

I sailed from Mandalay in a paddle-steamer which clanked noisily downstream. The river was wide, muddy and full of sandbanks on which we frequently stuck while on either side the mountains and jungle were said to be full of bandits who would attack if we delayed too long. At best we went at walking pace and it was very hot. For my own safety, so I was told, I was locked in a small triangular cage in the bows guarded by a platoon of armed guards. Having had a different mental picture of river boats, especially paddle-steamers, and the gracious life led on them, I had brought no food or drink with me so that for two days I ate nothing except two bananas which a friendly but mischievous passenger fed me through the bars pretending, amusingly I suppose for the rest of the crew, to be afraid that I might bite. Thirsty, I arrived at Pagan, the amazing deserted city which was the first capital of Burma from the 11th to the 13th century until conquered by the Mongols in 1287. Traces of 5,000 pagodas, stupas and temples can still be seen scattered across the great dry plain, but all the other buildings of the once-mighty city have long since disappeared, as they were made of wood.

On a mattress in the back of a low, old dogcart, with an even older horse, I dozed as we wandered through the vast area of huge pagodas built like flat-topped Egyptian pyramids and about as big. Inside were colossal gold Buddhas and frightening little steep flights of steps leading to the top. I slept and looked, sweated and ate watermelon and remember it all as a dream.

Not far from Pagan was an oilfield, which I reached in the evening and where I was transported rapidly back into the industrial world. I stayed in great comfort with the English manager and his wife and flew the next day on his private plane back to Rangoon.

From there I wandered by bus and train through Indo-China, spending a few days alone among the now desecrated ruins of Angkor; Thailand, Malaysia and Borneo, where I was to visit the Niah caves, an unsuspected foretaste of the great caves of Mulu which I would see twenty years later; on to Hong Kong and a magical month hitch-hiking through pre-industrial Japan in the spring. I then needed to cross the Pacific somehow without paying.

It was not easy to obtain a 'workaway' passage on a ship and for two weeks I haunted the dockland of Yokohama, dodging the guards aboard ships of all nations and trying to reach the captain. Sometimes I was caught and thrown off; sometimes I succeeded in saying my piece and was then thrown off. I found it hard to decide on the best approach – rough working clothes and an honest desire to work hard in return for my keep and passage; or a smarter turnout and an intellectual approach to the skipper based on my recently acquired university degree and a consequent desire to see the world and experience all sides of Life. As I was not a member of a seamen's union my options were limited and success depended on timing my arrival to coincide with the defection of a member of crew and the need for an instant replacement outweighing bureaucratic considerations. At last I was lucky and a formidable Norwegian captain admitted that his carpenter had jumped ship in the Philippines and he was short-handed. 'But I want no troubles and there will be no special treatment. You will be lowest member of crew and you will work hard all the time. No money, but food and the carpenter's cabin. In Vancouver you leave. We sail tonight.'

I brought my bags on board the *Varda* and was immediately accosted by the First Officer. He was drunk and had served in the German Navy in the war. The prospect of having the company for six weeks of a fresh-faced young Englishman who admitted to having studied philosophy at university amused him. His first assault was fortunately an intellectual one and he forced me into the wardroom where he began to grill me on my views as to the relative merits of the ideologies of Kant and Hegel. Did I not agree that the concept of a master race was patently valid and that he and I were clearly superior in all ways to the riff-raff who made up the rest of the crew? The Captain came in and ordered me below decks forbidding me to associate again with any of the officers. 'You take orders from the bo'sun and he takes his from me!' It was not a good start, since I was now universally mistrusted and the bo'sun had *carte blanche* to be as foul to me as he pleased, something I could see he was looking forward to.

Fortunately, there was another 'foreigner' in the crew, a gigantic genial Pole, known simply as Pol, who decided to befriend me saying, 'All Norwegians bastards, England-Poland OK. I chuck bo'sun in sea one day.'

We sailed to Hokkaido, the northern island of Japan where white snowy mountains came down to the water's edge and we called into a little harbour town. There we loaded timber and were given twelve hours shore leave, to end at midnight. Pol and I visited the three bars in town and drank a lot of beer and saké. By 11 p.m. the snow was very thick in the muddy streets and I was finding it hard to walk through. A small wet puppy followed our tracks into the warmth and crouched under my stool. The ship's siren blew calling us back on board. I asked the barman for food for the dog but he kicked it out of the door into the snow. We returned through the sleeping town to the last bar where I tried to persuade the proprietor to keep the puppy but he shook his head and gestured that we should drown it as it had no owner. On impulse I put it under my sweater and went back to the ship.

I was young and rather frightened. After my careless wanderings, this, I felt, was real life. A job where I would have to compete on equal terms with men. Their livelihood was sailing while I knew that I was a bad sailor and preferred, when on board a ship, to lie on my bunk and read or sleep. Accepting the puppy was in part bravado, a small gesture of defiance to an unfamiliar, disciplined world where eccentricity was clearly frowned on; partly, too, I needed a friend and companion whose loyalty I could trust, and who better at such a moment than a small, fluffy dog?

Fortunately I had a small cabin to myself. The *Varda* was a modern ship with a crew of about forty and our quarters were clean and comfortable, with a large communal galley and dining room where we sat in the evenings playing cards and relaxing. Bridge was the most favoured game, and the fact that I was a moderate player helped to raise my status a little in the eyes of the Norwegians. But not much. On the whole I was regarded with some justice as a rather tiresome joke who had to be shown how to do everything and whose main usefulness was as a source of amusement when something particularly unpleasant had to be done. We started work at 5 a.m. when decks were swabbed down for the first time. As we were taking the northern route across the Pacific and it was early in the year, this was a cold and dark business with frozen spray constantly spoiling my efforts. The deck was littered with unexpected obstructions for cracking shins and forehead on and always smelt of stale fish and diesel fumes. However, it was at least in the open air and better than coiling rope in the claustrophobic fo'c's'le locker where the movement of the ship was exaggerated and I had to fight down waves of nausea. Worse still for me, but fun for all the rest, was when the aerial linking the two masts iced up and I was sent up the rigging to clear it. In addition to being a rotten sailor, I suffer from vertigo and in heavy seas it felt as though the masts were going to dip into the waves as they lurched from side to side.

Meanwhile down in my cabin I had my small furry friend who was full of character but disliked being at sea almost as much as I did. As he was an illegal stowaway I had to keep him hidden from the rest of the crew, and could only take him for short walks on deck in the small hours and out of sight of the bridge. He was, I soon learned, not in the least cabin-trained so that when I was not swabbing the decks I was swabbing out my cabin. Both of us found the food on board unfamiliar, especially the strongly flavoured brown cheese which one scrapes off in slices with a scoop with a slit in it and of which the Norwegians are peculiarly fond. I shall always associate the smell of it with that voyage. There was, however, always plenty of it and it was easy to slip titbits into my pockets for my cabin mate.

It was almost a relief when the Captain sent for me again and, fixing me with a stern and penetrating glare, said, 'You have a dog in your cabin, *ja*?'

It was not a question but I answered, '*Ja*, sir.'

'I know about the English and their little madnesses,' he said. 'I know how it is with them and dogs. But I will not tolerate a dog on my ship! Before we reach Canada he must go, *ja*? Otherwise I am liable to a heavy fine from the immigration people.'

I agreed at once and apologized for being a nuisance but, clutching at straws, asked if I might be allowed to keep him until we reached Canadian territorial waters. '*Ja, ja*, OK,' he said, 'but then – overboard – you understand?' I understood.

Now the dog became legitimate and could accompany me at work around the ship. At first the Norwegians were predictably scornful. 'Bloody Englander, bloody hound,' they muttered as we got in their way. Then one day he attacked the hated First Officer, worrying his trouser leg, and hanging on like a burr. The Officer cursed and kicked, the puppy growled and tore the material, the crew laughed. Still saving a tiny piece of blue serge in his mouth, he flew across the deck and landed in some fresh paint. The news at that time was dominated by reports of the first Russian satellite and he was christened 'Sputnik'. Gradually the crew warmed to him and at mealtimes he was surreptitiously stuffed with choice scraps of bacon and cheese. Elaborate games were devised, a small rubber ball was found and Sputnik made a lot of friends. Even the bo'sun was seen to bend down and pat him before swearing at me to get on with my work.

Sputnik worrying the first officer's trousers in mid-
Pacific on the *Varda* in spring 1958.

The crossing took six weeks and by the end I was feeling strong and fit and able to answer back in Norwegian. The crew were treating me as a human being and Sputnik as a demi-god. I had said nothing of the captain's ultimatum and waited until the last night before mentioning it. Then, while Sputnik was in high spirits, having learnt a new trick involving having to decide who was sitting on the piece of cheese he had been promised, I told them.

'Perhaps now, while he is happy would be the best moment to drop him overboard,' I said as I picked him up by the scruff of the neck.

There was a moment's silence before a dozen deep Norwegian voices said, 'You put Sputnik down! You not throw Sputnik overboard.'

I explained that I had given my word to the Captain and that much as I would like to take him with me on arrival in Canada, the immigration authorities would never allow it.

'You leave this to us,' they said, 'Sputnik belong here.' I was ignored for the rest of the evening as they muttered in groups. By midnight they had come to a decision. An ultimatum was delivered signed by every member of the crew from the bo'sun down. It said, simply, if Sputnik were destroyed they would all leave the ship at Vancouver and fly home. Moreover, if he should slip ashore and the Captain become liable to a fine, they would pay it. The poor man had no option but to accept with good grace. I was not given the small *ex gratia* payment which I gathered was usual after a workaway passage, and he glared after me as I walked down the gangway for the last time.

For the next 12 years I kept a look-out for the *Varda* whenever I was in a large port. Pol wrote to me once enclosing a photograph of Sputnik who had grown to a remarkable size, developing into a fine strong dog looking like a cross between a husky and a chow. But I never saw him again.

Then one day I was lecturing at the northern Norwegian port of Trondheim, talking about the jungles of Brazil while the black snow of an Arctic Circle winter's night swirled outside. After the lecture one of the audience came up to me and asked if I was the same Robin who had worked my passage once across the North Pacific. He had been a member of the crew of the *Varda* and told me what had happened. Sputnik had travelled the world from Canada to New Zealand, the Far East, Africa and the Caribbean. He was known to ships' pilots all over the world and had seen three captains come and go. Then, a bare six months previously, he had gone ashore for the first time in the Philippines. Within minutes of stepping on to dry land, unsteady on his sea legs and unused to traffic, he had been run over by a lorry. They buried him at sea with full honours.

At the height of my London and Oxford life, in amongst all the parties and frivolities, I had met Marika. She came to stay with a group of other friends in Ireland, and during my last year at Oxford we became inseparable companions but more like brother and sister than potential lovers. During my travels I began to experience the extraordinary pulling power of correspondence. At first our letters to each other were merely affectionate and light-hearted like our relationship. By the time I had circled the globe we were neither of us in any doubt that marriage was what we wanted.

Our love had matured and we had come to know each other far more through our letters than we had when seeing each other virtually daily. I never again looked seriously at anyone else until she died 26 years after we first met.

From then on, through all my travels, as well as keeping a daily journal, I wrote with almost equal regularity to both my mother and Marika. Both kept all my letters and, looking back through them now, I can see how down the years it was this link which made me long to return home rather than keep on travelling. I am often asked why I do it; why, when I have a comfortable home and a full life in Cornwall, do I keep making these uncomfortable journeys. Perhaps part of the answer is the bitter-sweet contrast of absence and reunion, of homesickness and *Wanderlust*.

When I left university, home and friends, I had seen no further than the great need I felt to travel through the world without a schedule, time-limit or particular end in view. If I thought about the future at all, I alternated, according to my mood, between imagining that I would find the perfect place to settle and make my fortune and seeing myself as a perpetual wanderer.

South America was always the continent which represented for me the ultimate both as a place to which to escape and as a place where real exploration might still be possible. As I hurried down Canada to Mexico and began to learn Spanish, while visiting as many of the Aztec and Mayan ruins in the Yucatan and other remote parts of the country as I could cram into each week, the attractions of deep roots and a home in familiar surroundings began to seem more appealing. I realized that for me travel would never be a full-time form of escapism, but rather a necessary contrast to the permanence and discipline of home life.

What I learnt from those early travels was something which no one could have told me and which I would not have listened to if they had tried. My mother always encouraged my desire to travel. Perhaps she believed that I would 'get it out of my system', although I know she never got it out of hers, and I would not really wish to either. Had I been prevented from going, for whatever reason, I know that I would have resented it for the rest of my life and I would never have felt content. The excitement of arriving in a strange land among strange people never lessens for me, whether I am on an expedition or on holiday. But since those early wanderings I have gradually learnt that such talents as I have as a traveller and the satisfaction I derive from my travels come not from the journeys themselves but from the fact that I have strong roots in my own country, know my place in the world and the priorities which govern my life. The whole business of travel may then become a useful exercise instead of a selfish pursuit.

3

The Last Continent

'Better die than kill an Indian!'

Marshal Mariano da Silva Rondon,
Founder of the Serviçio de Proteção aos Indios (SPI)

Richard Mason had been writing increasingly enthusiastic letters to me, which caught me in unlikely places in the Far East. We were planning a Great Expedition, one we had dreamed up together during the long nights at Oxford. Poring over maps of the world we had conceived the idea of attempting to drive across the South American continent at its widest point, the last continent where this had not already been done. The great routes from Cairo to the Cape, Peking to Paris, Alaska to Tierra del Fuego, had all been pioneered long before. Richard believed passionately that if we could only succeed in being the first to conquer this last transcontinental journey we would not only be hailed as true explorers, but we would have done something important and significant.

His letters became a flood as he neared the end of his medical degree course (four years instead of my three, which was why he was still at Oxford) and we began to appreciate quite how many difficulties lay in our way. Meanwhile, I was wondering whether I had not had enough of travel for a time.

In the end I resolved all the uncertainty by flying home unexpectedly in July 1958, almost exactly a year after I had left England. Being a deep-dyed romantic I took Marika to Oxford, where Richard was having a party, persuaded her to come out in a punt with me, although it was a damp night, and proposed to her on my knees with her engagement ring ready in my pocket. We fixed the date of our wedding for six months later –

January 1959. I then told her that I would be spending the whole of that time on an expedition, beyond contact, in the jungles of Brazil, Bolivia and Peru and that I was leaving again in a few days.

It was a cruel and thoughtless thing to do and the wounds took many years to heal. Marika even sent me a telegram telling me it was all off but it never reached me and, not wanting to hurt my feelings, she went through with the wedding on my return. But until she started coming with me many years later, she always feared my expeditions more than I realized. She feared the danger for me, but no less the danger long separations can spell to a marriage, and she never wholly forgave my absence during our engagement.

Richard and I were starry-eyed about making our expedition 'worth-while' – the word appears constantly in his letters about our plans. I suppose what we meant by this was that we wanted no one to think we might be doing it all just for fun. Instead we believed that our shared desire to do something epic under distant and dangerous conditions would somehow counteract the jaundice with which we both viewed the world.

Without wars to fight or empires to build, such urges are natural and I see them all the time today among the vastly increased number of young expeditions from schools and universities which approach the Royal Geographical Society for advice and assistance each year. Now it is the pursuit of scientific knowledge which almost alone is used as the justifica-tion. But the spirit of adventure, the thrill of danger, the excitement of seeing new and different parts of the world are no less strongly felt. Most of the time spent on an expedition should properly be hard and uncom-fortable perhaps, to give a proper sense of achievement, and the few, brief moments of joy should be enough reward, but I do not believe that this in itself can ever justify all the effort and heartache, let alone the great generosity so often lavished on travellers. The concept that an expedition must have a useful outcome, if only in terms of pointing the way for others to benefit from the experience, has stayed with me ever since. But then the achievement of a real expedition still lay ahead for us. Richard thought that all my adventurous wanderings around the world during the previous year would have equipped me as an experienced explorer, wise in overcoming daunting difficulties and stalwart in the face of danger. I knew that all my journeys so far had been no more than 'real' travel; a step up from tourism certainly, but a long way from true exploration. What we now proposed to do was undoubtedly the real thing, an epic 'first' journey which, if we succeeded in pulling it off, would go down in the annals of travel as a great expedition.

The Director of the Royal Geographical Society, later to be knighted as

Sir Laurence Kirwan, a formidable figure of whom young hopeful travellers stood in fearful awe, never thought that we could do it. He told us so in no uncertain terms, making sure that the Society had nothing to do with us since he thought it likely that we would perish in the attempt. Our desire to prove ourselves in his eyes drove us on and was eventually to be rewarded by his magnanimity on our return.

Without exception those we consulted about our proposed journey said it was impossible and the nearer we came to our departure the more gloomy became the forebodings. In Europe the interior of South America was regarded as impenetrable. In Brazil it was thought to be positively hostile, full of savage Indians, dangerous animals and crippling diseases. Anyone wanting to go there must be mad.

For weeks we struggled in Rio de Janeiro through a maze of bureaucracy, persuading reluctant officials to issue the permits, documents and visas without which we could not travel. As every real traveller knows, this is the hardest part of any journey, requiring infinite patience and an iron will. We persuaded the Ministry of Culture that we were doing it all for the glory of Brazil so that they gave us official letters of recognition, which were very useful. Best of all we managed to 'borrow' from the manufacturers the first ever Brazilian-made jeep, a splendid machine fitted with special long-range aero tanks on the roof and all sorts of extras. The only snag was that it had to be returned to them at the end or we would lose massive guarantees, and so once again there could be no question of failure. It is not a bad thing to have such sanctions hanging over an expedition, as it stiffens the sinews at bad moments when it might otherwise be easy to give up.

We drove up the coast to Recife, the easternmost point on the continent and from there headed inland, due west. Our objective was to reach Lima on the Pacific coast by the most direct route possible, making our way across country from one river settlement to another and travelling far north of any roads. The nearest vehicle route across the continent lay 4,000 km to the south, between Buenos Aires and Santiago. Our theory was that adjacent villages, even if hundreds of miles apart, would be likely to have some direct contact, if only faint foot trails, which we would try to follow yard by yard, overcoming obstacles as we met them. And that was what we did, reaching Lima some five months and 10,000 km after setting off, about half of it across country never previously visited by vehicle.

Breaking new ground in the interior was extremely hard work and very exciting. We never knew what to expect next, our informants at each place we reached *always* telling us that the next stage was impossible and that the natives were hostile. We were virtually self-sufficient, only needing to find petrol. Across our route lay the mighty tributaries of the Amazon, running from south to north, the Rio Tocantins, the Rio Araguaia and a network of smaller rivers. These posed quite a challenge, but we became adept at building rafts from fallen trees, usually given added buoyancy by a couple of canoes, and floating the jeep across. Here we sometimes met river boats from whom we were able to buy a surplus drum of fuel.

For a few miles on either side of the rivers there was usually dense jungle through which we had to cut and push our way, weaving the jeep between the forest giants and chopping down trees which were too big to knock over. Here it was often wet so that we would regularly become stuck, having to dig and pull ourselves out for hours on end. Between the rivers, however, the country was often open scrub covered in long grass and 'apple-orchard'-like scattered trees. Here the danger came from the rock-hard termite heaps, some as much as six metres high, like strange pointed huts dotting the landscape. The small ones, just hidden in the grass, did terrible damage to the jeep, abusing the suspension and chassis with violent jolts no matter how slowly and carefully we drove.

Our basic diet was porridge, a food I have found to be excellent on expeditions. It is light, nourishing and quick to make. This we supplemented with game we shot and fish we caught along the way. We had an impressive armoury of guns, mainly for this purpose, but also, it must be admitted, because at 22 years old and having seen too many cowboy films we both found it great fun to wear .38 revolvers in holsters suspended from heavy bullet-studded gunbelts. We practised our draws against man-sized cacti. There were constant stories of bandits, but we noticed that they were always to be found in the next village but one, and we found it entertaining how often when we visited bars in remote settlements everyone treated us with exaggerated respect as we strode in wearing our guns. Only once did our bravado nearly get us shot. We stumbled on an illegal cane-spirit distillery when lost and far from any track. As we stepped out of the jeep, innocently meaning to knock on the closed door of the house and ask the way, a rifle was poked round the door, we heard the sounds of a bolt being drawn back and we were curtly told to drop our gunbelts. This we did as fast as possible, explaining in our very best Portuguese that we were 'actually English explorers and a bit lost'. It seemed a sufficiently far-fetched excuse to be believable and we were eventually shown around with a gun still in our backs before being sent on our way with a complimentary bottle of moonshine.

We also had a repeating .22 rifle and a 12-bore shotgun with which, although game tends to be extremely scarce in South America by African standards, we were usually able to shoot a deer or a duck when we needed extra food. Fishing was much easier and we developed an excellent technique with piranha which, though rather bony, reminded me strongly of the perch of my childhood and made good eating. Not nearly as savage as their reputation, so that we swam among shoals of them without ever being bitten, they were nevertheless quite easy to work into a feeding frenzy by throwing the intestines of a bird into the water. Then, using a strong hook on a length of fencing wire attached to a pole, we could pull them out as fast as each captive was removed. This was the dangerous part as fingers could easily be lost to the savage snapping jaws. We resolved that problem by simply chopping off the head and throwing it with hook still embedded straight back in when it would promptly be taken again as bait by its cannibalistic brethren.

There are universal lessons about life to be learned on an expedition. Discomfort, frustration, hard work are inevitable. Life would be very dull without these with which to contrast comfort, pleasure and rest. An expedition simply emphasizes the contrast and can therefore be useful in teaching one to grasp the nettle of unavoidable unpleasantness cheerfully and get on with the job. Of course any paragon who succeeded in following this policy continuously on an expedition would certainly be strangled by the other members before the end, but Richard and I managed an excellent compromise, ruthlessly smiling in adversity when the other was in a bad mood and as a result we never had a row even during the worst moments of stress.

Then at the end of a long, hard day, when we were filthy with dust, mud and oil, bitten all over by red ants, cut by thorns and blistered from wielding the axe and the spade, we would occasionally come across one of those rare camps which make it all worthwhile and which I believe are the secret drug to which all true explorers are addicted. After one especially bad day, during which several punctures were added to our problems, causing us to use up all our water so that we were very thirsty by evening, we came unexpectedly on a clear, cool stream which, just at that point, opened into a deep, inviting pool with a sandy beach.

Tearing off our clothes we plunged in and swam and washed ecstatically as the sun set. By then we had our camping routine down to a fine art, needing only one tree to which we attached our hammocks from either end of the jeep's roof. A hammock is the perfect expedition bed, being comfortable, compact, and inaccessible to snakes and all but flying insects. With a military jungle hammock these too can be avoided, as can the rain, but comfort is sacrificed.

On a clear, mosquito-free night in the tropics there is nothing better than stretching out aching limbs, clean from a good wash, in a soft cotton hammock, while one's companion brews excellent coffee over the fire to round off a filling meal of venison stew, porridge and bananas. The sense of utter contentment such moments bring is in itself reward enough, and the slight element of danger from what almost everyone else regards as a hostile environment only adds spice to the tranquil beauty of the night. Once we woke to see the spoor of a large jaguar on the sand beneath our hammocks and easily traced how it had stopped to sniff each of us before continuing on its way down to the river to drink. I was reassured in my belief that wild animals will very seldom attack unless provoked.

The most remote and exciting part of our route began when, contrary to expectations, we managed to raft the jeep across to the island of Bananal, thereby becoming the first vehicle ever to reach the largest inland island in the world. It was a wonderfully wild and unspoilt place in those days, having been settled in only a couple of places in all its 18,000 sq.km; there was a small American Protestant mission at the north end and a recently built pioneer farm or two near the south. The rest was the undisputed territory of more than 2,000 Karaja Indians generally peaceful now but with a warlike history.

As we burst through the undergrowth and emerged in the mission clearing at Macauba, Indian women dragging their children ran terrified to their palm-thatched huts assuming we were an aeroplane crashing. They had never seen or heard of a motor vehicle. A blond, crew-cut American remained to greet us.

'I thought I heard a plane awhiles back,' he said, when we had introduced ourselves. 'Then the darned thing changed gear and I said to myself, "I've never heard a plane do that before!" '

He was the first of many American fundamentalist missionaries I was to meet over the years and from whom I have received hospitality and shared meals but found no common ground for discussion or belief. At first I was impressed by their dedication in devoting their lives to the Indians, but I have always been rapidly disillusioned by their preoccupation with using their authority to forbid the Indians from practising their traditional customs rather than giving practical help.

We had already met some groups of Indians who had begun to teach us about the hazards for them of contact and contamination with various types of Western culture.

The first had been the Xerente, one of whose villages we had visited before crossing the Rio Tocantins. Formerly they had been one of the great Indian nations, occupying a huge area of land between the Tocantins and the Atlantic. But as the interior had been opened up from the coast they had found themselves sandwiched between the waves of settlers and their traditional enemies to the east, the Karaja, Xavante and Kayapo. As a result they had been successfully 'pacified', losing in the process their land, their hunting grounds and, most important of all, their pride. We were profoundly depressed by the squalor and hopelessness of what appeared to be a crushed group of tattered beggars. As we walked among them trying to talk with them and to take some photographs mothers snatched their screaming children away as though we were going to attack them, and the men were surly and nervous. We asked if they ever celebrated their feasts, danced or made feather headdresses and other artefacts but they only stared at us with blank, uncomprehending, hostile eyes. They were the first South American Indians either of us had ever seen and they have always remained for me the model of what our much-vaunted Western civilization will bring if it is imposed crudely on other cultures.

The mission Indians at Macauba were hesitant, humble, attempting to ape Western ways and ashamed of their own culture. The missionaries had taken them over completely, banning the use of tobacco, forcing them all to wear ragged clothes to 'cover their nakedness' and undermining their self-confidence.

After a welcome but rather sterile meal of imported tinned meat and dried milk pudding interspersed with prayers and hymns, we tried to discuss the Indians' problems with our hosts. They were attempting to translate the Bible into Karaja and I asked if they were also translating the words of Indian songs and myths into English. 'Oh no,' they replied, apparently rather shocked at the suggestion. 'We understand what they are all about and the subject-matter is quite disgusting. We have forbidden them to sing those songs any more and are teaching them hymns.'

'But surely,' Richard persisted, 'it would be helpful to know their stories and legends in order to understand their view of the world if you are to help them?'

'You are wrong,' they said, with the smug conviction of religious fanatics. 'They are disgustingly preoccupied with sex, magic and the human body. They must be made clean.'

We suggested that the same might be said of all romantic poetry, not to mention Chaucer and the Bible itself, but they refused to argue, saying that once 'saved' like them, it would all become clear to us.

Continuing down the island we arrived after some 150 km at another Karaja village called Fontoura. These Indians had not yet been mission-ized, although they had for some years traded with settlers along the Rio Araguaia, and they appeared at once much stronger and better able to face the future. The men stood tall and proud, looking us in the eye and permitting us with great friendship to sling our hammocks in one of their open-sided thatched huts. Most of the men wore shorts and the women cotton print dresses but they were all also decorated with paint and feathers as one of the great annual Karaja feasts, in honour of Aruana the god of the river, was about to begin.

It was a solemn and dignified occasion as the two pairs of shamans, draped in elaborate straw robes reaching to the ground to make them look like moving haystacks, danced backwards and forwards across the clearing between the thatched communal huts, their arms linked as they received offerings of bowls of food from young girls.

While trying to film the ceremony I stepped too near and was sharply prodded back into line by one of the young warriors. Later almost all the Karaja went down to the river and slept on sandbanks as they had always done, away from mosquitoes and surrounded by the water which supplies their livelihood of fish.

When I revisited Fontoura 13 years later I was to see the shamans dance again, this time on the orders of the government official in charge of the village and in the presence of the Protestant missionary who had 'saved' them. A 'main street' had been built as a mark of progress where the Indians slept in strictly nuclear families in squalid, stuffy, square brick boxes. Young Indians in dark glasses and gaudy shirts who had been taken out to Belo Horizonte and given 'moral and civic instruction' to make them into Indian Guards, responsible for 'maintaining order in the Indian communities', mocked and jeered as the old men shuffled about in an embarrassed way. Around the village was a barbed-wire fence and it was forbidden for any Indian to sleep outside. . . The Karaja population had by then dropped to 800 and there were 8,000 Brazilian settlers on the island.

Richard and I were also able to cross the Araguaia and visit the remnant of another once great tribe which had been massacred, the Tapirapé. Two remarkable Basque nuns had rescued the handful of survivors from extinction some years before and settled them at the mouth of the Tapirapé river where they were relatively safe from attack by settlers or by other more powerful groups of Indians. Although only a handful of families, they appeared to be prospering, the children looking fit and healthy. The nuns were away when we stayed there and I never had a chance to speak to them, but we were well looked after by the Indians and impressed by the apparent strength of their self-confidence and hope for the future. It was one of the first inklings I was to have of the relatively beneficial approach of some of the more progressive Catholic missionaries. They recognize the deep importance of a tribe's symbols and, instead of trying to undermine or forbid all the rituals which the people have practised throughout their history, accept that everything can be a sacrament and so attempt to adapt their own ritual to be as acceptable as possible to the tribe. While I doubt if any proselytization brings benefits to people of totally different cultures and beliefs, the dedication, self-sacrifice and love of many good people who have devoted their lives to helping others should not be lightly disregarded. Often they are the only protection a tribe has against alien diseases and against men who would happily kill them as animals. But I have often wished there were more people with the urge to help others without believing it is essential to make them Christians at the same time.

It was as we made our way down the island towards its southern end that disaster struck. The jeep, which had been taking a terrible pounding from poor tracks, tree stumps and termite heaps for more than a month, suddenly fell in half, the chassis breaking completely through on both sides and depositing the engine on the ground. Although I have been in much more dangerous situations in my life – after all we could always try to walk out if we had to – I don't think I have ever been so near to total failure. The financial implications alone of giving up were horrendous as we had given bigger bank guarantees than we could afford that the jeep would be returned.

The area we were in was an uninhabited no man's land between two mutually hostile tribes of Indians, the Karaja and the much-feared Xavante just across the Araguaia on the Rio dos Mortes. The nearest town where we could expect to find a garage with repair equipment was nearly 1,000 km away to the south. In all other directions the jungle stretched unbroken for two or three times that distance. There being nothing for it but that one of us should go and try to get help while the other stayed to guard the jeep, we tossed a coin. I lost, although staying alone for a matter of weeks living off the land was not a wholly desirable alternative. Taking my passport, my gun and some money I started walking, leaving Richard cutting down some trees to build himself a house. After a few hours I came on a track which led me to a small *fazenda*. The owner, with that great generosity towards strangers which is the most attractive characteristic of the inhabitants of the Brazilian interior, agreed at once to lend me a horse, riding with me for the first day to show me the way. Driven by my extreme anxiety at the seeming hopelessness of the situation, rubbed raw by the unfamiliar Western saddle and rocking with exhaustion from lack of sleep I covered almost 300 km in three days, changing horses *en route* and riding through one whole night.

With the unbelievable luck which sometimes comes at moments of great crisis, I arrived at the nearest large *fazenda* with a vehicle track to the outside world on the day when a lorry had arrived to collect the annual harvest of large fish from a lake nearby. It was the only occasion in the year when such an expense was justified. Normally everyone went in and out by horse. I perched on top of the rather unsavoury load, which was beginning to go off, and so arrived at last at Anapolis, a small frontier town close to where the great new federal capital Brasilia was about to be built. I always enjoy, when I visit that impressive bustling city of skyscrapers and wide boulevards, telling Brazilians who ask me proudly if it is my first visit that I rode through there on a horse before the city was built. Although not strictly accurate, it's worth bending the truth in order to watch their expressions.

My problem now, having located the only garage in town, was to persuade its owner, a delightful Greek immigrant called Alexander, that he wanted to go on an exciting picnic into the interior, taking some welding gear with him. This took me a couple of days to achieve, regaling him with tall stories about the huge fish in the rivers, the herds of game to shoot and the beautiful Indian girls he would see. At last we set off, but after three days' driving, by which time *his* jeep was falling apart, he was beginning to lose patience with me. Moreover, the strain of trying to find my way across uncharted country seen only once from the back of a horse was beginning to tell on my nerves. Alexander announced that he had had enough, missed his wife and was going home immediately. I argued, threatened, blustered, begged, all to no avail. Then I burst into tears. You must remember that for ten days I had had next to no sleep, my greatest friend was, as far as I knew, at that moment defending himself with his last round against a horde of attacking Xavantes; the jeep and equipment, into which we had put all the money we could raise, was lying perilously close to being abandoned in the bush, and my fiancée was preparing in England for our wedding a bare three months away.

The effect was instantaneous. Alexander's kind and susceptible Greek heart melted and the possibility of turning back was not considered again.

Eventually Alexander and I reached the familiar stretch of river near the breakdown and I fired a signal shot. A wild figure with matted hair and a body almost black from the sun paddled into view seated in a small dugout canoe. Richard had been sleeping badly, eating little and had a painfully swollen foot, but our greeting was the epitome of British *sang-froid* and had Alexander chuckling for days.

'How did you get on, then?' asked Richard.

'Oh, all right,' I replied. 'I've got everything.'

Richard had been living rough, paddling the canoe, which he had found abandoned and had repaired, along the many creeks and lagoons which networked that part of the island. For two days he had been delirious and in excruciating pain after stepping on a stingray which had jabbed its highly poisonous barb into his ankle. I had been away for nearly two weeks but it seems never to have occurred to either of us that I would fail to bring help and a second vehicle on to Bananal and we had made no contingency plan for what Richard should do if I never came back.

After a couple of days' hard work on the jeep the repairs were nearly completed and so Richard and I went off in his dugout to explore his domain. It was an idyllic place teeming with wildlife and we glided for miles along silent galleries of light and shade. Richard knew the best places to look for some of the strange wild inhabitants of the river and we came upon a pair of huge tapirs standing on the bank. These are much fancied by Brazilians as food and they carry a lot of meat, but we had plenty and so just watched them as they jumped into the water and, submerging like hippopotami, vanished below the surface. We also saw several capibara, the largest rodent in the world, which scampered up the banks like gigantic fat rabbits and disappeared into the undergrowth.

There is no better way of seeing wildlife than from a canoe, and we forgot time as more and more wonderful sights met us round each bend in the river. Giant jabiru storks, with their top-heavy beaks, stood in the swamp, gazing intently at the water between their long legs; turtles and small, unwary crocodiles slept in the sun as we slid past with hardly a ripple, and of course a constant swarm of insect life, from gaudy butterflies and dragonflies to a host of sparkling smaller fry, shimmered and glinted over the stream. It was an enchanted world and, content for once not to shoot with either camera or gun, we were allowed to drift through this Garden of Eden.

All at once we both realized that the atmosphere was changing and the noises from the dark woods beyond each bank were increasing to a crescendo. Without our noticing, dusk had fallen and the changeover between day and night creatures was causing frantic activity. It was as if the rest of the animals had also lost track of time during the peaceful afternoon and were now having to hurry home before darkness fell. A group of small spidery red monkeys careered overhead like a troupe of trapeze artists, so that they had swung themselves across the trees which met over the river almost before we had heard their excited chatter and looked up. Flocks of noisy green parrots rocketed past in tight formation, screaming abuse at each other, while brilliant blue and yellow macaws, and once a vivid red pair, flapped past more sedately and always in twos like elderly couples going for an evening stroll.

We decided to spend the night collecting some caiman, the South American variety of crocodile, as payment for Alexander since he could sell the skins for good money back in Anapolis. Sunset gave way to darkness with the speed of the tropics and was followed by that magical hush when one feels that the daytime animals, not sure if their sleeping quarters are really so safe now that they cannot see, crouch motionless so as not to give their presence away, while the nocturnal creatures, their eyes still dazzled by the day's glare, look out from their lairs for a moment to assess the situation. For a few seconds the world is breathless before the first tree frog breaks into song to be followed by a rising crescendo of hoots, howls . . . and screams.

We entered our first lagoon leading off the little river and shone the torch around. Deciding to try for only the very biggest crocodiles we carefully assessed the eyes that watched us. There was something eerie about paddling quietly towards these red-eyed monsters who seemed to be encouraging us to come a little closer to their 'gently smiling jaws'. They always seemed to be looking straight at the torch but seldom became alarmed at its approach so that we were able to come quite close before they would vanish in a swirl of mud. This meant that we could lay aside the noisy shotgun, which threw the jungle in a turmoil each time it was fired, and use the light .22 rifle.

For a couple of hours we prowled around the lagoons collecting half a dozen monsters, the largest nearly four metres long, and then we camped on the ground stretching out on palm fronds by a roaring fire. Sleeping this way in the jungle without a hammock is, I found, perfectly possible if one is utterly exhausted, as we were then. Otherwise it is not to be recommended as the tremendous variety of night noises and activity will keep one awake, while insects of great variety, mostly quite harmless, investigating every part of one's body are hard to ignore.

On my return journey 13 years later I was to have a chance to revisit and canoe again through a part of this wonderland. Now fully settled by Brazilians, almost all the game of Bananal had been destroyed. Caimans were virtually extinct, tapirs unheard of and the habitat of most other birds and animals burnt and cleared to make way for ranching scrawny cattle.

Alexander was delighted with his skins, accepting them as full payment for his trouble and, after seeing him safely back to the track leading to civilization, we continued on our separate ways. Rafting the jeep across the Araguaia and heading west to the Rio dos Mortes, we now entered the heart of Xavante country. No local settler would have ventured so far into the territory of these legendary warriors, but two years previously an Italian in São Paulo had staked a claim to a large stretch of land there. Under Brazilian law such land had to be actively farmed in order to secure title and so he had sent two young families to live there. Shortly after their arrival a hunting party of 150 Xavante men had arrived and settled at the farm. They had been friendly and appeared only to want to feed and rest. After a few days the two settlers had decided it was safe to go off and round up some cattle together. When they returned they found their wives and children killed and their farm looted and burnt.

We heard that two more young men with their families had recently arrived to rebuild the farm and we decided to visit them. As we drove through the open country west of the Rio Araguaia we spotted a group of

Indians watching us from the bush, but decided it was better not to stop. At the *fazenda*, a simple thatched building open along one side, we saw at first nothing but Indians everywhere and for a moment were afraid that history had repeated itself and we had arrived at the scene of a massacre. Then a fair-haired young Paulista came out and greeted us warmly, inviting us at once to stay as long as we wished, since he was glad of the extra protection for his family.

The Indians, all male – we understood their women and children were some distance away in the forest – were naked and unpainted, with fine muscular brown bodies, open friendly faces and long hair cut in a fringe in front. They were a boisterous, cheerful crowd who clearly expected hospitality as a right, but did not abuse it by stealing from their hosts, and contributed as much as they ate by way of large fish speared in the river and other game. Their presence did however undoubtedly make a lot of extra work for the two young Paulista wives. The only article worn by all the men was a thick woven cord of white cotton tied neatly round their necks, with the ends fluffed out. In the back was a feather or a piece of bark, stuck on with beeswax. Two of the Indians with whom we became friendly, admiring their bows and arrows, took off their cords and tied them round our necks, thereby, according to the Paulistas, making us

With the Xavante warriors at the Paulista farm near
the Rio dos Mortes in 1958.

Richard Mason with his Xavante brother.

Xavante and so less likely to be killed. We noticed they always wore the cords they had been given, as did we thereafter – and I have mine still.

Richard particularly enjoyed meeting these Indians and had a great gift of communication without any common language. The enthusiastic use of signs and an expression of deep interest in everything he examined, combined with a ready sense of humour, made him instantly popular. In the evening we all bathed together in the lagoon near the farm, splashing each other like children, fighting and rolling in the water. The mood could change instantly if something went wrong, probably because we were all a bit tense remembering, as undoubtedly the Xavante did too, what had happened two years before. If we gave one of our particular friends a fish-hook, for example, the others would all crowd round demanding one too, so that we would have to cause a diversion by perhaps trying to shoot an impossibly distant bird, as we had nowhere near enough hooks to give one to all the hundred or so Indians.

The Paulistas had not been able to check their cattle for some days and so one afternoon I drove one of them to look for the cattle in the jeep with about 20 Indians who climbed on at the last minute. Richard stayed with the other settler to guard the wives. On the way back, after dusk, we became stuck in a deep gully too far from the farm to walk back easily. Instead we all curled up in a tangled heap on the ground. A feeling of great security enveloped us and we had no sense of danger – two white men alone and unprotected in the jungle with wild Indians! Instead we were just people huddled together for warmth and very much united against the night spirits surrounding us.

At the farmstead the Indians also slept on the ground. Four lay in a row underneath the shelter of my hammock, slung on the verandah. When I looked over the side there would be a flash of white teeth as one of them grinned up at me. Their prowess with bow and arrow was impressive, shooting flying birds and moving fish with apparent ease. Their self-confidence and independence of spirit reminded me of the nomadic horsemen who played with me in Afghanistan.

Today no Xavante live nomadic lives, hunting freely for weeks on end.

---

on following pages

Richard Mason shaving in the wing mirror of the jeep at a campsite, Central Brazil, 1958.

Karaja Indian shamans dancing at the feast of Aruana on the island of Bananal in 1958. Traditional house in background.

Karaja Indians living in little boxes on Bananal in 1971 following contact by missionaries and government officials.

Caught by the rains on the Brazilian–Bolivian border.

All are settled in villages and practise agriculture. In spite of several massacres and constant abuse from those stealing their land, however, they have retained their spirit to a quite exceptional degree among Brazil's Indians. One of the reasons for this is that they are exceptionally good football players and in Brazil that excuses even being an Indian!

We had a hard time reaching Peru and many more adventures on the way. The rains caught us in Bolivia and we had to borrow oxen to tow the jeep the last stretch before the foothills of the Andes where roads began again. But in the end we made it just in time for me to fly back for my wedding, while Richard drove the long way round by Santiago and Buenos Aires to return a very battered jeep to its owners.

The jeep being towed out of the Bolivian swamps by
borrowed oxen.

On our return Sir Laurence Kirwan most generously acknowledged publicly that ours had been no mean feat. We were given one of the Royal Geographical Society's awards and our reputations as serious explorers were made.

I settled down to married life with Marika. We agreed that we did not want to live at the farm I had inherited from my mother when I reached the age of 21, a bleak and treeless piece of land on the coast of Norfolk. Instead we sold it and bought Maidenwell, a deep wooded valley with rough farm and eccentrically altered 14th-century farmhouse on the edge of Bodmin Moor in Cornwall. This became the very centre of our lives and into it we poured every penny we earned, turning it into a beautiful and original home for our children to grow up in. I forswore exploration for ever and fully intended never going on another expedition, a promise I was to keep for nearly four years.

Richard and John meanwhile, with the full support of the Royal Geographical Society this time, set off together on another great venture. This was a major joint expedition with Brazilian experts. I can well remember Richard, shortly after he, too, had arrived back in England from our first expedition, saying, 'Well, you and I know what we did wasn't all that difficult. On the other hand, if we had been able to get *there*, that would really have been something!' He pointed to an empty area in the very heart of Brazil round which we had been forced to detour in our jeep. Somewhere in that tangle of unexplored rivers lay the headwaters of the Iriri, one of the longest unexplored rivers in the world. It was their plan to discover the source and chart its entire length by canoe.

Tragically, Richard was to be ambushed by a previously unknown group of Indians and killed. His death caused a sensation in the European press, grieved the many people who loved him, and was a dreadful waste of a fine man. I can do no better than reproduce, with his permission, John Hemming's letter to Marika and me written just afterwards.

Cachimbo Air Base, September 9th 1961

Dear Robin and Marika,

I am still in the first stunning shock of Richard's death, trying to grasp the full reality and meaning of his going. As the turmoil of thoughts and memories about him begins to fall into shape, I realize what an enormous vacuum he has left for so many people.

During the past months Richard has been at his very finest – you have been on an expedition with him and know how all his courage and passionate determination comes to the forefront when he is grappling with physical difficulties and struggling towards a clear objective. I think much of his love of exploring came from his wish for a definite goal towards which he could devote all his extraordinary ability and strength of character. He certainly believed very strongly in the value of what we were doing, and I am sure that he was right. Had the expedition succeeded it would have been a great personal triumph for him, for Richard had conceived the idea and gone on to overcome every sort of obstacle to make it a reality. His leadership once we were in the jungle was really magnificent. He always carried more or worked longer or harder than anyone else, partly to fire our difficult group of men with some of his own enthusiasm, and to lead by example, and partly to give away some of his physical resources with his usual great generosity. He never let himself complain or indulge in any pettiness, despite the very hard conditions, but always tried to remain cheerful and encourage or praise others. As a result of these qualities and of his determination and strength of character, he succeeded in winning complete obedience from the group he was leading. But you know Richard as well as I did, so I will not try to list the many qualities and facets to his character – his intelligent enthusiasm about so many different subjects, his generosity, courage and infectious good spirits. During this trip we have experienced all these combined with a remarkable talent for leadership.

Richard's death was a wretched killing by a group of Indians, probably of the Kayapo tribe. He was walking alone along the 25 miles of *picada* that we had cut between Cachimbo air post and our camp on the Iriri. At a place where the path runs through a clearing and plunges back into the dark of the forest the Indians jumped out on him from behind. I am certain that he knew and felt nothing of what was happening. The Indians stole some of his possessions and left warclubs and arrows beside the body.

There had been no signs of Indians in this area and they had left no warning signals to show hostility. We had been in the area for many weeks and this familiarity bred a sense of false security. All the members of the expedition often walked alone, hunting or carrying, and many had passed this particular place on previous occasions. It was tragic fate that Richard should have been their victim.

We are now awaiting the arrival of a doctor to go in and carry Richard's body out.

The irony of it all is that everything was ready for the descent of the river, except for a parachute drop of more food which I was bringing from Rio de Janeiro. Richard had led the expedition through its most difficult part: the cutting overland, finding the river, carrying supplies forward, and making canoes. The success of his expedition was not so very far from realization.

Knowing how I feel at the mounting void left by Richard's death, I can try to sympathize with you both. I am enclosing some photos that I had developed while arranging the parachute drop in Rio. When I see you in England we can talk about him at length, but I cannot begin to put what I feel about him into words – we have all lost such an extraordinary person and such a wonderful friend. I will let you have more photos later.

Yours,
John

After his death the press, radio and television were obsessed with the story of a young Englishman being killed by Indians in the Amazon. It seems to be an idea which excites people, and yet it is not really so strange that Indians who have been hunted and massacred for centuries should occasionally retaliate. Oddly enough it never seems to have occurred to any of the many friends who mourned Richard to blame the Indians. Perhaps we all knew enough of history already to understand where the blame really lay.

Through examination of the clubs and arrows left by his body, other neighbouring Indians were able to identify the tribe they belonged to. This was the Kreen Akrore. Their name had never been heard by non-Indians before, but the tribes around knew of them and feared their fierce independence. None had ever been seen so far west, they said. For the next 14 years efforts were made repeatedly by Brazil's finest explorers and Indian experts, the Villas Boas brothers, to contact the Kreen Akrore. These efforts were intensified when it was learned that a road was planned to run through their territory. The British film-maker Adrian Cowell made an excellent movie about this work called *The Tribe that Hides from Man*. When at last they were successfully contacted, Brazilian politics removed the Villas Boas brothers from the scene, preventing them from ensuring that the Indians' health was taken care of at this critical moment of exposure to foreign diseases. Instead the Indians were left to the mercy of a corrupt functionary who sold the women as prostitutes to the road-workers. Eighteen months elapsed before anyone was able to expose this abuse and, by then, out of the 800 proud and healthy warriors and their families, only 35 wretched, weak, diseased survivors remained. They have since been moved to the Xingu National Park and their numbers are again increasing, but would anyone dare assert that their 'crime' in killing Richard Mason, which so preoccupied our press, has not been exceeded a hundredfold with barely a mention?

In 1965 I was approached by Sebastian Snow to go on another South American expedition. He had been part of a team who had discovered the true source of the Amazon a dozen years before and he had then rafted its entire length, acquiring subsequently a considerable reputation as an eccentric traveller. His idea now was to attempt to bisect the South American continent from north to south by river, another continental 'first'. As the sole survivor of the first land crossing from east to west I persuaded Marika that I could hardly refuse, especially as the necessary finance had been raised. Once again the distance involved was to be some 10,000 km and much of the route would be through uncharted territory.

We chose to go in an inflatable rubber dinghy powered by two outboard motors. It was an uncomfortable means of transport which required constant labour to keep it afloat and moving. Air leaking out had to be replaced with a foot pump. Water leaking in through the floor had to be removed over the side with a hand pump, while the two engines had to be manipulated to steer the craft, the driver sitting on the edge and permanently soaked with spray. It was like operating a one-man band, only with no audience.

We set out from the mouth of the Orinoco, a huge river where our little orange craft was thrown about by great waves like a cork. 1,500 km upstream, after negotiating rapids and shallows, but at last on calmer water, we were able to turn into a sidestream which, incredibly, runs out of the main river to wind up eventually as a tributary of the Amazon. This

Sebastian Snow in our inflatable rubber dinghy on the
Orinoco in 1965.

is the unique Casiquiare Canal, which links two great river systems,
effectively running over the watershed to do so.

Sometimes we employed a guide to take us through the rapids or to
avoid getting lost in the complicated networks of islands which broke up
the major rivers. One such guide was Manolo El Tucuman, a tiny old
Indian who sat hunched in the bows for several days, soaked with rain and
spray as he guided me through the São Gabriel rapids at Uapes and on
down the Rio Negro; Sebastian, unable to move, his head splitting with
the pain from a sickness which destroyed his sense of balance, lay
groaning in the stern. Between were heaped our few possessions: hammocks, cooking gear, tools, camera equipment and the two 50-gallon
rubber petrol tanks which gave us a range of 800 km.

After three weeks Sebastian was clearly too ill to continue and had to fly
home from Manaus. I went on alone, going slightly crazy myself, as I slept
out night after night alone in my hammock on the riverbank, miles from
any other human and surrounded by the terrifying sounds of the jungle.
Every daylight hour I drove at high speed along the endless corrugated
routes of wave-tossed twisting rivers, singing to myself at the top of my
voice and terrified that at any moment I would strike a hidden snag,
puncture and sink without trace. My ability to endure solitude was honed

to a fine degree during the next three months as I headed south for Buenos Aires.

Round some formidable and impassable rapids on the Rio Madeira south of the Amazon, I had to have the boat deflated and carried on an old steam railway line. For two days the passengers were subjected to constant incineration from flying sparks which settled on their clothes, burning black holes. I persuaded the driver to let me travel in the cab where I helped fill the boiler with logs, keeping a gun ready against much-discussed attacks by Indians or jaguars. What I would have done if Indians had attacked the train I do not know, but we saw none and the journey passed peacefully.

Along the Bolivian border I was negotiating ever smaller waterways where I was assured by the occasional rubber gatherer I met that the danger from attack by uncontacted Indians was very real. Where possible I slept on islands in the stream, tired enough to sleep well after a day of intense concentration and physical labour driving the boat, but starting awake with every crash or footstep. Usually these proved to be falling branches or lizards scrabbling in dry leaves, but the tension was always there.

After a short portage between the headwaters of tributaries of the Amazon and Paraguay rivers I was on the last downhill stretch to the South Atlantic. During the years after Richard was killed I had a recurrent dream in which he turned up with some far-fetched story about the adventures he had been having while we all thought him dead. Something in my subconscious persistently refused to accept that he had gone. Now, as I approached the point at which I was to cross the route of our transcontinental journey, I half-believed that he might appear.

The small ferry we had used to carry the jeep across the Paraguay river south of Caceres was in midstream as I arrived. Once again there was a jeep on it, but this time the passengers were two very attractive girls with their mother. I was an unusual sight as I cruised alongside in my battered little rubber boat with the Union Jack on the bows, and they invited me to have a picnic with them on the bank. They were returning home from college and were fascinated by my tall stories of my adventures so that we had a very jolly time, but there was a sense of unreality to the scene. Richard would have enjoyed it immensely and I felt his presence. When I mentioned his name while describing our previous journey one of the girls said, 'Oh yes, Richard Mason. I have heard of him. He lives down in the Pantanal swamps and makes his living hunting jaguars!'

I had to hurry on and the mystery remained unsolved until I learned that there was indeed *another* Richard Mason, a young Englishman who, after serving as a mercenary in Angola, had gone to Brazil where he led hunting safaris. Years later I met his mother in Cornwall and she confirmed his existence, but I have never met him. To compound the coincidence even further, I did on another occasion meet the bestselling author of the same name and spent an evening drinking with him. Not surprisingly, perhaps, the Richard Mason who was my friend still sometimes appears in my dreams.

Apart from the constant dangers of breakdown, sickness or sinking, there were a few occasions on that journey when I was very frightened. Nights alone in the jungle represented a special and rather enjoyable kind of fear, but when the discomfort and loneliness built up to almost unbearable proportions, I did long for it all to be over. Once it rained so hard all night that everything I possessed, except for the film and cameras in their sealed container, became soaked. Too cold and wet to sleep, I spent the whole night wading in my bathing suit up and down the muddy bank trying to stop the flooding river from sweeping my camp away.

Mostly those I met along the rivers were charming to me, fascinated by what they saw as my excessively eccentric behaviour in wishing to travel alone and so far. They feasted and fêted me generously as they examined my unfamiliar craft and possessions, and never stole a thing from me. When asked where I came from I used to say at first 'the moon', and indeed my odd bulbous orange dinghy must have looked to them as though it had dropped out of space. Everyone enjoyed the joke and I learned again that no matter how remote and strange the community, people tend to find the same things funny and respond to the same overtures of friendship. Some of these lonely river settlements were visited by outsiders no more than once or twice a year. Their populations were *mestizo*, people who were a mixture of Indian from long-vanished tribes, black from the descendants of escaped slaves and white from frontiersmen, trappers and prospectors. Less friendly were some of the cowboys I began to meet as I approached the Brazilian border with Paraguay. They watched me greedily from the bank as I passed and I felt that it would not be wise to linger.

However, I was also hesitant about continuing, as ahead I faced the very real danger and embarrassment of imprisonment and the confiscation of all my possessions. The difficulty lay in the fact that I had no proper papers entitling me to drive a boat alone through Brazil. I had entered the country illegally across the Venezuelan border without any problem and had only found out later that I should strictly have had a Brazilian 'pilot' on board and a mass of documentation to explain my business. On the lonely waterways I had been following this had been no problem but there was only one way out of Brazil by river and that was heavily guarded. Being where Brazil, Paraguay and Bolivia meet, it was a region best known for the amount of smuggling practised there. Travellers who could not explain their presence satisfactorily tended to get shot. My informants along the riverbank, all of whom were eager to help with advice as to how to hoodwink the authorities, told me that it would be no good giving myself up and trying to sort the thing out as the authorities were all corrupt and would certainly steal everything I had unless I paid huge bribes. I was already outside the law and the answer was to stay there.

As I meandered through the hot, shadeless maze of the great Pantanal swamps, bitten by mosquitoes and tortured by anxiety about what I should do, I heartily wished that it was all over and that I was back at home. I missed Marika and Maidenwell, clean sheets and cool country air, hot baths, regular mail, newspapers every day, and company. I seem to spend a good deal of my time on expeditions thinking about these things, but never more desperately than then. It all seemed very pointless at that stage and I would gladly have given up if I could. What I distinctly remember fearing most was the shame and inconvenience I would cause if the British Embassy had to become involved and bail me out. I felt desperately tired after several sleepless nights.

Still, as there was no other way out, I ploughed on towards my nemesis, gathering every scrap of information I could along the way about the various hurdles I would have to overcome if I was to escape with my life. With both the outboard motors at full power I could plane the boat at high speed, though absolute concentration was required to avoid snags which could puncture the inflatable hull. In the heart of the swamp I fell asleep and the boat crashed into an island of tangled roots and vegetation, ending up on its side, the contents spilling out and the engines roaring in the air. For the rest of the day, too shattered to care about piranha or crocodiles, I waded about waist-deep in the weeds rescuing everything and repacking the boat. Miraculously, nothing was too badly damaged, though there were fresh leaks and the tempo of my one-man band had to be increased as I pumped wearily to keep afloat and inflated.

I crossed my Rubicon at Corumba, the main frontier town where the customs and immigration people never saw my passport and non-existent documents as I glided past the waterfront using only one motor. Everyone seemed to be drunk and I suddenly realized it was Saturday night. The whole town was *en fête*, music blared over public address systems, I glimpsed dancing through the brightly lit doors of bars and no one stopped or hailed me. Next came the Brazilian Naval Station at Ladario where I was again ignored and around midnight the final customs post at Pôrto Esperança, where I passed under the bridge carrying the railway which crosses Brazil – the first bridge since leaving the Orinoco. The customs were asleep.

So far so good, but the final hurdle was much the worst and still lay ahead. The border itself, at the point where the river passed between two hills, was guarded by a fort where guards patrolled all night with searchlights to ensure that no one got through, neither smugglers nor invaders from Paraguay downstream. I planned to cover my boat in weed and drift past pretending to be an island of floating water-hyacinth, but the whole plan seemed to me less and less likely to succeed with every hour that passed.

All night I drifted towards my doom, not daring to use the motors for fear of alerting the military to my presence, straining my eyes to see ahead, until at dawn I pulled in behind an island just short of the fort and hid the boat under a mound of rotting vegetation. For the long hot day that followed I lay in my hammock sweating, worrying and very frightened. It was almost a relief when at dusk a patrol boat with three heavily armed soldiers on board cruised past and spotted me preparing my craft for the escape run. They tramped ashore covering me with their machine-guns. I welcomed them with a broad smile, offered them coffee and explained that I was a British explorer who had come all the way from Venezuela.

At first they refused to believe me, in particular expressing amazement that anyone should even consider travelling alone and camping on an island that was well-known to be infested with snakes and jaguars. The nonchalance I affected impressed them and instead of being clapped in irons I was taken back to the fort as a sort of hero to be shown off in the officers' mess after dinner. I managed, whenever the issue of permits and papers was raised, to change the subject and they were too polite and too interested in my journey to press the point. They even gave me a generous supply of petrol and gathered on the ramparts of the fort to wave me goodbye. Believing that at any moment they would realize that no one had seen my papers and come after me, I drove as fast as I could into Paraguay and flung myself into the arms of the Capitan of the Port at Bahia Negra, the border post, explaining that the Brazilians were after me. Nothing could have been better calculated to endear me to the Paraguayans and he assured me that I was now quite safe.

I finally reached Buenos Aires to find that my prolonged absence had caused diplomats and journalists to worry about my safety. Press conferences were arranged and I was made much of briefly on television and in the papers, dubbed El Intrepido and recognized everywhere I went. It was February 1965; Sir Winston Churchill had just died aged 90 and the British were enjoying a period of exaggerated popularity. A hero was just what was needed. The Argentinians were also enthusiastic about the implications of being linked directly by river with Venezuela.

Later that year I was invited to lunch with the Queen at Buckingham

Palace. Prince Philip, on whose left I was sitting, grilled me penetratingly on the economic implications of the river route I had pioneered. This was not an aspect to which I had given much thought and I felt myself floundering. Then I had an idea.

'Of course, Sir,' I replied, 'since many stretches of the river were only a few inches deep due to sandbanks and rapids, the perfect craft for opening up the interior of South America would be one of these new Hovercraft I've just been reading about.'

He turned to the man on his right, whom I had not yet met, and said, 'Mr Cockerell, there's a young man here with a good idea. You should give him one of your machines!'

Mr Cockerell (later Sir Christopher Cockerell), the inventor of the Hovercraft, was not amused, but from that conversation a series of strange expeditions were later to take place which were to introduce me for the first time to group travel.

Although I can hardly take the blame for the disastrous effects, in both human and ecological terms, of the massive Brazilian trans-Amazon road programme, it is rather ironic that my first South American expedition should have pioneered the first major penetration and traverse of the area by vehicle, while the second pointed, almost by accident, to a development policy, using the existing rivers, which could have been much cheaper and less harmful than the destruction which has followed in the wake of the roads. Unfortunately the idea came too late and would probably never have been adopted anyway as it provided far fewer opportunities for entrepreneurs to cash in on 'opening up the west'. Nevertheless, I have always felt that, apart from introducing me to the little-known interior of South America in a unique way, those two trans-continental journeys gave me a special and very personal insight into how development might still be planned better.

4

The Mark of Nomadism

The mark of nomadism, that most deep and biting social discipline. . .

T. E. Lawrence, *The Seven Pillars of Wisdom*

Desert and desert peoples have always attracted me. The glimpses I had had of hard, dry places and the hard, tough people who lived in them on my early travels had made me want to return. During the 1960s, once the myth that I would settle down exploded, I made several long and usually solitary journeys across parts of the Sahara. All I needed was an excuse and this I found in the search for rock art in the almost unexplored mountain ranges far to the south.

Deep in the heart of the Sahara, a thousand miles from rivers or greenery, is an oasis called Djanet, which means paradise. Above it towers a craggy, mountainous plateau, the Tassili N'Ajjer, among the dry gorges and cliffs of which the largest collection of prehistoric paintings in the world lay forgotten for thousands of years. These were discovered and recorded by Henri Lhote, the great French archaeologist during the late 1950s, and he revealed them to the world in a series of exhibitions and books. Believing that they would not reproduce on film he had taken with him artists who, struggling with high winds and sharp rocks, traced and coloured the innumerable designs and animals on sheets of paper. The results were sensational, showing that a succession of cultures must have occupied this now almost totally arid region which was then fertile and even at times lush. Great herds of domesticated cattle were cared for by nomadic pastoralists. Hunters with bows and arrows pursued long-vanished animals, elephants, giraffes and hippopotami. An unknown race daubed giant white figures with round heads and fish-like bodies.

The paintings were described as 'the most unexpected art find of the century'.

A young French photographer Jean-Dominique Lajoux, who had accompanied Lhote's expedition, returned alone and proved that the paintings could be photographed. I was so captivated by the illustrations in the book (*Merveilles du Tassili N'Ajjer*, Editions du Chêne, 1960) that I planned to go there and make a short film on the subject. During the Algerian troubles travel in the southern deserts became impossible, but immediately after Independence, and although the country was still unsettled and foreigners suspect, I decided to try my luck.

August was the only month I could get away that year and so although I was warned that it would be hot then – indeed the highest shade temperature in the world, 136.4 Fahrenheit (58 Centigrade), had been recorded not far from Djanet – I felt that if I were to experience the Sahara fully I might as well go at the worst time.

The young man I called on at the British Embassy had just returned from the desert and assured me that it was best avoided.

'I've just brought in the remains of a dead Englishman and it was not a pleasant job,' he said.

'Oh dear, poor chap. . .' I began.

'You don't understand,' he interrupted. 'He'd been dead about thirty years. Crashed his plane trying to fly across the Sahara. They only spotted the wreck a week or so ago. Hellish place to get to. Ruined the Embassy Land-Rover. Actually, it's all a bit of a nuisance. You see, nothing decays in the desert so there were all his papers and things in a satchel on the seat beside him. The trouble is the letters tell a strange story and I'm not sure what we ought to do about it. There are several to a lady who was clearly not his wife saying that when he arrived home he was going to get a divorce and marry her. Might cause a bit of an upset if we sent them to the widow – she'll be quite an old lady by now anyway – on the other hand I can't very well just tear them up. Nasty business.'

The authorities in Algiers told me that I was quite mad to want to go to Djanet.

'The fort is abandoned, the French have left, no lorry will go there before the winter, if then; there are no more planes, there is no one there.'

'But surely,' I replied, 'the Tuareg are still there?'

'Who knows?' answered my informant. 'Anyway, they do nothing at this time of year but sit and wait for it to get cooler. If you should arrive there you will die! Besides, Algeria is very dangerous at the moment. Armed bands of robbers wander the countryside plundering and killing. Why not come back next year when things may be quieter?'

'Where is the nearest point I can reach to Djanet?'

'Well, there's a new oilfield at In Amenas, about 1,000 km to the north, but what will you do if you reach there?'

I muttered something about reaching paradise requiring an act of faith and hurried round to the oil company office.

The oil company plane slipped through a narrow pass in the Atlas Mountains, leaving the rain clouds and fertile valleys behind. We emerged into metallic sunshine over arid land where rocky slopes seamed by dried-up river-beds zigzagged down towards the desert. Gradually the terrain levelled out and the parched, twisting rivers became like the innumerable fingers of a giant hand clawing out into the encroaching sand. It reminded me of stories I had been told of the last movements made by a man dying of thirst. He will crawl a final yard and then lie still. Only his hands will for a while continue to scrabble at the ground.

Then came the sand rippling in a bowl of space, the plane a dot above a vast, yellow, circular world until the sun set. Four hours later the orange flares of burning gas broke the blackness and we landed at In Amenas.

By one of those impossible-to-plan coincidences which lift travel from the mundane to the sublime, the Sous-Préfet of Djanet was there and left in his Land-Rover the morning after my arrival. He had been on his annual two-day visit to the oil town. No other vehicle had travelled the route for the previous six months and none would for at least another three. I went with him.

After three days bumping across rock and sand, Djanet in the dawn was indeed paradise. The sun rising behind the old white fort high above the oasis and glancing off the jagged black peaks of the Tassili N'Ajjer beyond transformed the landscape into a fairytale backcloth, complete with Beau Geste fort and romantic scenery. The palm trees and gardens below made the valley cool and welcoming.

The Sous-Préfet, an Algerian from the north, suggested that I make my home in the fort since it was empty and abandoned and, as he put it, 'Il n'y a rien ici dans le village.' He was right, there being no shop or café. I took my meals with him, climbing up through the darkness afterwards, away from the Tuareg night noises, to the utter silence of my thick-walled fortress where I would prowl the courtyards and terraces by moonlight, equally fearful of treading barefoot on a scorpion or horned viper as of meeting the shade of a murdered legionnaire.

Djanet was like a small port at the mouth of a great river. A sweep of green palm trees ran along the bottom of a narrow valley before debouching on to a great flat sea of orange sand. The square mud houses of the Tuareg clustered on the hillside above the few solid stone administration buildings left by the French which enclosed three sides of a square like harbour walls. The rock paintings lay 'inland' behind the sheer 600-metre cliffs guarding the Tassili plateau. There were four passes into the mountains, all steep and difficult. A meeting was called to discuss my plans. It was presided over by the young chief of the Ajjer Tuareg whose father had led the last pitched battle against the French in 1926. He was dressed in spotless white robes which left only a narrow slit for his eyes between turban and veil. He sat very still watching me closely, his hand on the red leather scabbard of a long straight sword. Around him squatted three old men wearing the more familiar indigo turbans of the Tuareg. It is the dye from these which, rubbing off on the skin, gave these people the name of the blue men of the desert. The old men were experts on travel in the mountains and they were unanimous in their opposition to my going there. The Sous-Préfet and I sat facing them and he translated for me from French into Tamashek, the Tuareg language.

'The Akba Tafelalet [the direct route] is too steep for camels.'

'Then I will go to the north by the Akba Assakao.'

'The camels are weak at this time of the year. It has been a long drought and they have no fat.'

'Then I will go on foot.'

'No man will accompany you without a pack animal to carry water.'

'Then I will go alone.'

After several hours of this the chief spoke for the first time.

'He says he will give you two camels and two men,' the Sous-Préfet translated. 'He also says that he does not think you will survive the journey and he does not wish to be held responsible. For that matter nor do I!'

I agreed to leave a letter behind exonerating them from all blame if anything should go wrong. I asked about payment.

'The chief says he will accept no money. If you are satisfied with his men you may give him something for them on your return. But you must not pay them before or they will rob and abandon you. What will you do for food?'

'I shall eat what they eat.'

'But how can you live on their food? They are very poor and eat next to nothing. I am told there is no water up there and if you run out you may have to go for days without any. A Tuareg can live for nine days on three dates after his water has gone. He eats the skin one day, the flesh the next and sucks the stone on the third. On the tenth day he dies. Could you live so long?'

'I very much doubt it but I intend to live as nearly as possible as they do. It will be interesting to see how I get on.'

At last everything was arranged. Since I wanted to traverse as much of the plateau as possible it was agreed that the Land-Rover would rendezvous with us in three weeks' time at the foot of the southernmost pass, the Akba Adjefane, some sixty miles south of Djanet so that I should be spared the long return journey across the desert.

My first *'ascension du chameau'* was an inelegant and chastening experience which took place in front of a small crowd who had come to witness our departure. When I admitted that, although I had ridden horses of all sizes almost from birth, this was to be my first encounter with a camel, I was beset with advice from all sides. One of our animals was laden with goat-skins bulging with water, a small sack of provisions and our bedding rolls. The other squatted on the ground, a magnificent throne-like saddle on its back and a supercilious expression on its face. I approached and climbed on board, at which it gave a blood-curdling roar and everyone began to shout and gesticulate pointing at my feet. I gathered that I was supposed to remove my shoes which, having climbed off, I did before remounting and having my bare feet placed correctly at the base of the neck in a semi-prehensile position. I grasped the cross on the front of the saddle which was made of wood bound in tooled leather and looked like the handlebars on a bicycle. Once again a chorus of protest broke out and I understood that this was against the rules as the cross was purely ornamental, being fragile and likely to break. Wholly unnerved I allowed my hands to be placed for me. The right one held a single leather rein which passed under the camel's neck and was attached to a ring in its nearside nostril. The left one grasped the back of the saddle below the base of my spine. Everyone clicked and hissed at which the camel began to rise. I was totally unprepared for the extraordinary series of jerks which ensued as an apparently random selection of joints were straightened, throwing me forward and backward at irregular intervals while the ground dropped several yards below.

I had handed my cine camera to the Sous-Préfet so that the incident could be recorded for posterity, but he was laughing so much that he forgot to press the button. The young chief stood aloof and gave off an aura of not being impressed.

Later I came to enjoy riding camels although during this particular journey we covered most of the ground on foot, using our single mount in turn only when we were tired. It had seemed important to me that I should leave in style, mounted on my status symbol. Instead my dignity was badly impaired and I was concerned that I had not yet earned the respect of my two companions. Muhammad, the guide, was almost blind and seldom spoke. He claimed to be seventy but was said to know his way through the Tassili. Hamouk by contrast was young and cheekily voluble. He showed a distressing tendency to laugh at me and so when, after we had gone a few miles, he asked me my name, I decided on the spur of the moment to tell him that it was 'Sir'. Clearly deducing that such a short name must be a familiar form of address he lost no opportunity in using it which gave me much quiet satisfaction as well as preserving my anonymity should any other Englishman pass that way in the future.

In the evening Hamouk baked rock-hard bread in the ashes of the fire and made a millet stew. At first we had some camel meat and onions to mix with this, but in time only our sack of dates was left. Water, however, was our main concern. Gradually the goat-skins shrank. Through transpiration the contents keep cool, but there is a constant small seepage. We drank astonishingly little, surviving on thimblefuls of hot mint tea three times a day and perhaps a pint of water in addition. The goat-skins were freshly made so that the water tasted strongly of goat and was stained from the lingering shreds of meat. This helped to reduce its palatability but even without that I found less effort needed to control my thirst than I had expected. Of course I dreamt of ice-cold beer and longed to plunge into a cool, clear stream when the midday heat was at its worst but by and large I found myself more frustrated by the apparently interminable distances we covered when range after range of rocky hills succeeded each other without our arriving at our next objective. Muhammad's sole unit of measurement was 'a day's journey' so that I could never comfort myself with the thought of only a few more hours.

At night we lay and watched the stars until the moon rose. They stretched in an unbroken kaleidoscopic pattern from horizon to horizon. Once, when I saw one moving slowly in an erratic course across the sky, I asked Hamouk what it was.

'I don't know,' he replied. 'It is something new. I have seen it also over Djanet.'

Of course, it was a satellite and the irregularity was accounted for by the heat refraction of the earth's surface. I found it distasteful that even there in the remotest of all possible places in the world there should be evidence of modern man's tampering with the nocturnal order of things. Untold millions of people who have gazed for years up at a familiar night sky must have been disturbed by this incomprehensible intrusion.

By morning the camels had always disappeared. We turned them loose at night so that they could forage on the occasional spike of dry grass or thorns. Since these were few and far between we often had to walk several miles before we found them. During the heat of the day the desert appeared quite lifeless, but at this hour before the sun came over the horizon, when all wild animals seemed to be at their least watchful, I was surprised by the amount of activity I came upon. Fat, round hyraxes popped up to stare at me, whistle, and vanish into their holes. Lizards glided a few yards as though running on rails before stopping to stare malevolently over their shoulders. A black and white bird like a diminutive magpie, common all over the Sahara, hopped inquisitively from rock to rock beside me, while another shyer and plainer little bird sang sweetly from a distance. Once I surprised a ridiculous Alice in Wonderland hare with head and ears far too large for its body. It looked at me with such a horrified, incredulous expression that I burst out laughing in the silence and it hopped away apologetically as though it had just remembered a previous engagement. Gazelles were always shy and nervous and to my regret I never saw one of the few moufflon which are said to survive in the Tassili. Shaggy wild sheep with distinctive long beards and magnificent curved horns which reach back over their heads, tapering from a very thick base to sharp points, they are almost the only living link we have with the prehistoric people who inhabited the region. They, too, must have found them as beautiful and fascinating as we do today, for paintings and engravings of their horns are found in large numbers.

We were able to replenish our goat-skins once after a few days from a well, but thereafter we found no more water. A day came when, down to our last few pints, Hamouk and Muhammad awoke looking very grave and said that I should search diligently for water as well as for the camels during our morning stroll. Leaving them to follow the most likely directions for the camels to have gone I set off into some tall rocks where I hoped to come across more paintings. As it happened, after half an hour or so I stumbled across a guelta, a small pocket of water left over from the very infrequent rains which every year or so reach the high plateau. But instead of running back rejoicing with the good news I sat for a while looking at my find and thinking. I'm not normally squeamish about what I drink and have never taken precautions with water from Amazonian rivers, African lakes or Oriental ponds, working on the theory, which has never so far let me down, that building up my own resistance to disease is a better safeguard than any artificial protection. But this little pool struck me as going beyond the pale of sanity. About a yard across and eighteen inches deep it lay in a rough trough in the solid rock at the base of a deep cleft. It was all too apparent that a great many camels and wild animals had visited it during the months or years since the water had been fresh. Now it was dark brown and stinking, the distillation of endless days of hot sun evaporating what had once been a sizeable pond to leave behind a shallow murky sediment in which nameless objects floated. I could smell it from where I sat.

Returning to our camp I found the two men and camels waiting. They asked if I had found water. I denied it, mentally justifying the lie on the grounds that no sane man would call what I had found water. But

Muhammad insisted that he had heard of water there and that we should have another look. Inevitably they found it and I had a short reprieve when it seemed that only the camels were to be watered. They were led as close as possible, their spindly legs slipping on the bare rock and straddled wide as they reached down. Our one bowl, in which we cooked, and in which our remaining millet was stored wrapped in a cloth, was dipped into the *soi-disant* water and held up while in turn they noisily slobbered and sucked it out. After a time they were pushed protesting back and the goat-skins were filled one by one. Occasionally a lump of camel dung was removed from the bowl, not, I felt, so much for hygiene's sake as so that it should not block the narrow neck and so cause some of the water to spill. I tried to save the one remaining skin with some old water in it but was chided for my incomprehensible fastidiousness and that one too was filled. Once its origins were forgotten the water tasted fine, did us no harm and in fact almost certainly saved our lives since we found no more.

The ostensible reason for my journeying was to look at the paintings. My memories of them are personal rather than instructive and while I am glad I had the opportunity to see the pictures in their natural state before others came and washed them away so that they are, I believe, today almost gone, I have nothing to add to the speculation about their antiquity and origins. Some are said to have been painted as long ago as 10,000 BC and the giant round-headed men are attributed variously to artists who were bushmen, spacemen, Romans or Nubians. I only know that they were artists. Certainly successive waves of people occupied the once-fertile plains of the Central Sahara, travelling first in pursuit of the vast herds of game which must have wandered there, then bringing fat, healthy dappled cattle with large udders and curving horns which, from the affection with which they were drawn, must have been cared for deeply. Many of these peoples come from untraceable origins and vanished in time leaving no other record than these pictures behind. Others may have moved on, as the desert dried out, to evolve as the Peuls and Fulani of the Sahel who still herd cattle, and the few remaining Bushmen far to the south who still hunt in the same way today as those seen on the rock walls of the Tassili did thousands of years ago.

Many of the paintings were of a sensational beauty and I am grateful to those distant artists for having painted them. The first I saw and the one I will remember best was at a jumble of rock called Tin Tekelt. I had been staring at a likely-looking cliff, frustrated at knowing that somewhere near were pictures, since Lajoux's map said so, but unable to make out anything among the natural stains and colours of the rocks. Suddenly there was my giraffe, about nine inches high where I had been looking for something larger, yellow and ochre where I had been expecting red, invisible until I saw him, then clear as if framed alone on the wall of an art gallery. He stood on long slender legs, his graceful neck stretched out in an elegant curve as though he were about to pick a succulent leaf off a high branch. Once I had seen him I became aware of others all around. Now that my eyes were focused properly, cattle, people, wild animals leapt from the rock on all sides. Day after day from then on I reached new sites, many undoubtedly already recorded, some perhaps unseen for millennia, but I never found another which moved me as much as my first giraffe. For me he will always be the most beautiful painting in the plateau.

We reached the base of the Akba Adjefane on the appointed day. Our camels' feet were bleeding and we were all exhausted. We collapsed on the unfamiliar soft sand of the Admer Erg and wondered whether we could make it back to Djanet if the Land-Rover failed to arrive. At dusk, when hope was almost gone we heard a motor and, trailing a cloud of dust, it sped towards us. Out of it leapt a white-robed figure which ran with great strides across the sand towards us. Swooping down like a bird of prey the chief of all the Ajjer Tuareg embraced me in his arms before shaking me repeatedly by the hand and congratulating me on my safe return. I realized that he must have been worried.

The Sahara is full of unexpected pleasures. The hardness of existence in the desert, the loneliness of space and distance, the solitude and silence make the relief of momentary comfort, a rare full belly, unexpected encounters, into pleasures whose enjoyment is sharply accentuated.

Later, with John Hemming, I crossed the Libyan desert, riding high on an Arab lorry. This was the route used by General Leclerc to bring his forces from Chad to Tripoli in 1943. We explored the harsh Tibesti mountains together finding innumerable rock carvings and gazing down into the Trou au Natron, the most spectacular volcanic crater in the world.

Another time I tried to reach the western Adrar des Iforas mountains from Timbuktu and Gao in Mali, sailing along the Niger river but was prevented from entering the desert where the Tuareg were in conflict with the authorities.

It was more peaceful in Niger, and the camels in the Aïr were said to be the best in the Sahara, the most highly prized being white. The *chef du poste* of Iférouane lent me his white camel and at last I felt the freedom of fast, smooth travel in the desert. By day there are heat and dust, sweat and flies to mar the enjoyment, but at night I know of no feeling to match it: the clear, fresh air of the desert mountains and the silence and peace all around. No people and no noise for mile after mile, just the soft scrunch of the camels' cushion-like feet and the stars overhead. Riding fast along a

Riding high on an Arab lorry across the Libyan desert in 1964.

dark wadi with the scrubby thorn trees and acacias big and black on either side, the sand of the long-dead river-bed swishing below felt like being in a boat on a long, dark river, a swift canoe, gliding and undulating over rapids.

But making camp was so much easier than from a boat. No clearing of a space on the bank; no deciding what to unload from the inevitable superfluity of clutter on any motorized transport. The camels had to be unloaded anyway and their saddles and saddlebags made the shelter of the camp. A fire from tinder-dry sticks boiled the black pot of millet and goat stew, followed by liqueur glasses of sweet mint tea as my Tuareg companion and I gazed into the flames, at peace. Gradually my face, scorched by the sun during the day, began to burn from the heat of the fire while my feet began to freeze as the temperature dropped sharply. I crawled into my down sleeping bag, sole concession to comfort and always in use as a saddle cushion, mat or bed. A flash of light like a hurried glow-worm travelled along the metal zip from the static electricity when I pulled it up and I lay on my back and watched the stars.

No words can describe the peace of desert nights. A familiar atavistic unity with space, a return to the time when man was part not only of the universe but also of nature, evolving with all other kinds of life, in competition and yet still in harmony with them. Today we are separate and different, frightened and superior, driven at all times to keep up our guards and standards lest we should slip back to the level of animals again. But in the desert, at night, the peace and contentment which steal over you remove the problems of life or at least cut them down to size so that you feel complete and alive. I am making no demands on the world and, for a while, it is making none on me. The feeling is so good that I found myself once again believing that if only the harassed statesmen of the world could spend a little time like this occasionally, they would find their problems a lot easier to resolve. That, I was beginning to realize, was why I had come to the desert. The pictures were only an excuse.

Arambé was an old soldier, an ex-*goumier* who had served for a time under the French. Tall, upright and, to judge from the respect with which he was treated and the deliberation of his movements, quite elderly. I never saw his face properly. He ate turned away from me, passing his food under the lower half of his veil. Occasionally, he smoked a cigarette in the same way. Later I was to glimpse a fine, aquiline nose and a leathery, scarred face.

He carried a rifle, rusty and antique, his proudest possession and never far from his hand. The single round of ammunition which circumstances and the *chef du poste* allowed him did nothing to reduce the status which this weapon gave us. As a Tuareg he knew camels, the desert and the occasional nomad we met. He was doing what his people had always done and if I wanted to follow a peculiar route and keep stopping to scramble among the rocks looking for prehistoric pictures, that was fine. As an ex-*goumier* he could match my halting Tamashek with a few words of French, while as an old soldier he had come to accept the strange ways of Europeans and did not allow taking care of them to become too onerous. I wanted neither servant nor intimate friend and Arambé was a good companion.

We came to a well called Tedekelt where a woman and her daughters were drawing water for their herd of goats. The well was in the bed of a wadi, about five metres deep and reinforced round the base with some pieces of wood. With no other water for many miles around, I was most struck by the orderly behaviour of the goats. They stood gathered tightly together, affecting an aloof lack of interest as the two girls filled a wooden trough and led up two or three at a time to drink. Gracefully the elder girl, a mature beauty of sixteen or so, swung out the goat-skin bucket, cleverly designed with a wooden frame round it, so that it sank and filled instantly. Without a pause she leant out over the well and began to haul it up again.

Watering goats at the well called Tedekelt in the Aïr
Mountains in Northern Niger, 1966.

Her younger sister, lithe and coquettish with sparkling eyes and an enchanting smile, brought us water and dates as we settled in a patch of shade to rest and watch.

The men of the family were away, as is normal with the Tuareg, conducting the serious business of trade, travel and tribal diplomacy. With the progressive introduction of heavy trucks to replace the old camel caravans, the decline in the trade routes across the Sahara, the abolition of slavery and the suppression of fighting, such manly pursuits were becoming harder to justify.

The pretty Tuareg girl who gave us
water and dates at the well.

The terrible Sahel drought has made survival more and more difficult each year so that many Tuareg have died or been forced to become refugees in the camps on the edge of the desert. But when I was with them, in 1966, life was still supportable and the bright joy and laughter of that small family of women gave no hint of the starvation and degradation which have almost certainly befallen them since.

Their camp was close by and Arambé persuaded me that we should stop and take it easy for once. The chance of fresh meat and milk was too good to miss and so we hobbled the camels and turned them loose. That night we feasted on bowls of sour goat's milk; maize meal; a leg of kid grilled over charcoal, and passed from hand to hand; finally, sweet mint tea close to the fire as the night became colder and the mother and grandmother came to talk: the refreshing courtesy of people who made no demands on me as a stranger. If I chose to try out my few words of Tamashek or attempted to extend my vocabulary, they helped me politely. When I stretched out to write by the firelight, they carried on their conversation without embarrassment.

The night was less peaceful and pleasant. The goats, corralled in a solid smelly mass behind a thick thorn hedge beside us, made various disturbing noises ranging from hysterical bleats to sudden explosive farts. The dogs set up a chorus of barking when the moon rose, and Arambé's camel felt lonely and tried to join us. In the icy cold half-light of the false dawn I watched the younger girl milk one of the camels into a wooden bowl. Then, picking up a burning log from their fire, she carried it over and lit ours from it, leaving the milk beside us. It tasted just like a camel smells, but was warm and frothy and stimulating.

Such luxury was, however, rare. On our own, we often started before dawn so as to cover as much ground as possible before the heat. Wrapped in a blanket with only my bare feet cold on the camel's neck, I left Arambé behind so as to have a better chance of coming on wildlife unexpectedly. The camels jogged along at a steady trot, making almost no sound except for an occasional snuffle when a fly landed on the nose of one of them and it would shake its head up and down, blowing out its flews to dislodge it. This was the best time of day to see gazelles, fragile and afraid in the vastness of rocks and sand; ostriches, so big and clumsy by comparison, pacing off in a scatter pattern to confuse pursuit; a troop of long-tailed monkeys, the females clutching babies to their chests as they ran off on all fours over the rocks, while the males stayed behind guarding their retreat; once, in the half light, a jackal.

Henri Lhote says of the rock drawings of the Aïr Mountains, 'they reveal a certain decadence'. Certainly I saw nothing to compare with the beauty of the paintings and drawings of the Tassili N'Ajjer nor with the tableaux of energetic battle scenes and hunters in the high Tibesti. But at a pile of broken rocks called Djangeran and near a mountain called Arrarhous, by the wadi Taroué and at other nameless sites, I saw figures of giraffes and ostriches, large, dappled and horned cattle, horses, deer and sometimes elephants. Many were effaced and hard to see and often, after climbing high among the rocks to reach a promising gallery, it turned out to be no more than nature chipping the stone into weird shapes by the action of sun and sand, heat and cold, wind and tempest over the centuries. By now this barely worried me. The frustration of searching, the excitement of dis-

covery had both cooled. My ambition with regard to the prehistoric art of
the Sahara had become tempered since I had come to realize that the
search itself was what I had been seeking, not the intellectual satisfaction
of becoming an expert in the subject. Besides, the Aïr Mountains were
without doubt the most congenial of the Saharan ranges, with just enough
patches of sparse vegetation to temper the harsh aridity of the desert,
encourage wildlife and allow a few scattered flocks of sheep and goats to
survive. For the first time, I felt I could stay in the environment and be
content. The savage joy of icy, clear dawns and blazing noons; the gentle
peace of firelit silent nights and canopies of stars had become familiar.
Paradoxically, with this the need to strive evaporated and, almost to my
surprise, I found that I had proved to myself something unexpected and
quite other than my original aim. Growing to like the desert rather than
love, hate or fear it, removed the necessity of being there. Like an old
friend whom one may not see for years, it would always be there if I
wanted to return. It is the people of the desert who matter and whom I
mourn. Thousands have died in the worst drought in their history. As a
result, much of their knowledge of how to survive in the desert has been
lost and their confidence in their ability to do so has been undermined.
Most now live in refugee camps, dependent on government handouts
from the countries in which they find themselves. Few advisers suggest
that they will ever be able to return to the apparently barren wastes they
alone know how to live in, so that these lands with all their potential for
sustaining life will become empty and abandoned. Desert and marginal
lands like the Sahara and the Sahel do not respond easily to the applied
agricultural technology of the industrial societies. Only in very rare cases
and in extreme circumstances is the desert made to bloom.

Many years later, in 1980, I was to walk across part of the Kalahari desert
with a Bushman. The group I met of small, yellow-skinned, round-headed
people had become ragged, frightened and consciously poor as they clung
to a bore-hole which had come to represent their only source of water.
Gradually they had forgotten how to live out in the dry scrub, sipping
water up from the sand and storing it in ostrich eggs. They told me they
were frightened to travel now as they would die of thirst. As a result they
seldom ate meat and were finding it hard to scratch a living.
    Ebenene, however, was not frightened. Through the Tswana inter-
preter who had led me to the group from a nearby prospectors' camp I
learnt that he regularly walked long distances to visit other groups and
that he was a celebrated hunter. I asked if we could walk together across
the empty space on the map between the Gemsbok National Park, on the
edge of which his camp of simple *scherms* lay, to Ghanzi, the remote central

settlement of Botswana served by an all-weather road. He asked how we would communicate since we had no language. I replied that language was not so important since we understood and trusted each other.

'When we want to walk, we will walk,' I said. 'When it is time to stop we will stop, or sleep, or eat. We do not need to talk. You will show me what to do.'

When this was translated Ebenene and his family and friends clapped, laughed and danced as I had heard the Bushmen did. Before dawn next morning we set out together, each carrying an ostrich egg full of water, a little food, my sleeping bag, and a few clothes. We walked each day in amiable silence, stopping only when Ebenene spotted wildebeest, buffalo, ostrich or elephant, when he would crouch and watch with a hunter's stillness. In the heat of the day we would rest under a thorn tree.

There was a project with which Survival International was involved, digging further bore-holes for the Bushmen. While it was sad to see how dependent they became on these and how they lost their skill and interest in desert travel, after being for so long the greatest experts in extracting nourishment from a land where no one else could survive, there seemed no other solution for them. Few if any lived wholly off the Kalahari in the traditional way, or wanted to. Life there was becoming harder each year as over-grazing by cattle and a sinking watertable made it ever more arid. But there was hope for the future. On one of the settlement schemes, where an enlightened Tswana administrator advised and protected but did not interfere too much, I saw a group of nearly a hundred Bushmen who had become excellent farmers, growing some of the best crops of vegetables I saw in the country. While being exploited and despised by their cattle-rearing Tswana neighbours, they had not had to endure the terrible sudden drought of the Tuareg, and while the change of lifestyle ahead of them was just as radical, I felt they stood a better chance of coming to terms with it.

It is easy to see the mistakes which have been made in the past, and are still being made, at the extreme fringes of habitable environments but the lesson is no less urgent in relatively more favoured ones. Meanwhile, due in no small way to the scorn in which their administrators hold them and the lack of any attempt to overcome the difficulties of the changing world, the Tuareg and the Bushmen are forced to leave the desert, and the Sahara and the Kalahari become truly barren lands.

5

Exploration for Its Own Sake

Because it is there . . .

George Mallory

My first experience of exploring with more than one companion came when I was invited in 1968 to take part in the first Hovercraft expedition. The plan was to convert a ten-ton SR N.6, normally used as one of the daily ferries to the Isle of Wight when it carries more than 36 passengers, to carry 20 expeditioners and their equipment. The craft was shipped out to Brazil where it was going to try and cover part of my previous route in reverse, going from Manaus up the Rio Negro, through the Casiquiare, down the Orinoco and across to Trinidad.

The members of the expedition represented a wide variety of interests and almost everyone seemed to be a 'chief' rather than an 'Indian'. It all looked like a recipe for disaster, but the opportunity to go was too good to miss and I signed on as camp-master, a very definite 'Indian' role, which made me general dogsbody responsible for everyone else's comfort and welfare. Dr Conrad Gorinsky, a brilliant ethnobotanist from St Bartholomew's Hospital, joined as 'cook and bottle washer'. We two, who became firm friends on the journey, were the only two clear 'other ranks', working night and day. We were also the only two who spoke Portuguese and Spanish, who had much experience of jungle life and who actually enjoyed being there. This gave us a huge advantage in becoming indispensable and gradually taking over the running of the show, as it were from underneath, and did not always endear us to the other members. I was particularly suspect, having been there before, since the whole project was billed as the Last Great Journey on Earth, which it clearly was not, while reports of our activities sent back concentrated on all the horrors and discomforts of life in Amazonas which I was supposed to be alleviating for the other members and which I also failed to appreciate properly.

The first objective was to demonstrate to the world in the most dramatic way possible that brilliant British invention, the Hovercraft, which glides over the surface of water and land alike and is thus able to operate in terrain unsuitable for all other forms of transport. This I believe we did, but the follow-up salesmanship was abysmal and not a single craft was subsequently sold in South America. We had a first-class crew headed by the Captain, Graham Clarke, who sensibly confined himself to the safety and efficient working of his ship; when these were in question he became very much the Boss, but otherwise he avoided discussion. The rest of the party was divided between three very disparate groups whose interests seldom converged. The organizers were the *Geographical Magazine*, then partly owned by IPC whose representative, David Smithers, an intense and Machiavellian Welshman, held the purse-strings and so ultimate authority. Ensuring full journalistic cover of the exercise were Douglas Botting, the excellent photographer and writer, and Arthur Helliwell, an almost legendary Fleet Street hand who was convinced that he was going to die on this great adventure and sent back appallingly lurid descriptions of our daily brushes with death, cannibals and tarantulas.

The ostensible purpose of the expedition was to conduct a team of botanists and geomorphologists. These formed the second group. They would have liked to have been allowed to stop for days at each new environment and found the speed and preoccupation with logistics very frustrating.

Finally there was the BBC film team who had put up most of the money for the exercise and naturally wanted to make as rousing and interesting a film as possible.

Conrad and I belonged to none of these categories and so were not usually included in the nightly discussions when contrary opinions were expressed at great length about what should happen on the morrow. Instead we found that whenever we arrived at a new campsite on the riverbank, everyone suddenly had urgent and unpostponable business elsewhere, leaving us to unload the two tons of stores, set up camp and cook dinner. Technicians serviced the craft; scientists dug for samples and collected plants; journalists and film crew recorded all for posterity. There was no overall leader and I learnt several very useful lessons about organizing large expeditions which were to stand me in good stead later.

It all began pleasantly enough as we roared up the wide, calm Rio Negro, with its white sandy beaches almost completely free of insect life owing to some quality of the tea-coloured 'black' water, after which the river is named. Camps were pleasant picnics and only man, as he competed for territory and status on board and ashore, was relatively vile.

In Manaus we took on a river pilot who was reputed to know every twist and turn of the Rio Negro for all the 1,200-odd km of it we would be covering. As we left the city to the cheers of the population, he was placed in the front seat next to the co-pilot. Peering ahead through slitted eyes he directed importantly with hand signals to show the route up the wide and deep stretches. Then we approached the first shallows. Ahead a yellow sandbank sloped down from the shore to appear here and there across the wide stream-bed as flat breaks where the surface rippled. Now our guide leaned forward directing the pilot urgently to the left where the narrow channel lay. Travelling at over 100 kph the Captain was not going to bother weaving about unnecessarily as he knew that the Hovercraft flew a metre or so above the surface of water or sand equally. I realized that the guide, used to shallow-draught steamers, had not been made aware of this and I watched his knuckles whiten as we hurtled towards certain disaster. When we glided safely over the sandbank with no diminution of speed his nerve broke completely and from then on he refused to play any part, saying that if the ship was so clever it could look after itself. As a result I had to stand in as navigator, relying on map-reading and my fading memories of the river's behaviour seen from the other direction some three years before. It was important for the Captain to know what lay ahead as, in order to conserve fuel, he needed to maintain a smooth and constant high speed, and so the sharpness of approaching corners was critical. The craft was powered by a 1,000-hp jet aircraft engine which made an appalling noise. Travel inside was hot, deafening and claustrophobic, but it did get us from A to B extraordinarily fast, though the effect on the fauna and human population as we passed must have been shattering.

I particularly remember seeing a small canoe in midstream far ahead, the Indian in the stern quietly fishing. As he heard our distant roar, his head came up and he looked around the sky for thunder clouds. Then he glanced in our direction to see a large boat heading for him. Believing he had plenty of time to paddle to the shore before the wash swamped him, he set off at a leisurely pace. Suddenly, seconds later, as we were almost on top of him he began to paddle frantically and I saw his anguished expression as he looked up, certain his last moment had come. Then we passed with a roar but scarcely a ripple. We wondered whether he would try and explain his experience to his disbelieving family or simply pretend that it had never happened.

At many of the places we stopped on the way I met people who remembered me and the strange little rubber boat in which I had been travelling on my trans-continental journey three years before. It was exciting to be returning in a much more dramatic and remarkable form of transport. Although it could travel about twice the speed of my original boat, the problems of making and breaking camp and giving the scientists time to do their work meant that our actual rate of travel was very similar to what mine had been, and we spent the night at many of the same places including Uapes, one of the large Salesian missions to the Indians of the Rio Negro.

These Indians, descendants of the rich variety of tribes who originally inhabited that generous and pleasant part of Amazonas, had long before lost much of their identity and self-respect. The Salesians, conscientiously seeking out and removing all children from their families to bring them up in the segregated mission boarding schools, had gained complete moral and physical control over the region. It had become almost a private religious fiefdom, sharing the administration with the Brazilian Air Force: an unholy alliance which anthropologists and the Indians themselves were beginning to question. It was also in glaring contrast to the new liberalism in the Brazilian Catholic Church which was about to start raising one of the very few voices in defence of Indian rights.

One contact I renewed pleased me particularly: Manolo El Tucuman, the wizened and good-tempered old Indian with a nutbrown wrinkled face and no teeth who had guided me through the São Gabriel rapids and on downstream. I knew that he lived at Uapes and, while there, I tracked him down humbly sweeping out the vestry of the big church. He seemed much older than I remembered him and at first he failed to recognize me and backed away from my grinning approach. Then his eyes opened very wide and filled with tears as he came and embraced me affectionately.

Still clutching my hand in his sinewy and claw-like grip he led me through the village, asking why I had not returned sooner as 'he had been waiting'. Proudly introducing me to his family in their simple thatched hut, he pressed coffee on me, and we sat and talked about the things we had been through together.

Although, as a distinguished visitor, I was treated with respect by the family, I soon gathered that poor old Manolo was now regarded as old and useless, that no one took him seriously any more, and it seemed to me that he had a fairly rough life. His eldest daughter and her husband had taken over the running of his small household and clearly found him an encumbrance.

As I walked back to join the rest of my party, who were comfortably lodged in the mission hospital, I began to think of a plan to do something to raise Manolo's prestige – at least with his family, if not with the whole village. The discussion that evening was all on the crossing of the São

Gabriel rapids which broke the river into a mass of white boiling water as it swept round a curve past Uapes. These rapids were nothing compared with those we had to face later on the Orinoco, but they were the first on our route since leaving Manaus and everyone was interested to see how the Hovercraft would perform in them. Graham Clarke, the skipper, well knew that they would present no difficulty, but for maximum safety had the rest of the members of the expedition go round on foot. As I had crossed the rapids during my previous visit, Graham invited me to go in the craft. I asked whether Manolo El Tucuman 'the finest guide on the Rio Negro' might come as well. Although the route which the Hovercraft should follow was quite clear on this occasion – and bore no relation to that which a boat would have taken – it was agreed that he could.

Now Manolo's finest hour arrived. A huge crowd had gathered on the beach below the rapids to witness our fantastic 'flying turtle' (as the Hovercraft had been christened locally) brave the rapids. Not fully understanding that it skimmed over the surface of the water rather than through it, many thought that we would be dashed to pieces on the rocks. But many more wanted to accompany us and clamoured to be allowed to occupy the empty seats. Stuart Syrad, the co-pilot, patiently turned all-comers away explaining that we must travel as lightly as possible.

Then Manolo made his way through the crowd and it divided to let him pass. He wore his Sunday best and carried a small bundle, as though going on a long journey. Graham Clarke shook his hand and led him to the front seat next to his own. In a cloud of spray, sand and noise we rose off the shore and roared easily out into the stream, over the turbulence and past a few rocks where the water broke white. From the bank the BBC camera team filmed our progress and the crowd ran to keep up with us, cheering wildly. Inside Manolo peered through the spray-spattered windscreen and gave the same steady and considered directions I remembered from the time when he had sat cold and exposed to the elements in the little rubber boat.

In a few minutes it was all over and we were being welcomed ashore above the rapids, congratulated on all sides and well pleased with our performance. Manolo was once more treated with respect and I like to think that this incident had a lasting impression on his family as well, so that his declining years might be a little more comfortable and dignified for him.

In Uapes I also acquired a beautiful and rare orange bird called a Cock of the Rock. An Indian had caught him as a fledgling in the Sierra de la Neblina and brought him home in a wicker basket which seemed to me too small for comfort. All I could see at first was one angry and determined eye glaring out as though daring me to poke a finger through. I did so and felt

myself seized and nibbled by a surprisingly gentle and knowing beak. Irresponsibly, because it would probably only encourage his owner to go and catch another one, but with a crazy idea that I might free him, I exchanged him for a few cruzeiros; but his wings had been clipped and when I opened his basket he just settled on the ground and eyed me belligerently. I placed him on my hand at which he fluffed out his brilliant feathers, doubling his size from pigeon to guinea fowl and erected his amazing crest until it came right forward over his beak to make a perfect circle of his head. At the same time he crouched down, sensuously digging his razor-sharp talons fore and aft into my finger until they met and the blood flowed. I never tried again to treat him like a parrot.

Chico was allowed to join the ship's company and when we crossed the equator the next day he was issued with a certificate signed by the Captain to say that he was the first Cock of the Rock to have done so by Hovercraft. It was also the first Hovercraft to glide across the equator.

Normally Chico remained silent, observing the passing world from his perch through bright yellow eyes and only lowering himself to burble gently as he crouched on the floor and did his sexy mating dance when I offered him choice pieces of pineapple and banana. To see this dance in the wild has been the lifelong ambition of many ornithologists but Chico, after we had returned to England, where he lived happily for several years in our kitchen, would perform the instant anything orange came within his field of vision. He fell passionately in love with Marika and her yellow apron; a bowl of oranges or even a duster was enough to set him off, clear proof that birds are not colour-blind.

It was when we turned into the Casiquiare, thus entering 'white' water for the first time, that the trouble started. I think of all the insect-ridden places in which I have travelled, the Casiquiare is the worst. The mosquitoes seem larger and the swarms of little black *jejenes* more numerous than anywhere else. Within an hour every face I looked at was being transformed as though a smallpox epidemic was raging. Suppurating sores erupted, scratched spots bled and tempers flared. Only Conrad

---

on preceding pages

A Bororo girl with feather painting on her face, hands at prayer as taught by missionaries.

Kamayura Indians, healthy and strong, outside their communal house in the Xingu National Park.

On top of Mt Roraima, at over 6,000 ft, weird rock formations provide no shelter against the rain and cold.

In the midst of a riverine dawn there is no more beautiful dwelling in the world than a single Choco hut tucked into a fold of the hills . . .

and I remained virtually unaffected, which did nothing for our popularity. When asked how I do it, I tend to reply that it's only a matter of not scratching and thinking pure thoughts, which comment can make the mildest of persons turn murderous. But I do believe there is some truth in my philosophy, and I have often deliberately 'willed away' bites while similar ones on others have festered. Genetics and an innate lack of allergy must, of course, also play a significant part and I recognize how lucky I am.

At this point the BBC decided that life had been too undramatic so far and insisted that, although we could have made it right through the whole 250 km of the Casiquiare to the Orinoco in a day, we must camp twice *en route*. It has always been my policy to make life as comfortable as possible on an expedition, knowing that discomfort and danger have their own ways of seeking one out. To go looking for them seemed sheer folly which would tempt the fates; and so it proved.

The first night went reasonably smoothly as we were able to use a recently abandoned Indian hut on the bank and, swathed in mosquito nets, the party dropped off to sleep without too much trouble. In the small hours of the morning the silence was suddenly shattered by an hysterical burst of screams from Chico whose cage was hanging on one of the corner uprights. I hurried over to him to see in the light of my torch a wildcat standing on its hind legs and groping through the bamboo bars with claws extended. Chico was having a hard task keeping out of range, leaping from side to side, but having the presence of mind to shout for help at the same time. After the cat had left it took a while to settle him and by then the other members of the expedition were awake and demanding their early-morning tea.

On the next night there was no hut and so I rigged as best I could the large and heavy tarpaulin we had brought for this purpose. Hammocks were strung between small trees and poles stuck in the ground underneath. All might have been well had it not rained, but the heavens opened as they do only in the tropics and there was soon unhappy bedlam as I hurried in my bathing suit from one miserable figure to another, mopping and comforting while the tarpaulin gradually collapsed.

I resolved that if I ever found myself in the position of leading an expedition, my first rule would be that all members are equal and equally responsible for looking after themselves. There is no room for prima donnas on an expedition, but human nature being what it is they will appear out of the woodwork on the least excuse. When people are tired, uncomfortable and a bit frightened by their strange surroundings, they will suddenly become petulant and demanding of their fellows, and behave in a way they would never dream of at home. This of course has a dreadful effect on morale so that everyone ends up screaming at each other – or more often at the camp-master and cook. Never again, I vowed.

Shortly afterwards, at Esmeralda on the Orinoco, it was sensibly decided to halt the expedition for a week or so while everyone went his separate way and the Hovercraft received a major overhaul. Conrad and I made two long journeys together by canoe which were to change my life.

The first was a nearly fatal visit to a remote group of Yanomami Indians. An old white-bearded Catholic priest, Padre Coco, who had a mission at the mouth of the Ocamo river, lent us a dugout canoe and outboard motor. With two Yanomami Indians from the mission we set off up the river. Conrad wanted to collect specimens of some of the plants used by Indian groups for healing purposes. One of the sources of the powerful hallucinogenic drugs made by and used by the Yanomami and of potential value to Western medicine was said to grow some way up the Ocamo and we were determined to find it. On the way we stopped to call on a group of Yanomami who had only recently arrived, having migrated from the hills to the east. Only Padre Coco had visited them before and that only once. Otherwise they had probably had no other contact with non-Yanomami people.

A Yanomami Indian watching the Hovercraft speed past on
the upper Orinoco in 1968.

The Yanomami live in circular thatched communal houses – *yanos* – with a wide open 'plaza' in the centre. When we arrived we were given a friendly reception and invited to stay. But we resisted the temptation to look around this fascinating dwelling, deciding to carry on upstream in search of Conrad's plant and then return for the night. When we arrived back in the evening, having successfully completed our mission, we found everything changed. There were no welcoming Yanomami on the river-bank and our guides urged us not to stop. I told them not to be silly and ran up the bank, bursting through the low entrance to the *yano* to see one of the strangest sights of my life. The atmosphere was no longer relaxed and peaceful, but charged with an almost tangible antipathy tinged with what I later realized was grief. The Indians' bodies were no longer a pale beige, blushed pink with a light colouring of *urucu* but now were decorated in violent patterns of red and black. The men stood in a row holding their two-metre bows and arrows aloft and stamping their feet. In the centre of the plaza a fire was burning. As I raised my camera one of the Yanomami guides, who had hurried after me, grabbed my arm and began to drag me back to the boat. The Indians ran after us and, as we pulled away from the bank, fired a few token arrows over our heads.

We heard later, back at the mission, that a young girl had died during the hours between our first and second visits. Assuming quite naturally, but in this case erroneously, that our unexpected arrival might have caused her death, the Yanomami wanted nothing more to do with us, especially during the preparations for her funeral.

In search of a quite different medicinal plant, one with reputed blood-clotting properties, we next went for several days up the Ventuari, one of the largest tributaries of the Orinoco, about 250 km downstream from the Ocamo. The Piaroa tribe were the traditional users of this medicine, trading it with other groups. Having heard it referred to over a wide area Conrad felt that it should be collected and analysed in order to identify and isolate any active ingredients.

These long journeys by dugout canoe involved many hours sitting still, only occasionally interrupted by the need to jump over the side and help the craft over shallows or through rapids. During this time we talked, or rather Conrad talked and I listened. Conrad's belief was based on the simple premise that the Indians knew and understood the jungle better than we ever could. Before it became fashionable to do so he condemned the industrial world's profligate use of resources and wasteful destruction of the remaining wildernesses, especially the tropical rain forest. His special interest was the Indians' knowledge of the uses and potential of plants for both food and medicine.

He showed with innumerable examples that almost all modern foods and drugs have not been invented by scientists working in isolation in laboratories but are simply adaptations drawn from the immense source-material of other cultures. The cultural diversity and the irreplaceable knowledge represented by the heirs to so many different biological adaptations and experiments are the first victims of environmental despoliation and the inevitable social changes which accompany it. The indigenous inhabitants of the region supposedly being 'opened up' represent the specialist knowledge which is vital if proper use is to be made of unfamiliar biospheres. Without this knowledge and the clues it provides, options are severely limited, resulting in the all-too-familiar cycle of mono-cultural exploitation, which itself leads to abandoned, useless wastelands. Without diversity our own economic future is threatened.

And yet, ironically, wherever cultures differing from the accepted Western norm exist, immense effort is still being expended to change them; to wean the 'ignorant savage' from his foolish ways; to bring him enlightenment, both spiritual and material; to introduce synthetic cures for diseases he has successfully withstood for centuries while at the same time striving, usually unsuccessfully, to cure those much more lethal epidemics which contact with outsiders has unleashed; to teach him to become totally dependent on one dangerously pest-prone crop and abandon the complex and precisely balanced mix of gathered wild food and rich variety of domestic plants; to force him to forswear the pagan gods whose demands so nicely match the requirements of their particular environment, imposing instead a set of prohibitions and imperatives devised for a prehistoric desert race, and resulting in the Judaeo-Christian work ethic.

We decided that an organization should be created to oppose these short-sighted policies; that it should be based upon principles which take into account the Indians' own desires and needs rather than our society's prejudices; that it should strive to protect the rights of Indians to their lands, their cultures and their identity; that it should foster respect for and research into their knowledge and experience so that through being recognized as experts they should be allowed to survive and we should learn from them and so contribute to our own survival. Thus the concept of Survival International was born. When, a few months later, exposure in the European press of the atrocities perpetrated in Brazil against the Brazilian Indians by the very agency created to protect them, roused public opinion, we were ready to join in the slow process of raising money and building an organization.

An immediate example of what Conrad was talking about was present-ed to us when we eventually reached a Piaroa group living up a small tributary of the Ventuari. In due time we raised the subject of the particular plant we sought.

'Yes,' they said, 'we used to trade in that.'

'Can you show us the plant from which the medicine was derived?' we asked.

'Ah . . . Only the shaman would know that. You would have to ask him.'

We then learned that there was no longer anyone who admitted to being a shaman. The last one had died a few months before, shortly after the arrival of a medical 'dresser' whom the government had sent to establish a clinic for the group. He was a nice enough young man with some very basic medical training and his 'little white pills' were undoubtedly effective against some of the obvious health problems the group were then facing – colds and infections brought in from outside. But the result of his arrival had been so to undermine the authority and self-confidence of the old shaman that he had retired to his hammock and died, taking with him, as Conrad put it, a whole library of irreplaceable knowledge and experience, the accumulated wisdom of centuries of experiment by successive shamans – almost the whole tradition of the tribe. This had been passed down to him by word of mouth but he had never passed it on.

The dangerous climax of the Hovercraft expedition came when we reached the dreaded Maipures-Atures rapids on the Orinoco. Massive waterfalls, whirlpools and giant waves succeed each other along 60 km of the river. There is a lorry track round the rapids, via which all goods and people travel both up and down the river, as I had done with my rubber boat. No one had ever negotiated the rapids and lived. So formidable was their reputation that the chief of the Venezuelan Armed Forces declared that he would eat his hat if we survived.

Although I knew no more about the rapids than anyone else, not having even seen them from the road, I was once again asked to do the navigating. With the Captain and co-pilot I flew in a helicopter down over the rapids and back again, marking a large-scale map according to Graham's instructions as to which side of islands we should pass and where the possible routes down waterfalls were. From the air rapids always look deceptively innocuous, but Graham was not fooled and knew it was going to be very difficult and dangerous. However, since the river was falling and the conditions were likely to become worse he decided we should go right away, sending all our stores and the rest of the team round by road.

Driving a Hovercraft under severe river conditions requires three people. The navigator chooses the route, telling the co-pilot who watches out for conditions ahead in the medium term, leaving the pilot to wrestle with the controls and deal with immediate obstacles. Setting off over the smooth surface of the wide river, while the helicopter, now carrying the BBC film crew, hovered overhead, we approached the line on the water which, going downstream, was all we could see of the first waterfall. Taking a perfect line to the point where the bulk of the water funnelled down the main channel we suddenly found ourselves plunging as though on a roller-coaster towards a great wall of water some three metres high. Crashing into this, the Hovercraft stopped dead and almost disappeared beneath the surface. From above, it looked as though we were gone and the cameraman believed he was filming a disaster. Inside there was bedlam as water poured in through a smashed window beside me, swamped us and dissolved my carefully marked map. Slowly, with full power, we rose above the waves and Graham, his teeth gritted, headed on since there was now no turning back. I had no map but I did not want to add to my Captain's worries and so pretended that I could still read the heap of pulp on my lap, guessing wildly as the co-pilot snapped urgently, 'Which way now?' every few seconds. Only once did they begin to suspect that I knew even less than they did about where we were going when Graham passed the laconic message across to me: 'Ask Robin to check the route again. We are now going upstream!' We had turned up a tributary.

But after an extremely tense and nervous hour, since if in any of the successive rapids we had struck a rock, the craft would have disintegrated and there would have been no chance of any of us swimming to shore, we made it to the other end. I don't think I have ever been more frightened. This was not just a fear of drowning (I always secretly believe that I will be the only survivor) but arose from the combination of having no control whatsoever over our destiny and having to carry the burden of knowing that my contributions were worthless.

That night there were great celebrations, and a chocolate cake in the shape of a hat was baked for the Venezuelan General. Our festive welcome at Port of Spain, Trinidad, a week later, when steel bands played and the whole city seemed to turn out to congratulate us, was almost an anti-climax.

In spite of my reservations I did, as things turned out, take part in another Hovercraft expedition the next year, 1969. This time I was made Deputy Leader, under David Smithers, and was sent ahead to obtain political clearances and reconnoitre part of our route between Dakar in Senegal, via Timbuktu, the River Niger, the Benue in Nigeria and Cameroon, Chad, the Central African Republic and the Congo (now Zaire) before reaching the Atlantic again at Matadi.

The craft's ability to pass from sand to water and back, as well as to go through dense reed beds made it particularly well suited for exploring Lake Chad where there is a vast shallow expanse of water, interspersed with innumerable low islands, the shores hidden behind mile upon mile of papyrus and rushes. The main danger, we were warned, was from bilharzia (Schistosomiasis) with which its waters were riddled so that the disease was endemic throughout the lakeside population. This meant that we were prevented from swimming or even wading in the water, which limited our activities.

The islands to the south of the lake consisted of semi-floating beds of reeds on which lived a nomadic population of fishing people, using papyrus boats. They looked like miniature replicas of the Ra in which Thor Heyerdahl crossed the Atlantic, and in fact his first boat was built by a boatman from Lake Chad. We stepped ashore on some of these islands, feeling the ground roll and swell below us like a quagmire in the bogs of my youth in Ireland. Cutting through the tangled mass of thorns and weeds, we were directed by the botanist of the party towards various rare plants he wished to collect and which he alone could see from his perch on the roof of the craft.

Surprisingly, we sometimes flushed herds of deer in the undergrowth who leapt into the water to escape and swim to the next island. Immense flocks of birds used the lake, ducks and waders on the water itself and every sort of migratory finch and warbler in the lush vegetation around the edges. This is the last place where they can rest and feed up before undertaking the 5,000-km flight to Europe, riding high on the trade winds over the Sahara. For a time I helped our ornithologist to catch, weigh and release birds in mist nets morning and evening. I found it astounding to learn that a warbler can double its weight during the three weeks before the flight, rising from twelve grammes to twenty-four grammes only to lose the lot in three to four days' hard flying and arrive weighing twelve grammes again. Imagine a twelve-stone man building himself up to twenty-four stone only to lose it all again in three days!

The northern part of the lake is dry and sandy where the Sahara continues as it has done for thousands of years to eat into what was once a gigantic inland sea. Now only a fraction of its former size, the lake is shrinking daily and will one day disappear unless a new Ice Age comes or man does something catastrophic to the climate. The water is dotted with rows of little sandy islands, the tops of emerging ripples in the earth's surface. Seen from an aircraft high above, they look like a mackerel sky reflected in the surface.

Many have some vegetation on them and it was rumoured that on one there was an elephant. Apparently some years before a herd of elephants had wandered across the lake, swimming and wading from island to island in search of food. For some unaccountable reason a splinter group had decided to remain on this particular island and, perhaps afraid to leave, had died one by one. There was said to be a lone survivor and we set out to find him with a guide. On board were, again, about 22 people, almost all different from the South American party. We had also with us some French scientists from the research station in Fort Lamy and a couple of Chadian officials.

The island seemed too small to hold an elephant and all we saw at first was the heap of white bones on the shore belonging to one which had died and had been picked clean by the vultures. Then the survivor rushed out of the small clump of bushes in the centre of the island to see what the noise was all about. Trumpeting in amazement, he ran along the shore level with the Hovercraft, roaring back at this noisy creature which had come to disturb his tranquillity. Then as we slid ashore in a cloud of sand and spray, he hurried back to hide in his bush.

There was a moment of deflation as everyone climbed out, cameras and tripods were set up, the clapperboards of the film crew clapped and nothing happened. The elephant remained in hiding.

I felt that something should be done about it and decided to help by slipping round to the back of the bush to drive the elephant out. I thought, in my eagerness to be useful, that I would simply make a loud noise and the elephant, alarmed, would run out to give everyone some nice pictures. It was not until I had groped my way into the bush that it began to occur to me that the elephant might take exception to my action and instead of being afraid and running away might turn and flatten me. I moved slower and more cautiously, parting the grass ahead.

With a shock which made me hold my breath I suddenly realized that I had arrived before I had made up my mind what to do and, the elephant having retreated nearer to the far edge of the bush than I had expected, I had reached it. Indeed, the two tree trunks looming before me through the grass and on one of which my hand rested before pushing them apart, were the elephant's hind legs. If I had approached quietly enough for the elephant not to hear, my retreat was mouse-like and took much longer. Once in the open I ran like hell until in sight of the waiting group again when I attempted to stroll nonchalantly. I was too ashamed, as much of my foolhardiness as of my cowardice, to tell anyone that I had actually touched the elephant and so pretended I had just been for a walk. No one ever believes that story but it is true.

The trouble about spending a fair proportion of one's life pursuing what is popularly called 'travel and adventure' is that one is expected to return burdened with endless breathless tales of danger and excitement with which to keep dinner guests enthralled. In fact, people are so nervous of unleashing this flood that I find no one ever asks me where I have just been and what happened to me there. Instead the inevitable question is: 'Where are you off to next?' I have never been sure whether this oft-repeated inquiry is asked out of genuine interest or to steer me tactfully away from reminiscences. In fact, real-life incidents are seldom dramatic when they happen but only become so with the telling. More often, like my encounter with the elephant, they are private moments of shame and embarrassment from which one shrinks guiltily away, cloaked in the realization that if they had gone wrong they would have caused others grave inconvenience. I know no real traveller who travels in search of excitement; that is incidental to the deeper desire for self-awareness and enlightenment which some find easier to reach out for in the wilderness.

Travel in harsh and alien environments is also much more satisfying if it has a clear purpose. One may, as I did in the deserts, secretly enjoy the experience for its own sake, but the ostensible reason validates it at least to some extent. Worse, one may find that the mechanics of travel, the distractions and tantrums of one's fellow travellers may so detract from the original purpose that each would have been better on his or her own.

On these expeditions by Hovercraft I learnt a lot about what an expedition should not be and began to make my own secret plans for how I would do it if I ever had the chance. Travelling with several others had been a new experience for me and I had enjoyed for the first time the pleasure of being a member of a group while having my eyes opened to the dangers of mob rule, even when the mob was a highly intelligent one. Leadership seemed to me to be the key and I wondered if I had the necessary qualities and if I would ever find out.

6

True Men and Not Beasts

The Papal Bull, *Veritas ipsa*
'Solemnly recognizes those Indians as true men . . . and that the said Indians and all other peoples who at a later stage might come to the knowledge of the Christians, even if they should be outside the Christian faith, should not be deprived of their freedom, nor of the enjoyment of their possessions, and should not be reduced to slavery. . .'

Pope Paul III (1537)

For the four centuries following the discovery of Brazil in 1500 by Pedro Alvares Cabral the Indians were almost ceaselessly subjected to the most appalling oppression. In what must count as the cruellest and most effective of all wars of extermination, untold millions of Indians were butchered, flogged to death, flayed alive and mutilated. The pain they suffered in this extended orgy of killing rings down through the ages and I still wince when I see contemporary illustrations of gentle, welcoming people having their hands cut off at the wrists or being burnt at the stake simply from sadism or to punish them for not wanting to work hard enough.

Everyone who met the Indians in those early days commented on their beauty, health, cleanliness and friendliness. Their freedom from inhibitions about nudity and sex were what struck the repressed Conquistadores most forcibly – and even today, when virtually all modern thinking and outlook should recognize the benefits of such an attitude, it is still this which primarily preoccupies those with whom the Indians have most contact – settlers and Protestant missionaries. The Portuguese were also impressed by the Indians' generosity and good manners. Anything admired was instantly pressed on their guests. Headdresses, necklaces, bangles – whether made of feathers or of gold – were handed over with equal spontaneity to the greedy and acquisitive arrivals. Perhaps it was the deeply felt, but instantly rejected, sense of inferiority given to the Europeans by such open-handedness which led to their incredible sadism. For the purpose behind the brutality was greed, a desire for cheap labour to work the timber mills, plantations, factories and mines of the colonists; to kill off the labour force was improvident. And in spite of the hundreds of thousands slaughtered, millions more died from disease. Epidemics of pestilences nurtured in the mediaeval slums of Europe and unknown across the Atlantic to a people isolated for tens of thousands of years from the rest of mankind and who therefore had no resistance to foreign diseases, were unleashed to race from tribe to tribe through the forests and across the savannas condemning whole peoples to extinction. Measles, smallpox, whooping cough and even the common cold were fatal to the Indians and still are today. Forcing them to wear unaccustomed clothes and live in crowded, unhygienic conditions, totally unfamiliar physically and psychologically to people accustomed to hunt daily in the rich forests and move their villages regularly, compounded the effects and hastened the spread of infection.

Later, when slaves were shipped across from Africa, they brought another set of diseases. Malaria, yellow fever, leishmaniasis, yaws and, more recently, bilharzia and African river blindness probably all came from the dark continent to cause more deaths and debility. John Hemming, in his definitive book on the history of Brazil's Indians, *Red Gold* (Macmillan, 1978), makes an interesting point about this fatal impact. Both continents probably had about the same number of inhabitants in 1500 – perhaps 10 or 20 million each; but while the native population of Africa has survived and multiplied so that almost all the colonists have been expelled, the indigenous peoples of South America have declined, in the case of Brazil's Indians to near extinction. Instead of repossessing their country they are now an oppressed and despised minority, perhaps 100,000, not enough to fill a large football stadium.

The ignorance and prejudice about Indians that still exists in Brazil and other South American countries, and indeed in Europe and America, constantly amazes me. Even educated people still ask me when they see pictures of Indians, 'Do they have a religion? Do they believe in God?' as though, were my answer to be 'No' (which of course it isn't), this would somehow excuse what has been and is being done to them. Do most of those who ask such questions believe in God themselves? In any case, to quote Claude Levi-Strauss on the subject of Indians and God: 'Few people are so religious . . . few possess a metaphysical system of such complexity.'

Over the years occasional efforts have been made to bring justice and respect to the Indians. The earliest French missionaries gave the most vivid descriptions of Indian reactions to European invasions, and the French prided themselves on their sympathy with Indians. Some of the Spanish priests championed the Indians, notably the Bishop Bartolomé de Las Casas who underwent a conversion to the Indian cause in 1514 and spent the rest of his life in their defence, threatening to excommunicate anyone who enslaved or mistreated an Indian. In 1537 the celebrated Papal Bull was issued which declared that American Indians were true men and not beasts. Even tribes that were not yet converted to Christianity 'should not be deprived of their freedom, nor of the enjoyment of their possessions, and should not be reduced to slavery'. But few listened and the uncontrolled slaughter continued, only slowing down because there were fewer Indians left to murder.

The newly created Jesuits, bursting with missionary zeal, arrived in Brazil determined to fight slavery and defend the Indians. While successful in gaining a virtual monopoly over all the Indians under Portuguese rule, their efforts were, if possible, even more disastrous. Collecting whole tribes and confining them in insanitary and unfamiliar conditions which would certainly be described as concentration camps today, they found to their surprise that they almost all died. Their response was to bring more and more Indians from even further afield, flogging them to death if they tried to escape, fully aware that the same epidemics were likely to carry these off too in a horrible rotting death, but obsessed with maintaining numbers in the missions and so justifying this most profligate way of saving souls.

Paradoxically, throughout the whole of the first four centuries of contact, while the slaughter and torture continued, there was a constant and widespread fascination in Europe with the Indians as perfect human beings with the secret of happiness and innocence. In the 16th century Thomas More's *Utopia* praised the Indians' disdain for possessions; in the 17th century Hugo Grotius described their simple, communal life; Jean-Jacques Rousseau created the romantic political theory of the noble savage in the 18th century and many many more writers and philosophers referred to their simplicity and nobility. By the 19th century, the Indians became less valuable as black slaves from Africa became cheaper and a mood of Victorian sentimentality was allowed for a time to surround them, even in Brazil itself. José Bonifacio declared in 1823, 'We must never forget that we are usurpers in this land, but also that we are Christians', and the rights of Indians to their land and the produce thereof was embodied in the first Brazilian Constitution of 1824 and in all six succeeding ones to date.

Then, at the end of the century, came the rubber boom. Amerindians were found to be better than Africans at searching the forests for the wild rubber trees, and all the atrocities began again with renewed vigour. For over a decade, while there was an insatiable demand for rubber only obtainable in Amazonas, huge fortunes were made and the wild extravagances of Manaus were fuelled by the indiscriminate slavery of tens of thousands of Indians. The floggings and tortures were crueller than ever and it is said that one company alone, the notorious British-registered Peruvian Amazon Company, murdered 30,000 Uitoto Indians. Roger Casement's report on the conditions on the Putamayo river in Peru, for which he was knighted, caused a sensation in Europe and a new crisis of conscience in Brazil. It also coincided with the collapse of the rubber boom caused by competition from the new plantations in Malaya, grown from seeds stolen from Brazil. I have always had a secret, almost guilty, admiration for Casement. An Anglo-Irishman like myself, passionate in his defence of the Indians, he was eventually shot as a traitor by the British!

Determined that Indians should never again be exploited in this way, the Brazilian Government created an Indian Protection Service (SPI), the first such body of its kind in the Americas, with noble ideals and led by the great Marshal Rondon, himself an Indian. While the SPI's philosophy was to integrate Indians into Brazilian society, an ideal which Rondon himself turned against on his deathbed, the humanity with which this ultimately mistaken and unworkable policy was applied did at least stop the slaughter. Unfortunately it did little to slow the decline of the Indian population, as efforts were now directed at contacting remote tribes in the course of running telegraph lines across the country. Indians who had previously fled from the brutality of the slavers were tempted out with gifts and kindness, only to die in their turn from disease.

On 23 February 1969 an article was published by Norman Lewis in the *Sunday Times* Colour Supplement which was to have far-reaching effects. It was entitled 'Genocide' and arose from a rare piece of public self-examination by the Brazilian Government. The article described the contents of an official report into the workings of the SPI, in which it was revealed that the Service, having become almost totally corrupt, had been dissolved and there was to be a judicial inquiry into the conduct of 134 functionaries. The Attorney-General of Brazil was quoted as saying that he doubted if more than one per cent of the one thousand or so employees would be fully cleared of guilt. At a press conference he had supplied more of the report's findings. Under the auspices of the Service Indian lands had been stolen, whole tribes had been destroyed, bacteriological warfare, bombing with dynamite and starvation had been used against them, children had been abducted and mass murder had gone unpunished. He catalogued some of the tribes who had, through the direct activities of the Service, been reduced almost to extinction, starting with the Munducurus, believed to number 19,000 only 30 years before and now down to 1,200 and ending with many groups reduced to a single family. After some moving first-hand descriptions of massacres of Indians, the article ended with the prediction of Professor Darcy Ribeiro, the leading authority on the Indians of Brazil, that there would not be a single Indian left alive in Brazil in 1980. I believe that it is partly due to what happened next that his gloomy forecast has so far been averted.

The following week there was a letter in the same paper signed by Nicholas Guppy and Francis Huxley, both authors of good books on Amerindian tribes,* saying that an international organization for the protection of primitive peoples should be formed. Conrad and I immediately made contact with them and during the summer a series of meetings took place in my London flat to which many of those interested in the subject came and a great many ideas were exchanged. Among them were John Hemming, who was just finishing his great book *The Conquest of the Incas*, as well as other anthropologists such as Audrey Colson and James Woodburn; Teddy Goldsmith, who was about to start the *Ecologist* magazine; Adrian Cowell, recently returned from making his award-winning film in the Xingu, *The Tribe that Hides from Man*; and many others. When over 30 people began to turn up and there was barely room to squeeze everyone in, it was decided to take premises and form a proper charity.

Largely thanks to Nicholas Guppy's efforts, distinguished sponsors were persuaded to support us. The legal groundwork necessary for creating a charity was done and The Primitive Peoples' Fund was formed. It was not a good name. Although there was a courageous minority who wished to prove to the world that 'primitive' should be recognized as a favourable and accurate term identifying the very qualities and differences from materialist society, most people, especially in Africa and the USA, could not escape from the pejorative overtones of the word; and so we decided to change our name to Survival International.

Our first objective was to raise money so as to get the organization off the ground, arouse public opinion to the plight of those we wished to help and initiate practical field projects. This was, and has continued to be, a major headache since the beneficiaries of our 'charity' fell into none of the conventional pigeonholes for aid. They were not all starving, or children,

---

* *Wai Wai* by N. Guppy (John Murray, 1958); *Affable Savages* by F. Huxley (Rupert Hart-Davis, 1963).

or old, or ill. They were just dying out and with the problems of the population explosion elsewhere everyone could understand why there were those who suggested this might not be a bad thing. Nor could the Indians be simply left alone, desirable though it might seem at times, since the world was encroaching on them irrevocably and they needed help in coping with it. Ironically, support would have been much more readily available had we not been concerned with human beings, and very complex, different and sometimes strange ones at that. The World Wildlife Fund, whose President, Peter Scott, was one of our sponsors, had grown out of all recognition in the previous few years and was doing an invaluable and admirable job, but we were dealing with an even more difficult and tricky subject than the preservation of species of fauna, and the results were much more difficult to achieve or even hope for. Although our first job was to work for the physical survival of the people we were concerned with, it was also necessary to look beyond that at the survival of their culture and pride, their skills and talents, so that they should not just enter our society at its lowest level, with no hope of rising any higher, but should at best be given the chance one day of joining us on equal terms, with a sense of identity with the past and a useful contribution to make to the future.

Some positive action to illustrate what our work was all about was badly needed and within a year a golden opportunity was dropped in my lap. Constantly under attack in the international press since the release and subsequent suppression of the report on the corruption of the SPI, the Brazilian Government invited me, as Chairman of Survival International, to visit their country, assess the position of the Indians and consider the possibilities of co-ordinating international aid for them. The previous year a Medical Mission of the International Committee of the Red Cross had undertaken a 'survey of the conditions of existence and health of the indigenous populations in a number of different regions of Brazil'. They had confined themselves largely to medical matters, but the news they brought back was disturbing.

A new government agency responsible for Indian Affairs, the Fundacão Naçional do Indio (FUNAI), had been created to replace the discredited and disbanded SPI and there were high hopes in some quarters that a new broom was now about to sweep away all the corruption. Once again Brazil would lead the world in idealism and practical concern for its Indians. But there were ominous signs as well. FUNAI was still only a small and ill-funded department under the Ministry of the Interior, whose specific brief was to open up the west to settlement and development by colonists and prospectors. The trans-Amazon road programme with its network of endless interconnecting swathes across the forest was gathering momentum. At one time the old SPI had been directly responsible to the President and so able to devote its efforts to the welfare of the Indians without other considerations and we had hoped that FUNAI would be given the same freedom, but it was not to be.

Most sinister of all was the fact that the celebrated official report into the SPI had vanished, the offices where all the files were kept having mysteriously burnt down shortly after the scandal hit the press; the judicial inquiry had never taken place and not a single SPI functionary had been prosecuted or punished in any way. It was widely believed that the new FUNAI was largely staffed by those who had escaped justice.

For the first time Marika came with me and, after twelve years of marriage, we found that we made an excellent expedition team. Her excitement and enthusiasm at all the new sights and experiences, her sharp and accurate judgement of character, whether of a Brazilian general or Indian chief, above all the fun and companionship we shared more than complemented the work I was doing, struggling to understand complex issues involved, in laboured Portuguese, and treading a delicate tightrope between the intolerance of prejudice and a too-eager idealism.

One of our first meetings in Brasilia was with the recently appointed head of FUNAI, General Bandeira de Mello, previously of the secret police, an all-too-familiar route into the Indian Service. A short, stout man with narrow eyes and a shock of white hair, he appeared to take an instant dislike to me and he launched into the attack right away. Since we were official guests of the government there were moments when he had to be polite and at all our meetings he alternated confusingly between abuse and flattery.

After a charming speech of welcome in his luxurious office he turned on me and shouted that there was no Indian problem in Brazil and no outside help was needed. Standing by a large wall-map dotted with coloured pins to mark the locations of different tribes, he began to move these about in a frantic and apparently haphazard way saying he was going to resettle remote groups nearer to civilization. Then, he said, their children could be taken from them and educated and the adults would live much longer than in the wild. I asked, perhaps a little provocatively, if any surveys had been made of the ages of groups of uncontacted Indians and he roared at me that everything necessary was now known about all the Indians in Brazil so that anthropologists were no longer needed.

Then suddenly the atmosphere changed completely while we were formally presented with black wooden Nambiquara wedding rings wrapped up in little boxes, tied with ribbon and containing a prettily worded message from the President of FUNAI welcoming us again formally to Brazil.

Immediately this was over I was violently attacked again on the subject of Orlando and Claudio Villas Boas. These remarkable, almost legendary brothers, among the handful of SPI employees to be praised in the famous report, had for 30 years worked unceasingly to create a sanctuary for the Indians at the headwaters of the Xingu river. Entirely due to their efforts, a large park had been created which was at that time regarded internationally as a model of its kind. The Royal Geographical Society had awarded the brothers a Gold Medal and, as a Council Member, I had been commissioned to deliver their citation. We had also arranged through Survival International for them to be nominated jointly for the Nobel Peace Prize which would help to bring our cause to the attention of the world as well as honouring two universally admired, courageous and dedicated men. The General was furious about this, telling me that the Villas Boas were no better than 'any other low-ranking' FUNAI officials. My gentle remonstration that such a prize would bring credit on Brazil as well was dismissed with an angry shrug.

Later, in the presence of his boss, the Minister of the Interior and a minister from the Foreign Office who were both charming, courteous and sensible about the issues, he behaved even more strangely. We had been discussing the rates of integration which might be considered possible for Indians and agreeing that at least two or three generations were necessary for people to come to terms with a totally new culture and set of values when the General interrupted. Monopolizing the conversation he delivered a tirade on the subject, declaring, 'It is no longer necessary to use the old slow process. Now we have new psychological [at this point the phlegm flew] methods for doing it in six months!'

I asked him what these were and he replied, 'We have applied psychology to the subject and we resettle them as quickly as possible in new villages and then remove the children and begin to educate them. We give them the benefit of our medicine and education, and once they are completely acculturated we let them go out into the world as completely integrated citizens like you and me and the Minister here.'

I protested. Surely it was not quite as easy as that, and would at least take longer than six months? But again he insisted, 'We can now bring totally isolated Indians into a state of full integration in a period of six months. We do not need the advice of so-called experts.'

He then began to attack me directly, saying that all I wanted to do was put the Indians in a zoo and treat them like animals.

The Minister then intervened, which was just as well as I was in danger of losing my temper, and said that surely in many cases the whole process would need to take as much as three generations. At this the General interrupted and insisted, 'No! We can do it in six months', and the

Minister went on to say that of course it was necessary that the process should be as rapid as possible. He also said that it was an internal matter for Brazil to work out. To this I replied that, although the situations were totally different, the same could be said of South Africa, but that did not stop people in other countries being concerned.

'Although the United Nations is not yet very involved in the problems of primitive peoples,' I went on, 'a huge amount of concern and a deep desire to do something to help does exist in Europe, the United States and elsewhere. All I am trying to do is to see if this concern can be put to good use, rather than destructive criticism.'

Although we had been promised every co-operation, including a small airforce plane and *carte blanche* to go wherever we wished, the General attempted to put every possible obstacle in our path, refusing to countenance any deviation from the first tentative itinerary and declaring that it was quite unsuitable for a woman to go to such places.

It was a huge relief when we were at last able to leave the skyscraper world of Brasilia bureaucracy and fly off to the Xingu.

During the next three months we were to visit 33 tribes of Indians, ranging from shy people who had barely seen an outsider before and groups still retaining their pride and self-respect to wretched beggars living abject, diseased lives in squalid slums. We were to be embraced and felt all over with affection or curiosity or aggression on arrival. Marika, encountering this unfamiliar treatment for the first time, had to overcome her desire to scream and run away. We were to weep together as we left people who in a few days had charmed us with their love and trust so that we felt as close to them as to any friends in our familiar world. We were to argue endlessly with all sorts of people about the future: dedicated people whose lives were devoted to the Indians; fanatics who wished to impose their own religious or civic values on them; intellectuals who viewed the subject dispassionately as though we were discussing the fate of fishes; cynics whose sole idea was to exploit both Indians and environment to the limit.

We were condemned to an evening with a gross example of the last sort before we left Brasilia. His name was Sam, he was from Texas, and he was building up a chain of vast ranches in the Mato Grosso. Smoking a fat cigar he showed reel after reel of film of himself getting in and out of his small plane carrying crates of beer and Coca-Cola at various remote airstrips. He admitted that although he flew his aeroplane regularly to inspect his properties, he seldom, if ever, spent a night there. Some Xavante Indians were, he said, 'allowed' to live on a corner of his land but he said they would have to go soon as he needed to clear the jungle there. He was proud of the way he treated them, saying that every month or so he gave them a sack or two of rice and beans – and the current edition of *Playboy* magazine, which he showed pictures of them looking at, among hoots of laughter from the rest of the audience. He claimed to admire the Xavante, saying that they were very tough guys who were independent and had no wish to be assimilated, but he finally destroyed his credibility with his next remark.

'You can buy the land out there now for the same price as a couple of bottles of beer per acre. When you've got half a million acres and twenty thousand head of cattle, you can leave the lousy place and go and live in Paris, Hawaii, Switzerland or anywhere you choose.'

It seems a pity that the opening up of Brazil's interior should be in the hands of such men.

It would be hard to find a greater contrast than that between Sam and the man with whom we were to spend the next three weeks. Since then Claudio Villas Boas, growing old and ill after a lifetime of incredible physical hardship and deprivation spent almost entirely living in the interior, has retired and left the Xingu National Park which he and his brother created. Orlando, still fighting for the Indians, has been attacked by politicians, criticized by anthropologists, and disowned by other

In the Xingu National Park medical teams regularly visited the
Indian tribes living there, inoculating them against fatal
Western diseases.

workers for the Indian cause. The Villas Boas approach to defending Indians by isolating them from the influences of missionaries and 'progress' has been branded paternalistic by many of the Indians themselves, and times and policies have changed. But I cannot ever deny the debt I owe to Claudio for convincing me utterly of the rightness of our cause. His humility and gentleness, combined with an absolute fearlessness in the face of physical or moral danger, had the effect on me of forging for ever my commitment to the people to whom he had devoted his life.

The foundation of his philosophy was that different ideals should be applied to the Indians' problems as to the rest of Brazil's population. The 'Indian' problem, he said, did not arise from the existence of the Indians but from the desire to change them and incorporate them in some vast gesture towards progress that would help neither them nor anyone else. Without this desire to interfere there really need be no problem. If Brazil would only wait until the rest of the population were sufficiently mature to understand the Indians' values, then they might well find that the problem no longer existed because the land on which the Indians lived was no longer needed and the Indians themselves, instead of being regarded as a liability, would come to be regarded as a national asset. It might then be possible for the Indians to take their rightful place in Brazilian society and play a useful part in its future.

Claudio said, 'The Indians are our ancestors and we owe them honour. Human beings are of much greater value than the moon. We have forgotten this and now we struggle with vast problems of our own making, ignoring the things which make our lives worth living.

'Why do we not solve the one human problem which lies within our power to solve?

'No man could integrate the Indian into our society. Into what sort of society could the Indian actually integrate? Into the society of frontiersmen and farmers and prospectors opening up the interior of Brazil? No! Into the *favelas* of Rio and São Paulo? They would come out even lower.

'Trace any process of integration which has taken place and watch the destruction of the people concerned. You cannot integrate an Indian by modern technological means. It has never been done and must always fail. At least give the problem time and let us try to learn. There is no need for hurry.

'The Indian is happy, he is complete, he needs none of our culture for his happiness; only medicines to protect him against our ills.

'In ten to fifteen years the Indians will vanish, not just as a culture but as human beings. They will physically die. The Indians should never be involved in other development programmes. They should be left alone and only given the help they need and want.

'The Xingu National Park is the only place left where you will see Indians living as they did before and always have. Elsewhere they are changed or broken into little groups. What good would it do to remove the park? It will turn into three or four large *fazendas* which will contribute nothing to the national economy.

'The best that integration could offer the Indians would be to make them small-time farmers farming their own property – a fine aspiration for our own poor people, but no step up for the Indians. Can anyone honestly say that the Indians would be any better off like that? Let us wait ten or twenty more years until we have a society fit for the Indians to integrate into and ready to receive them. The trans-Amazonian roads need put no pressure on the Indians if the park and other Indian areas are avoided.

'To improve the Indians' lot beyond their wildest dreams would cost next to nothing. Give them all they need – isolation, medical help and all the clothes, fish hooks and tools they want. If there were three million Indians then Brazil might have a problem, but there are so few. It would not only be in their best interests but also much cheaper to leave them be and take care of them than to try and change them.'

Claudio said he saw a new type of world coming, after Capitalism and Communism had both failed. It would arrive out of an awareness that we had over-exploited our world and that further exploitation would only bring about our own destruction. A new respect for cultural diversity would create a world in which the ways of an individual or a group would be respected and it would not be necessary to conform to certain rigid principles. It would be a world in which the Indian would have a place in society.

I asked him what sort of society this would be and he answered, 'You are the first sign of this society which I see coming.'

To have been allowed to sit at the feet of such a man was a great privilege. To listen as he described his own feelings and thoughts, the result of more years of practical work with Brazil's Indians than anyone else could claim, was fascinating. To realize that his views as a field-worker in constant dialogue with the Indians matched those of Survival International's founders, based as they were on mainly anthropological experience and idealism, convinced me that we were on the right track.

Marika and I described the months we travelled through Brazil in our two books written at the time (my own *A Question of Survival* and Marika's *For Better, For Worse*): the adventures and excitements we shared travelling vast distances by light aircraft, jeep, canoe, horse and on foot, the frustrations and obstacles, the discomforts and dangers. For Marika it was an eye-opening time of new experiences and at last she was able to share with me the magic of travel in the tropics and see and write for herself

Claudio Villas Boas with the Juruna Indians near the edge of
the Xingu National Park. Many were massacred a year later
by invading settlers.

about the exotic world with which I had become so familiar that I hardly
noticed my surroundings any more. For me it was a time of intense mental
concentration as I struggled to understand the issues, to decide what was
the correct attitude to take and to search for hopeful signs that our new
organization might, against all the odds, have a role to play. For us both,
our time in the Xingu passed like a dream. We were together and very
happy and excited. We were surrounded by some of the most beautiful
and apparently happy and unspoilt people on earth. We were filled with
hope for the future.

There was a strength about the different groups of Upper Xingu Indians
which I have not often seen elsewhere. In spite of nearly 30 years of
contact, settlement and administration by outsiders they appeared not to
have lost confidence in themselves and in their way of life. And however
much it may have become unfashionable and suspect recently among
defenders of Indians to dwell on the exotic and different, I have to say that
they were beautiful. There is a glow about bodies which have always been

naked which the habitually clothed can never acquire. Those for whom nakedness is natural do not look nude and there is nothing remotely vulgar or shameful about them. The men stood proud and tall like Greek gods and the women had smooth and honey-coloured skin which shone as though oiled.

For Marika visiting Indians
was a completely new
experience.

Because Claudio told them that I was there to try and help them in the future we were heaped with presents and we quickly learned to restrain ourselves from admiring anything or it would be thrust upon us. Even so we were unable to refuse quantities of finely made arrows, bows, feather headdresses, mother-of-pearl necklaces and some of the fine pots made by the Waura. Most are still with me in Cornwall. The Indians danced and celebrated a time of plenty. We talked and talked and felt privileged to be a part of it all for a time.

Our next stop, Bananal, was a sad shock. The lush rivers on the island I remembered from Richard's and my visit a dozen years before were now almost empty of fish and wildlife, their banks burned by the influx of settlers farming cattle. The Indians were confined behind barbed wire in huts where they were forced to live in single-family units. We watched,

'Civilized' Karaja Indians being forced to dance for visitors by
uniformed Indian guards.

sickened, as, forced to dance for the distinguished visitors, some of the
Karaja made a pathetic effort, jeered at by *civilizados* and FUNAI functionaries. This was one of the places the General had cited as being a
particularly fine example of successful integration. I remembered how
proudly the Indians had danced the last time.

As we travelled around Brazil we were to see many more depressing
sights. In the south, the once-proud horsemen warriors of the Kadiwieu
had been reduced to scratching a living from poor plots; the efficient
Terena, traditionally fine gardeners, were having their land stolen from
them; Levi-Strauss's noble Bororo were cowed into submission by
aggressive Protestant missionaries who had forbidden them to dance and
sing, decorate themselves or practise any of their traditional customs.

From time to time we met outstanding people working with dedication
for the Indians, usually against huge odds, prejudice and even danger
from the authorities, for derisory wages. There is something about the
Indians of Brazil which, when it does not bring out a desire to destroy what
is not understood, produces from time to time a level of selflessness and
dedication seldom found in any other sphere of life.

Outside Cuiaba there was a small country hospital for Indians. It
consisted of three rough thatched buildings; the generator seldom worked

and the equipment was limited. But it was without question the most valuable FUNAI service in the whole of that part of Brazil. This was entirely due to the diminutive Japanese-Brazilian nurse in charge, Dona Cecilia. Outwardly meek, mild and docile, she radiated a determination and forcefulness that made everyone, from puffed-up petty bureaucrats to angry, naked tribesmen, do exactly what she wanted without question. She was one of those rare people who held together, with the sheer force of her personality and strength of will, an organization that would otherwise collapse.

The hospital was constantly short of medical supplies and funds and had a skeleton labour force of only three or four. Yet it served a vital and perhaps unique role in Brazil in the fight to save the Indians from extinction. Valuable help was given by the Peace Corps who had provided two American girls as laboratory assistants. The approach road was very rough and sometimes impassable when the rains washed away the narrow plank bridges. Nearby was a corral where two milk cows were kept, providing the much-needed milk for the children suffering from tuberculosis but not enough for anybody else. Nearby was a vegetable patch where some recuperating Indians were working. As many as 70 Indians from the various tribes of the northern Mato Grosso had been cared for at one time there, although this must have made for terrible overcrowding. Our visit coincided with a serious measles epidemic among the Nambiquara groups along the Guaporé river, and so the hospital was very busy. In one group alone, the Sararé, it was estimated that half the tribe (25 out of 50) had died. Most of the deaths had been among women and children. This, of course, reduced the chances of the tribe surviving the disaster.

We saw several Nambiquara at the hospital. One man lay weak and emaciated on a bed, his apparently fully recovered small son lying beside him. The wife and mother had died the day before. On the next bed another man lay flat on his back staring at the ceiling. His wife and two children had died back in the Sararé village. An appallingly thin and wasted woman in a coma was being drip-fed intravenously. Her husband, a tall Nambiquara with a shaven head, was very agitated about the situation. While we were visiting the kitchen he came and took two burning logs from the stove and went to make his own fire outside the house. Once he had got this going he returned and tried to carry his wife out to sleep in the open beside him. Dona Cecilia explained patiently, but firmly, in sign language and a few words, that this was impossible, but that he could come into the ward and sleep next to her on the floor.

Something then occurred which Marika and I always said afterwards was one of the most moving experiences of our lives. We were standing together against the wall and we had our arms around each other. The Nambiquara in his agitated state was looking around desperately. He caught sight of us and for a moment his face relaxed into a smile as he clearly recognized us as an affectionate married couple. With great emotion he put his arms around both of us, expressing his grief at being unable to embrace his own wife. Alternating between gentleness and anger, moving rapidly with extraordinarily vivid miming and descriptive sounds, he told us in an unmistakable way how they had been brought to the hospital in an aeroplane, how he missed his village and would like to fly back there with his wife. Everyone watched in silence.

Going over to his wife he opened his cupped hands like a flower unfolding over her stomach to tell how she had borne three children and then drew the empty air around him into a circle of his arms to show how the children needed him now.

We both found this demonstration very touching, in particular the way in which his love for his wife transcended all other feelings, overcoming the strangeness of the hospital and the unfamiliar setting. We felt hopelessly inadequate and were grateful when Dona Cecilia allowed us to give glasses of water to some of the weak patients who needed help.

Often the only people working with the Indians were missionaries. There is no doubt that, in several cases, without their presence settlers would have moved in and killed or chased off the whole group. There is considerable fear of the Indians in Brazil. I was asked several times by people living in large cities whether I thought there was a chance of an Indian uprising. Considering the very small proportion of Indians in the population (less than 0.1 per cent), their very wide distribution over the large country, and the fact that they come from about 150 different and usually inimical tribes, the idea is ludicrous.

In the interior the fear is slightly more rational as clashes have taken place, and still do, in which both *civilizados* and Indians are killed. But cases of Indian attacks on farms or villages are extremely rare, though always given maximum publicity in the press. It is unfortunate that the Brazilian population pioneering the remoter territories usually consists of the least suitable representatives of Western culture. The splendid lack of racial discrimination which is such a striking feature of Brazil and which, even if not complete, puts most of the rest of the world to shame, sadly vanishes when it is a question of Indians. The desperately poor settlers on the fringe of civilization whose standard of living, physique and culture is patently worse than that of the members of a thriving Indian community, believe that those Indians are dangerous, unpredictable animals. And whatever other possessions he may lack, the settler is sure to have a gun, which means that he is militarily superior at any meeting. If he is lucky and

During three months in 1971 Marika and I visited and lived
with 33 different Indian tribes in Brazil.

finds that he has settled some of the marginally better land in the interior, he may be able to extract a living from it. If this turns into a surplus it is most likely that he will use the profits from selling this surplus to hurry back to the cities of the coast.

Indians, on the other hand, lacking resistance to the *civilizados'* diseases, need civilization's medicines to cure or protect them. So either they run further into the jungle, often taking the disease with them and spreading the epidemic to other groups, or they become dependent upon charity to be cured. If this is provided in an enlightened way, it may be possible for them not to be destroyed in the process, but too often the overpowering demonstration of technological or moral superiority that goes with it destroys the Indians' self-confidence and they, too, grow to believe that there is something inferior and wrong with them. Once this happens there is little chance of their ever entering Brazilian society as equals.

Some of the missionaries we met were fine men working passionately for the Indians' welfare, motivated doubtless by Christian zeal but interested in practical solutions to very real problems rather than proselytization at all costs. Others were so fanatically bigoted as to defy the imagination, so that Marika and I reeled away from encounters with them, appalled.

One of the best was a young Jesuit priest dressed in mechanic's overalls and riding a motorbike whom we met with the Paresis. Marika found him devastatingly attractive and watched jealously as we talked non-stop in Portuguese. He had travelled and worked among the Indians of that region for several years and was well known as an expert on them. We talked for several hours and I was most impressed by his unbiased and liberal approach to the problem. He was against taking children away from their parents to educate them in special schools, as both Protestant and Catholic missions had done, and said that it had never worked in Brazil. 'Far more important,' he said, 'is to educate the Brazilian people to understand the Indians.'

He said it was more important for us to learn what the Indians' needs were and then try to satisfy those needs than to impose change for its own sake. The Paresi Indians were in a mess because, in order to develop and exploit their reserve, they ought to introduce cattle and ranch them; this, he believed, was the use for which the land was best suited although I questioned whether he was right since the land was dry, barren scrub. But the Indians neither had the capital nor any knowledge of how to look after them. In spite of 50 years of contact they were still hunters at heart, and the changeover to an economy dependent on agriculture required expert advice and study. Since this was not forthcoming and game was increasingly hard to find, they had grown to depend on the road and to put all their confidence in it. But the road produced practically nothing for them except the sale of a few shoddy artefacts to lorry drivers, begging and prostitution and they were left worse off than their neighbours to the south and to the north – the Terena who were acculturated and beginning to cope with the situation and the Nambiquara, who, in spite of all their other problems, at least had much of their tribal culture still intact.

He also thought that urgent research should be made into the Indians as patients. At the moment they tended to run away when taken to hospital and it was difficult to treat them. Health, he said, was the first priority in the struggle to keep the Indians alive.

He was not afraid to criticize much of what his Church had done with the Indians in the past, although he did insist that the Catholic Church had done far less damage in recent years than the Protestant missions.

The attitude of the Protestant missionaries in Brazil has often been attacked by anthropologists and others. The International Red Cross team of doctors had also criticized the work of some of those we met and it had been officially announced after that visit that some of them were to be removed. A few were expelled for a time and prohibited from working with the Indians, but we heard that most, if not all, had subsequently returned. One American living in a luxurious house next to one of the most wretched Indian villages we saw told us over a large breakfast of pancakes, bacon, and maple syrup, while two Indian men scrubbed the floor on their hands and knees beside us, that this tribe, the Paresi, were like Jews, lazy and with no desire to learn. It was vital that they should do so as their only hope lay in education and, since they refused to do it the easy way, the only solution was forcibly to remove the children and educate them while making the adults settle and work. As far as his own efforts at evangelization went, he defended these by saying that what he was trying to do was not to change the Indians' beliefs but merely to alter them slightly. His theory was that they already believed in good and evil spirits but worshipped the devil because they regarded the evil spirits as stronger than the good ones. All he and other evangelists wanted to do was to make them change to worshipping the good spirits and gradually give them Christian names.

The power such men are able to wield, largely through intimidation, is appalling and the Indians under their control are rapidly reduced to abject servitude. Another Protestant fundamentalist, an Englishman, savagely attacked the Villas Boas brothers and the Xingu National Park as a den of iniquity. At first we could not make out what he was getting so agitated about, as he kept skirting around the subject with vague allusions to corruption and Satan. It was only when he showed us some of his own photographs that I fully understood the depth of his puritanical abhorrence of nudity. Wherever naked Indians were shown, their genitals had been scratched out so violently that the nib of the pen had torn the paper.

By no means all Protestant missionaries I have met have been bad and all Catholics good, though I have tended to feel more sympathy with the latter. One of the most charming Catholics was the German priest in charge of the Franciscan mission to the Tirio Indians in the far north of Brazil against the Surinam border. A park called Tumucumaque consisting of some 25,000 sq. km had been created there in 1968 and it was the only place we saw during our time in Brazil which compared with the Xingu in giving a sense of hope. Padre Cyrille Hass was a remarkable man of varied talents. Although a conscientious priest, whom the Indians seemed to like and respect, he should really have been an engineer. His great interest and obsession in life was with things mechanical, and he was a highly competent all-round handyman. It was through his abilities in this direction that he saw himself best able to help the Indians towards reaching a level on which they could compete with the modern world. Talking about the nature of the Indian he told me that he believed him to be more intelligent than the *caboclo*, the usually half-caste backwoodsman of the Amazon.

'He takes to Western equipment more quickly and more intelligently than the *caboclo* and, unlike him, does not take kindly to being pushed around, learning best by observation and example. I have taken great care not to force any change upon the Indians but to allow them to watch me at work and see that what I do is sometimes better than their way, so that they may choose to imitate me.

'When I first came to the village – this was ten years ago – I began by living in a house like theirs. Then I built a new house, still with a thatched roof, but with wooden sides which kept out the animals and insects and was more comfortable. Now you will see that about half the houses in the village have followed my example and about half have chosen to stay as they are. The Indians are choosing for themselves. One day the Indians may need stone houses and I am building one as a workshop down by the farm at the moment. My bishop wanted me to fly in cement and make concrete blocks to build this, but the Indians have no cement and it will be a long time before they will be able to buy any. So I am learning how to make bricks myself; they are learning with me and they will not forget.

'The same applies to bridges which we build, and the roads. At first, the Indians appear not to be interested, or they are scornful. But then they find themselves using our things and discover how much easier they make life. They are learning to work with my tools and to make things for themselves.'

A man of boundless energy and enthusiasm for new ideas, the priest told me that he was planning to install a water-pump so as to bring piped water to the village, and that he also had a much more ambitious plan to dig a canal some four miles long and develop a hydroelectric scheme. This, he said, would not only benefit the Indians directly by providing light for the village, but the dispensary would be able to sterilize its instruments, and other projects would follow.

The gravest threat that he saw to the park was tourism, something much in the news just then. He was violently opposed to encouraging tourists and said the idea should be quashed at once as it was the worst possible thing for the Indians.

'At present they are healthy and making good progress,' he said. 'Bring in tourists, and all that has been done for them will be destroyed. They will lose their self-confidence, their pride and their ability to fend for themselves. They will become beggars.'

We talked about integration and agreed that the Indians should be protected in their natural environment. He felt that the object must be to raise the Indian to a level at which he can compete with the rest of civilization and that this should be done as fast as possible, as the Indians might be faced with the need to compete at any moment. The Villas Boas brothers were not going fast enough, he thought, and so might be doing the Indians a disservice.

Although they were men of such very different talents, there was much in our conversation which reminded me of Claudio. The practical man and the philosopher, both in their separate ways, came to much the same conclusion concerning the Indians' welfare and needs. They had never met and I encouraged Padre Cyrille to go and visit Claudio in the Xingu. But I fear this meeting, at which I would have loved to be a fly on the wall, has not yet taken place.

The most important meetings and conversations I had were with the Indians themselves. Often with only limited language in common, little time to develop trust and sympathy and sometimes under the suspicious eye of a feared missionary or government official, it was not always easy.

---

on following pages

Bayano Cuna Indians with a magnificent draught of fishes from the river.

Toraja houses are among the most spectacular and beautiful to be seen anywhere in the world.

Marika and I entering the Hua Ulu village on the island of Ceram – only the second group of outsiders to do so.

One of the first To Wana boys met in the interior of Eastern Sulawesi in 1974. Despite his goggles and bathing suit we were the first Europeans he had seen.

But I acquired some useful talents in the process. The first was a 'nose' for atmosphere. Sitting quietly for a day or so with a contented group of Indians such as the Kamayura in the Xingu, watching the women and children at work and play, the men as they returned in the evening, made me sensitive to conditions which were not so ideal. And I found that the Indians themselves were far more aware of the problems that they faced, their causes, effects, and possible solutions, than almost anyone around them gave them credit for. I became, and remain, convinced that solutions are possible to most of the ills besetting Brazil's Indians, but that these can only be brought about by the Indians themselves. All they need is time to recover from the shock of contact and subsequent abuse, respect as equals so that they can restore their self-confidence and enough of their traditional land to support themselves. It sounds so little and yet the attitude of the Brazilians shows almost no sign of changing.

There were a few good and honest FUNAI functionaries whom we met, although they all complained that supplies, funds, even their small salaries were always months late in reaching them, and there was resentment of the top-heavy bureaucracy where most employees never left Brasilia or had any contact with Indians. Men of courage and character, prepared to stand up and fight for the Indians, were even fewer. One whom I liked and whose company I found stimulating, although I was doubtful about some of his ideas, was Apoena Meirelles. His father had pacified several tribes including some of the Xavante after whose chief Apoena was named. Apoena was in charge of the large FUNAI delegacy of Rondonia and currently preoccupied with making contact with a large tribe called the Cinta Larga. We had flown with him over some of their still uncontacted villages deep inside another vast, ill-defined park called the Aripuana, also created during the heady days of 1968. We had seen the Indians standing outside their huge communal houses, waving at our plane, in anger or friendship we could not tell – a strangely disturbing experience.

Apoena was young and fiery, fearless and outspoken one moment, shy, sensitive and even secretive the next. He felt very deeply about the Indians and it was clear that he had a remarkable gift of communication and sympathy with them. By all accounts he was the only person whom the Cinta Larga trusted and would deal with, and he was prepared to fight fiercely on their behalf. He had grand plans for the Aripuana Park and didn't want to create another model of the Xingu system, but to develop an economically viable unit where the Indians, thanks to their rich land, would be able to compete with the surrounding settler population. In this way he hoped that they would be able to bypass the worst aspects of shock and move gradually but directly from their present state to one in which

they were again self-supporting. This seemed to me an admirable ideal,
but I was depressed by his stated belief that nothing of the Indian culture
and way of life should or could be preserved. His eventual object was to
make them as like us as possible. We discussed at length the motives of
people who wished to protect the Indians and keep them as they were. He
was suspicious of any suggestion of human zoos or that the Indians
should be preserved as objects for study, and yet he clearly admired and
felt in harmony with their way of life and regarded them, as do so many, as
superior in many ways to the surrounding population. He was very
outspoken about the lack of idealism in most FUNAI employees, referring
to them as 'gigolos of the Indians', in that they regarded their employment
as a job like any other and, as a result, lived off the Indians as parasites
instead of having their best interests at heart.

After three months of travelling over much of the interior of Brazil we
were exhausted. Each visit had been much too short and packed with new
impressions and incidents, facts, theories and ideas. As one visit drew to
an end plans and preparations had to be made for the next one. There had
been no time to rest and no time to think or try and pull the whole jumbled,
confused picture into a coherent shape.

The devastation caused by open-cast tin mining deep in
Indian territory in Brazil.

Marika, who had been taking large quantities of photographs for an educational series on Indian domestic life, flew to New York taking our film with her to have it developed. I made a couple of flights to Indian settlements in Roraima territory from Boa Vista, the capital, but now I suddenly wanted to be alone for the week before the next international flight out of Brazil. Then I met a pilot who knew of a flat piece of ground near Mount Roraima. He knew, because he had recently dropped a party of Brazilians who were climbing the mountain and he was to pick them up again in a few days. If I was back in time, he would fly me out too.

This was a chance not to be missed, not only to climb a legendary mountain, but also to have a quiet period of intense physical activity and to give my mind a chance to unwind.

Roraima is not a particularly difficult mountain to climb. The main problem is its isolation and inaccessibility. It had been climbed before a good many times but always by parties supported by Indians carrying supplies. It had not been my intention to climb it entirely by myself, but the pilot had landed on a level patch of ground about 50 km from the mountain when he discovered that he did not have enough fuel to fly on to the Indian village, at which he had said I would be able to find Indians to accompany me. Rather than fly back to Boa Vista, I had overcome his conviction that I would instantly be eaten by one of the jaguars which he assured me abounded there and had persuaded him to leave me.

After the shaky little single-engined aeroplane had bounced across the stony ground, narrowly missed a shoulder of the hill in taking off and flown away to the south, I sat for a while, looking around. Above me towered a steep, green slope culminating in a sheer, grey cliff which circled the summit like a crown of lamb. Over this poured a thin stream of water, and a plume of cloud drifted away to the west. Near me a small river of clear water, ankle deep, splashed lazily over smooth rocks before disappearing into a green and shady copse. All around lay magnificent vistas. The wooded areas, elegant as if they had been landscaped, set off the hills and rivers that stretched into the distance.

Only to the west was the view interrupted, by a bank of cloud. Somewhere behind it lay the mountain after which the whole territory – four times as large as Switzerland – was named: Roraima.

Having expected to be guided by the Indians who would have carried my supplies, I was badly overloaded with hammocks and blankets as presents for them, as well as a heavy rifle I had been lent in Boa Vista. Taking only the bare essentials with me, machete, sleeping bag, torch, cameras and a bunch of bananas, I hid the rest carefully in a dense thicket on an island in the river and then, wading to the far bank, I began to walk towards the mountain.

There was a faint track, but it kept dividing or disappearing. With part of my mind I had to keep deciding which way to go. The other part wandered in a way that had not been possible for a long time. There was so much to be re-looked at, conversations to be remembered, thoughts to be put in order. It had been an exhausting time mentally.

Away from the need to plan, discuss, think and talk in Portuguese, my step lightened. I walked fast in this silent place. Insects buzzed around my head and birds cried in the patches of jungle.

It was hot and the sun beat down on to the hard, burnt ground. Beyond the immediate hum of insect life and the stirrings and rustlings of the undergrowth, an overpowering silence lay over the landscape. It was lonely, a little frightening.

Impressions came back to me. Memories of the silent Indians; the happiness and the despair, the rightness of their own ways and lives and the utter wrongness when our ideas and beliefs were carelessly and brutally imposed. I remembered the supreme peace of spending even a few hours in their world, where every act had a meaning and was part of a well-ordered but completely free system in which the simple joy of living was still something which could be embraced without shame.

I thought, too, of those who had been angry; the Brazilians who felt that the economic development and progress of the nation was all-important, and that bothersome Europeans, who had already destroyed the cultures in their own colonies, had no right to interfere in Brazil's internal affairs, and were impeding that progress; the frightening number of ordinary, decent people in the country who genuinely believed that Indians were inferior beings, lazy and dangerous, who had a limited use as labourers and were better out of the way altogether.

And then there were the rewarding conversations with those who had trusted me, and for whom my visit, and the fact that people outside cared and wanted to help, represented a new hope of success in what they were trying to do. 'Help us to fight for the Indians,' they had said. 'Teach the world to see what is best for them. Help us to prevent these people whom we love from being destroyed and vanishing off the face of the earth. Help them in the fight for survival. But above all help us with your voice which will carry weight in the world and make the world care.'

It was these conversations that troubled me most, these requests that made me feel afraid and lonely. The responsibility for what came next was mine alone, and was a heavy one. But through taking on the mission I had just completed I had acquired a burden of responsibility which would never leave me while there were still Indians in Brazil and people trying to save them from cultural and physical extinction. If I did nothing, or too little, I would be failing in my duty. If I did or said the wrong things I could easily do more harm than good. I felt inadequate to cope with such an enormous task, but then I had blithely accepted the chance of the journey and must now accept the responsibility that followed.

Towards evening I reached a thick belt of jungle marking one of the rivers I had to cross. I chose a flat piece of ground, hacked up some sandy earth with my knife to make it softer to lie on, laid the sleeping bag over the top and, after eating a couple of bananas, lay down and went to sleep. It was not necessary to use the torch to look around me, and so draw attention to my presence, as light clouds were trailing across the high full moon. I could see the outline of the hills across the valley. Once I heard the gruff barking of a jaguar, and a little later a few drops of rain fell.

As I was warmed by the first rays of the sun, I began to look forward to reaching the water as it was now some thirteen hours since I had last had a drink. I was still separated from the river itself by a steep and densely overgrown slope, and the thick belt of jungle on the far bank looked impenetrable.

I guessed that either this river marked the boundary with Venezuela or I had already crossed the border some time before. It seemed likely, from its size, that it was the Arabopo which is one of the sources of the Caroni river. This in turn joins the Orinoco shortly before it runs into the Caribbean. Mount Roraima is also the source of the Rio Cotingo in Brazil, which runs eventually into the Rio Branco, and so to the Amazon. On the Guyanan side of the mountain is the Mazaruni, which joins the Essequibo near Georgetown. The route to the top of Roraima is on the Venezuelan side, so that although the three-way boundary between Brazil, Venezuela and Guyana is on the top, only Venezuela has access to it. I understood that border patrols seldom visited the region, and hoped this was the case, as I had no current Venezuelan visa. It would be inconvenient to be arrested and taken to the nearest Venezuelan town as this was several days' walk away and would mean that I would miss my flight home from Boa Vista.

At last I reached the point at which a track led down to the water's edge and I was able to scramble down it. I waded across the river, waist-deep in places, and left my possessions on the far bank. I then stripped off my clothes and plunged in for a very refreshing and welcome swim. The water was cool, clear and fast flowing, and there were few mosquitoes and flying insects at that early hour. A light mist rose off the surface upstream where some flat rocks held back the current to form a deep pool. In front of me lay the dark, forbidding stretch of jungle. In its depths a bell-bird was calling monotonously. It sounded like a metal axe-head striking. The peace and solitude almost seduced me: I could gladly have stayed there for the day, avoiding the long journey ahead.

Following the faint track through the dense undergrowth was not easy and I took several wrong turns. But at last I burst into the sunlight again and saw ahead of me the path winding along a narrow ridge gaining height all the time. Here in the open country, it was clear and easy to follow. Roraima grew closer with every step and although I could not make out the ledge leading to the top, I began to hope that I might reach it before nightfall.

At last, the way up the mountain came in sight. A diagonal blur of green vegetation stretched across the cliff face, visible, once I had reached the right side of the mountain, from a good distance. As I came closer, I could see some streams of water pouring over the lip of the rock-face high above, barely checking as they passed through this green band, before continuing their sheer drop to the ground below.

Only the last half-mile or so before reaching the base of the cliffs was jungle, and here the ground rose steeply. I plunged into the undergrowth, following the now clearly defined path. I was glad that I was not having to make a path as I went. The water which poured over the edge of the mountain and the mists which swirled around it every day had created a rain forest at its feet. Everything was wet and overgrown, lichens hung from the twisted trees and the ground was very wet and muddy underfoot.

My legs and feet were very tired from walking. Now, instead of simply having to put one in front of the other in order to go forward, I had to climb. The temptation to stop at the bottom and postpone the climb until the next day was very strong. But I was afraid that I might be so stiff that I would never make it, and the top, directly above me, now seemed so very close. Besides, the Brazilian Expedition was up there somewhere and I looked forward to their company – to say nothing of the food they would undoubtedly have prepared. My one bunch of bananas had long since turned to pulp, and the idea of a square meal encouraged me.

From a distance, the ledge had looked like a regular slope. In reality the path ascended the side of the cliff in a series of switchbacks. Much of the time it was necessary to pull myself up hand over hand by creepers and tree roots before slithering down the next muddy slope. I was soon soaked through and filthy dirty. At the same time my thirst increased. I remember at one point lying on my belly in the mud and reaching in under the cliff to drink from a clear spring while the mist swirled wetly over me. It had begun when I was about halfway up, a solid, grey wall which moved along the side of the mountain, bearing rain and completely blotting out the sky, the view, and the sheer cliffs above and below. This, and the two or three feet of vegetation between me and the edge, made me forgetful of the fact that I had a gradually increasing sheer drop just to my left. Every now and then the rain suddenly poured harder for a few yards and I realized that I was walking through one of the waterfalls.

My legs ached abominably by the time I reached the top, and it was also beginning to grow dark. As I scrambled on all fours up the last rock fall, bare now of vegetation, two shapes loomed out of the mist ahead of me. They were the skulls, complete with curving horns, of two oxen which Marshal Rondon had carried up the mountain to feed his men on a boundary commission in the thirties. Below them were some signs painted on the rock, and beyond them the ground levelled off.

It was now late in the evening and I was very tired. My feet were sore and covered in blisters, my back ached, my shoulders ached and I kept getting cramp in my calves.

I had not counted on the fog. Actually, it was more like a cloud, swirling over the top of the mountain and drenching everything in its path with particles of water. It soaked through my clothes to the few parts of my body which had remained dry during the climb. With the mist and darkness came a dank chill and the rock on which I sat felt cold to the touch, making me shiver. Around me rose grotesque pinnacles and outcrops glimpsed fleetingly behind curtains of mist.

Climbing to the top of the highest point I could find, I stood and shouted, 'hallooed' and yodelled as loudly as my lungs would stand towards the four points of the compass. Silence, except for the faint fluting of the breeze on the rocks. Scrambling down from my pinnacle, I slipped and rolled the last few yards to lie in a shallow puddle, cursing my bruises and quaking at the thought of broken bones in the midst of such desolation.

I groped on through a mad, lunar landscape in which strange, distorted rock shapes leapt up on all sides; blank cliffs, their tops invisible, forced me to change direction; and water lay everywhere in pools whose depth it was impossible to gauge. My sleeping bag, though wet like everything else, was probably still dry inside. I considered getting into it and waiting the night out. But how to get myself a little drier first? And where to lay it when all around was wet, slippery rock and mud and water?

There were no caves and I could see no overhangs. An extraordinary rock, balanced upon the point of another like some gigantic toadstool, looked hopeful, and I scrambled up the side of it. But there was nowhere flat and nowhere dry. The angles were all wrong.

Before reaching the top of the ledge I had seen footsteps in the mud and knew that they must belong to the expedition. They had vanished on the bare rock of the plateau and, with little hope of success, I made my way back to where I had last seen them and began to try and track them further. By now I could only see the ground by the light of my torch, a small one with weak batteries. For 50 metres from the last footprint there was nothing but bare unmarked rock. Then came a narrow channel full of mud separating me from the next stretch. Casting along this, bent double, and examining the ground with intense care, I came to a place where the mud was slightly marked, as though a stick had been trailed through it. This gave me a line and brought me to the next patch where a small cactus had been crushed. A few hundred yards on I found a clear footprint and, as it was not my own, knew that I was on the right track – that is, unless I was following the trail of one of the expedition members who had gone off to walk the ten miles to the far end of the plateau.

For an hour I groped and searched, guessed wrong and retraced my steps. Never has an Indian tracked anybody with more care than I did, having convinced myself that my life depended upon success. Wet, cold and very tired, the twelve soggy hours to daylight seemed like a death sentence. What slimy creatures might not find me if I lay down now? Or was I near the edge and might I step over it at any moment and fall back 1,000 metres from the cliff? Fear kept me awake.

I must have crawled a kilometre before I thought of shouting again. This time there was an answer. A few minutes later I saw the light of a torch. The Indian carrying it looked at me as though I was an apparition from the dead or one of the spirits known to haunt the summit of Roraima. When I reassured him that I was not, he began to laugh and, giggling and shaking his head, led me to where the others were camped.

They sheltered in a shallow cave under an overhanging cliff. Over a roaring fire there bubbled a stew of spam and beans, more welcome to my nostrils than all the spices of Arabia.

The figures silhouetted by the fire rose as I came towards them. For a moment I hesitated, suddenly shy of human company and wondering whether I would be welcome. They looked at me in frank amazement and then we all began to speak at once.

As far as they were concerned, it was just not possible that I could be there. They knew that they were alone on the top of the plateau, and indeed that there was no one else in the region for several kilometres around its base. They knew that darkness had fallen over an hour before, and that there was no other camp on the top. So what was this Englishman doing appearing out of the fog?

It was impossible that I could be there. But they welcomed me generously, pushing a mug of hot chocolate into my hands, and listening while I told them where I had come from and how I had found them.

'But where is the rest of your party?' they asked.

It took some time to convince them that I was alone and had been since the beginning of the climb. This was the part that amazed them most, and in particular the fact that I had slept by myself in the open. For most Brazilians this is a situation to be avoided at all costs.

They were a tough lot that I now shook hands with, unshaven and wrapped in blankets against the cold. Byron, a farouche character with drooping moustaches and the clothing and bearing of a Mexican bandit, who was a lawyer from Boa Vista; Jaime, a *garimpeiro*, or prospector, who had spent most of the last 20 years looking for diamonds in the rivers between the Orinoco, the Essequibo and the Amazon. He was obsessed by diamonds and almost immediately started telling me how good the chances were of finding them on Roraima. He was wearing the jacket of a wet-suit, which surprised me, until he told me that much of his time in the river was spent deep below the muddy water at the end of a crude air-pipe, gathering stones from the mud at the bottom. The third member of the party was Raoul, a government geologist who was a powerfully built young man and looked as though he were always about to drop off to sleep.

Seeing them, and thinking of food ahead of me, I was once more filled with energy and, stripping off the soaking muddy clothes, I rubbed myself down with a dry towel. As I had no other dry clothes, I climbed as I was, into my sleeping bag. Lying as close as possible to the fire, I ate and drank my fill – they even had some wine with them! – and then stretched out on the half-metre or so of dry ground under the ledge, which was all the cave consisted of. The others climbed up higher, to a place where they said there was a deeper recess, but I was content where I was, near the fire with the Indians.

I slept little, turning over and over inside my sleeping bag on the hard ground trying to find a part of my body which did not ache. It was bitterly cold and several times I had attacks of cramp in my legs and feet. But the joy and relief of being in safety was so great that none of this seemed much to have to suffer. At least I was sheltered and dry. Outside, the rain sheeted down and the wind howled, making the mist swirl around us. It was a horrible night and I was glad and thankful to be safe.

The cold woke me. Although it was 8 degrees Centigrade (46 Fahrenheit), after what I had been used to it felt well below freezing. The rain had blown away and the clouds parted so that a shaft of early-morning sunshine was striking the rocks above the cave. A hundred metres below there was a deep pool of clear water. Its whole floor was covered in shining white crystals.

As I was still filthy from the day before, I hobbled down there, threw off my towel and, feeling excessively brave, plunged into the icy water. It was not quite as bad as I had expected since the air temperature was lower than that of the water. As I had soap with me, I had a thorough wash and scrub.

I looked up to see my Brazilian friends emerging from their blankets and looking down with some surprise at this further manifestation of insanity by the mad Englishman.

The wash and swim made me feel ready for anything again, and when I returned to the cave and found that they were cooking porridge for breakfast my joy in the morning knew no bounds.

We went our different ways to explore the top, I to the west, where I climbed on to an outcrop overhanging the yawning space to the green forest floor below. There I sat and looked out across to Kukenaam, Roraima's twin, and watched the clouds play hide-and-seek with it.

For the first time since setting out to climb the mountain I could relax. Now, too, the jumble of ideas and impressions resulting from the previous three months was at last beginning to fall into shape. Somewhere in the back of my mind a pattern was emerging, but the edges were fragile. If I tried to define it too sharply I lost it and again became confused. Putting the 'problems of the Indians in Brazil' into words and trying to spell out solutions in itself tended to cloud the issue.

The Indian is not motivated by the desire to acquire wealth and power greater than other men. He is content if there is game in the forest, fish in the river and crops growing in his clearing. He is not concerned with growing or killing a surplus with which to trade, and so build up wealth for himself or for a community. He does not desire to leave possessions to his offspring. The land on which he lives is enough. Therefore the land is fundamental to the Indian question. If we leave him in possession of his lands – and this means parks and protection – there is no need for rapid change. Medical protection is the only vital necessity. But if we are going to take away his land, then we must also change his whole psychological state by instilling into him the acquisitiveness and material ambition of our society. Can we honestly say that what we have to offer in our world is better?

During that time with Brazil's Indians I came to learn that unconsidered judgements were as dangerous as neglect. The squalor of drunken, hopeless and apparently degenerate beggars desperately in need of help contrasted with the beauty and romance of proud and independent human beings – or noble savages! The one inescapable lesson learned was that they were just people; special and different certainly, threatened and exploited, but by no means necessarily doomed since, given half a chance, they would solve their problems for themselves.

7

'Why Not Come and Live with Us?'

'. . . it is to be hoped that . . . we may at length be able to point to an instance of an uncivilized people who have not become demoralized and finally exterminated by contact with European civilization.'

Alfred Russel Wallace, *Malay Archipelago*, 1869

Following the publication of my Report by Survival International and our books on Brazil, a third mission was sent there by the Aborigines' Protection Society which included John Hemming and Francis Huxley. Their findings supported mine and although, inevitably, elements in the Brazilian Government attempted to discredit us and assured the world that everything necessary had now been seen to, I know that our criticisms and suggestions strengthened the hands of those within Brazil trying to implement humane, enlightened policies towards the Indians. Today, twelve years later, there are still Indians in Brazil and some are even increasing in numbers. Some of the credit for confounding the most gloomy forecasts of the last decade must go to our efforts.

The overall situation, however, continued to deteriorate. The road building and deforestation programmes were stepped up and new dangers of epidemics, attacks and relocation constantly threatened the tribes.

It seemed then to me that only by widening the focus of our concern and making the debate truly international could any major change of attitude be brought about. If it could be shown that these issues were not unique to South America and that in many other parts of the world similar problems were being faced, with similar successes and failures, then in time perhaps attitudes might change and some progress might be made towards solving what I all too often heard referred to in Brazil as 'the Indian problem'. I therefore decided to visit Indonesia, a country comparable to Brazil in size and population but with half a million people officially classified as 'isolated', about five times the number of the Indians in Brazil.

Just as we had to change the name of our organization to Survival International, another semantic problem arose right at the outset and has dogged us ever since. This is the question of what we should call the people Survival International tries to help. When dealing with the Americas it is relatively easy. The indigenous populations have been called, erroneously, Indians ever since the time of Columbus. True, some of the more emancipated and vocal North American nations do now object to this name, but at least they are in a position to choose for themselves, as they have every right to do, and for the rest everyone knows who we are talking about when we refer to American Indians.

But, while it all began with the Brazilian Indians, Survival International never intended to confine its efforts solely to South America. Just as Amnesty International concerns itself with the rights of political prisoners all over the world, irrespective of race, creed, colour or the political persuasion of the government denying them their rights, so Survival International would wish eventually to represent the interests of all indigenous minorities suffering oppression wherever they may live and however they are being exploited. But 'indigenous minorities' is not only cumbersome, it is also too general a term to identify the usually small threatened groups of people nearing cultural and physical extinction, who are the most urgent cases in need of help. 'Native', like 'primitive', has a disparaging connotation in some parts of the world; 'tribal' has quite different implications in Africa from South America; 'isolated' is useful but not by any means always accurate, and so on, the permutations being almost endless. On the whole we have come to use 'tribal peoples', but it is not perfect.

There was one other important similarity between Brazil and Indonesia, apart from size and population. In both countries dense concentrations in certain areas contrasted with vast, sparsely populated hinterlands, and both governments were making considerable efforts to encourage people to occupy the remoter parts. With improved communications and exploding populations, this had inevitably meant that the previously isolated and relatively undisturbed indigenous inhabitants of these areas had met an accelerating barrage of outside influences.

The biggest single difference I began to notice between the two cases was that, whereas in Brazil there had been a long history of concern both within and without the country over the dangers such pressures brought with them to the way of life and, indeed, to the very survival of the tribes affected, in Indonesia the whole question appeared to be a new one which was only then beginning to be raised and of which most people seemed to be totally unaware. Although in Brazil it could hardly be said that concern with these problems and their wider implications had done much to influence national policies, at least I nearly always found that these questions had been raised already and that people were, to some extent at least, aware of them. In Indonesia, perhaps because the country had been insulated for a long time from outside world opinion, ideas about the country's development and future were usually expressed in political, military and financial terms rather than scientific and environmental ones.

Another major difference between Brazil and Indonesia, from the point of view of my particular interests in each country was that, whereas in Brazil the Indians were a fairly easily identified section of the community, in Indonesia it was particularly hard to draw the line between truly 'primitive' peoples and others who were culturally sophisticated but relatively isolated and 'different'. The Indians of Brazil were a numerically small racial minority surrounded, threatened and governed by a vastly more powerful expatriate society originating from Europe, Africa, Japan and elsewhere who had colonized the country and regarded it as their own. Although a very great deal of miscegenation had taken place, both among the colonizing races themselves and between them and the Indians, the indigenous tribes which had retained their identity con-stituted a section of the community which was quite clearly separate from and outside the national identity. Persistent efforts to change this and integrate the Indians had been the main cause of the problems with which I was concerned there.

The Indonesian problem was not so clearly defined. There were small numbers of jungle nomads on several of the islands whose way of life and general situation bore comparison with some of the isolated Indian tribes of South America; there were the vigorous and numerous peoples of the Indonesian part of New Guinea, who are racially and culturally different from the Indonesians who govern them; and there were many other clearly individual peoples throughout the archipelago who had similar racial origins to, for example, the Javanese, but whose societies and cultures had developed in quite different directions. Moreover, the Indonesian Government had always been proudly nationalistic and, since the removal of the Dutch, Western-based social science research had been limited and often suspect.

Once more Marika and I planned to travel together and we were both again commissioned to write books on our experiences. For a year we researched the scanty material available on the remoter tribes of Indonesia. I did a crash course in Bahasa Indonesia and began to make contact with people who might be interested or able to help. The response was overwhelming and we were able to plan an exciting itinerary through the outer islands, which would give a useful general view of the situation. As usual, all but the most valuable and experienced contacts thought we were being wildly over-ambitious, warned us that travel away from recognized tourist routes in Indonesia was almost impossible and strongly urged us to confine ourselves to Bali. The echoes of Brazil were strong and once again we determined to prove everyone wrong.

I am never happy in cities and we spent the barest minimum time necessary in Jakarta getting essential permits. Marika was rather disappointed by this, as she enjoyed the exotic and exciting culinary adventures to be had there and we made a lot of delightful friends who tried to make us stay and enjoy ourselves. But I have one basic rule on expeditions (Tenison's law of travel) which is 'the longer you stay in a city the more things you will find which must be done before you can leave'. I therefore prefer to work as hard as possible preparing at home where I like to be best of all anyway, and then plunge into the interior with as little delay as possible and play it by ear. This means the maximum time is available for doing what I came to do, neither time nor money is wasted in expensive towns but can be spent instead on getting out of the trouble which will probably arise through not having delayed to obtain every conceivable permission.

Our eventual route took us to over a dozen tribes in Sumatra, Kalimantan (the Indonesian part of Borneo), Sulawesi (which used to be called Celebes), Ceram in the Moluccas and Irian Jaya (the Indonesian part of New Guinea). It was a very much harder journey physically than the Brazilian one had been and Marika became quite ill towards the end, her weight dropping to an alarming 5 stone (31.8 kg). Because the vast distances in Indonesia are between islands rather than overland much of our travelling was by very dangerous small coastal boats, overloaded with passengers and cargo, on which we tended to go very hungry. We were extremely lucky never to be shipwrecked, since there is a high wastage among such craft. Otherwise, as in Brazil, we flew or walked, travelled by dugout canoe or rode on horses to reach the people we sought. Some of these were strangely similar both in appearance and behaviour to some of the South American Indian peoples we had met; others were very different, but of their equal need for help I was never in any doubt.

The people we found most like South American Indians were the Mentawaians of the island of Siberut, 100 km off the west coast of Sumatra. We went there with a most remarkable German ex-missionary, Helmut Buchholz. After a decade working to convert the people to the tenets of his fundamentalist sect, the scales had fallen from his eyes and he had realized that he was doing them more harm than good through his teaching. Without losing his own faith, he had devoted himself more to their physical welfare and to fighting battles on their behalf, and less to proselytization. A sort of 'born again' human being, he knew more about the islanders' problems and was more liked and trusted by them than anyone else.

As a result we were able to travel far into the interior and were welcomed with great friendliness by the people. The island was much larger, we found, than it looked on the map. Some 130 km long by 50 km wide, it consisted of a series of ranges of low hills interspersed with swamps and rivers, all covered in dense rain forest. There were estimated to be 16,000 islanders, a proto-Malay race, probably among the very first inhabitants of any part of Indonesia. A gentle and attractive people, men, women and children wore flowers in their hair or in bead headbands round their foreheads: brilliantly scarlet hibiscus, delicate white day lilies with a heady scent, and bunches of feathery grass or velvet dark green leaves. All adults were tattooed on faces and bodies with finely traced, intricate patterns. Most men still wore bark loin-cloths, maintaining they were softer and more comfortable than cloth ones. Their skin was golden, their hair straight and black. They called to us as we passed them on the riverbank, 'Where are you going? Stay here with us!' And then, as we waved and carried on, or as we walked together through the forest, the lovely Mentawaian expression '*Moile, moile*', meaning literally 'Slowly, slowly', but in reality much more like 'Take it easy, what's the hurry?' or 'Go in peace', would float after us.

Their staple diet, both for themselves and the fat pigs they reared, was sago, a most efficient and labour-free natural crop. Sago palms grew wild and in profusion. Taking eight to twelve years to reach maturity, the stems were then cut down and chopped into lengths for soaking and grinding into flour or for feeding direct to the pigs. New shoots would grow from the stump creating an almost everlasting cycle. They lived traditionally in *umas*, where a whole clan would occupy a single communal house beautifully and simply made of hardwood and thatch. In the front was a wide verandah where men and women would sit and work on arrows or baskets. Behind was a large, wide room with a wooden dancing floor in the centre where ceremonies and celebrations took place and, further back still, stretching away into the darkness were the cooking fires and sleeping places for the families. The wooden uprights were usually covered in bas-relief carvings of crocodiles, gibbons, storks, deer and other animals, while from the rafters hung a rich collection of skulls, gongs, drums, feathers, bows and arrows, bundles of herbs and dried meat gently smoking over the central fire.

Here we would sit at night and, thanks to Helmut's fluency in their language, carry on long conversations with them about their problems. The gravest of these in the long run was undoubtedly created by the recent arrival of the several lumber companies who were exploiting the island's timber. We had seen some of the devastation near the coast where whole valleys had been turned into bare moonscapes. In theory the loggers were only allowed to export trees over 60 cm in girth, but this unfortunately did not mean that the rest of the environment was left undisturbed. The crawler tractors had to reach the trees and to do so they had to make roads. Much of the rest of the vegetation was smashed in the process and, since the roads soon turned to rivers and became impassable, while lakes formed in the hollows making new roads necessary, little was left standing except for a few bare trees rising up out of the mud. The soil was very weak and leached rapidly under the immense rainfall so that the destruction was permanent.

The effect of contact with the labour gangs from the Philippines and Korea was equally disastrous. Many Mentawaians were persuaded to become labourers and then found it difficult to leave. Prostitution, venereal disease, drink and social breakdown through living in labour camps and being made to practise unfamiliar work patterns were causing serious problems. With these changes, too, the taboos against hunting were being removed and the total eradication of many species of wildlife loomed. Since 65 per cent of the mammals of Siberut are found nowhere else in the world, this was giving concern to the World Wildlife Fund and it had, in fact, been through Sir Peter Scott that I had first made contact with Helmut.

More immediate threats to the people of the interior were brought by the police and the missionaries. The police, who were predominantly Muslim and from the mainland, had been very active recently. Virtual purges had been undertaken against the Mentawaians in an effort to Islamize them. Pigs had been shot so that the people could not go on living in the jungle, their houses had been burnt down and those who had refused to move to the new villages had been punished. On one occasion, all the men from a wide area had been invited to a feast by the police. When they had arrived at the police post in the north of the island, they had been told to leave their bows and arrows outside the village and to assemble in the centre. Then they had been surrounded by armed policemen who had told them that if they tried to run away they would be shot. Their long plaited hair which, in some cases, reached down to their waists, had then been cut off and taken away, it was suggested, for sale in Singapore. The authorities' obsession with long hair as a sign of decadence, whether worn by young Europeans or remote, isolated people, was very strong at that time and really quite extraordinary if one tried to understand the reasoning behind it. Only those living in sufficient isolation in the interior, beyond the reach of the police, had so far avoided forced change. If lumber companies now planned to extract the timber from these areas, the police would follow and they too would be forced to move.

The main trouble with the missionaries, as is so often the case, was that there were too many of them all competing with each other, saying different things and telling their respective flocks that the others were all manifestations of the Devil. Four main beliefs were actively being preached on the island; Baha'i, which was proscribed but apparently very strong in the region, Islam, Roman Catholicism and Protestantism. It is one of the tragedies of a situation like that to be found on Siberut that the tremendous energy devoted to missionary work appears to arise out of the challenge presented by a strange and fascinating people. Everybody fights over them and tries to alter them to their own particular way of thinking, creating confusion in the people's minds while combining to disrupt their own culture and beliefs. Once these are effectively destroyed and the people have become a sad, depressed and bored social problem, living in shanty towns around the coast, most of the missionaries move on to fresh fields.

Staying in one *uma* where we learnt we were the first outsiders, other than Helmut, ever to have been allowed to visit them, I found myself being questioned in some detail about my motives by all 30 members of the clan. Gathered around us in the darkness, relieved only by the flickering light of a few wicks burning in oil, we were conscious of being in the presence of a highly intelligent and alert audience who missed very little of what was going on. Whether I was speaking German with Helmut, English with Marika or Indonesian with the few Mentawaians who had learnt it, they seemed, through intense observation, to be able to deduce my very thoughts and so lead the questioning in directions designed to catch me out unless I was very careful.

They asked my advice as to whether I thought their *uma* was a better place to live than the rows of boxes masquerading as model villages which the government wished them to occupy on the coast. I answered with due seriousness that where we were was undoubtedly superior. They then inquired at length where I came from and I did my best to describe the vast distances and difference of my home in Cornwall. Was my life-style or theirs superior? they asked. Ingenuously I fell into the trap, saying that a communal life had many advantages over living in a nuclear family, their country was warm while mine was cold, etc.

'Then why not come and live with us?' they asked. As soon as I began, predictably, to explain that I too had my clan and family as well as a different cultural background, they all laughed for, while perhaps recognizing that what I said was true, they knew they had caught me out in a bit of rather patronizing double talk. With so many different groups of supposedly 'backward' or 'simple' peoples around the world, regarded by the surrounding population as ignorant and stupid, I have caught myself underestimating their acute wit and humour time after time. To suggest for a moment that they need help or advice in how to live is laughable. All they need is respect.

Later that same night I was able to ask them what, if anything, they wanted from the outside world, having explained at length that my purpose in being there was to see if there was anything I could do to help. They discussed the matter among themselves. Before answering they explained that if anyone else but Helmut had put the question for me they would have been afraid and would have said they needed nothing, but because of him they trusted me too and would answer truthfully.

Firstly they could use mosquito nets. With forest clearance the insects were getting worse, malaria had recently arrived and such fine nets were beyond their technology to make. Secondly, because of police harassment they had lost many of their brass gongs, which represented wealth, and china beads which were an important element in beauty and had traditionally been traded from the mainland. 'Finally,' they said, 'we wish that the police and missionaries would go away and not try to stop our world. Then our own religion and medicine would be strong again.' Time and again I have received similar answers from people who were speaking with trust, not trying to please me by saying what they thought I wanted to hear. The myth that all the less technologically developed peoples of the world live only to acquire more and more of our gadgets, toys and energy-demanding artefacts is one which we have created for ourselves to justify our own obsession with material things.

It would be a mistake to attempt to change the Mentawaians, either by criticism or by force. Rather, they should be allowed to realize in their own time that certain changes were inevitable and would help them to survive and even prosper under the different conditions which were coming. This was particularly true with regard to conservation on the island, the issue which had first brought it to my attention. On all the other, smaller islands of the Mentawai group almost all the people had settled in towns and, through hunger and ignorance, had ruthlessly destroyed most of the wildlife. By contrast, the scattered traditional population of Siberut, with an economy based on farming, fishing and periodic hunting represented a safeguard rather than a threat to wildlife. The Mentawaians used only bows and arrows; no rifles had yet been introduced. Most importantly, they were not enthusiastic hunters and killers of wild animals. Hunting was surrounded by many taboos and played a relatively small part in the dietary needs of the people, but a significant one ritually, since certain animals were required at certain feasts.

All killing was a significant matter, with spirits to be placated in advance whether the animal was a wild one to be hunted or a domestic one to be slaughtered. We watched a *kerei* or shaman sacrificing a cock and a pig before a healing ceremony. At first the animals were agitated and noisy when brought into the *uma*; then the old man, his eyes glazed and his voice high-pitched as he chanted the ritual, took them one by one in his hands and began to stroke them. At once they calmed down and lay still as he explained gently and apologetically, Helmut told us, that he was sorry but they had had a good life and were now needed for the ceremony and for food. Their spirits were not to be angry but should now get ready to depart and to come back as a new animal. Even when he cut their throats with one quick stroke of the knife, they never stirred, apparently lulled into a trance. The entrails were then removed and examined with great care to foretell the auguries.

The best way then, Helmut and I felt, to help both the people and the wildlife of Siberut would be to improve their existing sources of animal

A Mentawaian shaman on the island of Siberut off the coast of Sumatra in Indonesia examining the entrails of a sacrificed cock to read the auguries, 1973.

protein (pigs and chickens) as well as introducing improved methods of fishing the rich coastal and river waters. This would gradually reduce their need to hunt and so protect the island's rare and threatened species, already hard-pressed by the growing timber industry. Simply to impose reserves and regulations would only alienate the population, would be impossible to police and in the long run would be self-defeating as the hunger caused by the disruption of a viable and environmentally sound economy would drive the people to wipe out all the edible animals as had happened everywhere else.

A plan along these lines was drawn up jointly by the World Wildlife Fund and Survival International and in spite of all sorts of problems it has proved one of the most successful and interesting of our projects.

In Kalimantan, Borneo, we journeyed for several days far up into the interior on the Melawi river staying at a succession of increasingly traditional longhouses on the way. Most of the people we met there were Limbai and Ot Danum, two of the many groups of indigenous inhabitants generally referred to as Dayaks. All used to live in longhouses, but successive administrations have made efforts to break up these communal dwellings where up to a hundred families share one building. The Dutch administration of the outer islands as much as the present Indonesian one seems to have regarded longhouses as a barrier to progress. There is the puritanical belief that it is somehow immoral for families to live in such close association and that all sorts of licentious behaviour and disgusting orgies will take place if people are not separated by walls and space at night. It is assumed that the only normal, healthy way of life is the single family unit; that hygiene, social responsibility and work will suffer under communal living conditions. Finally, there is the often frankly admitted reason that such arrangements are harder to administer, police and keep a check of than regular rows of numbered houses near to a coast, road or river where numbers can be estimated at a glance and access to each family can be easily obtained. None of these assumptions impresses me as a valid reason for implementing resettlement programmes but the process is still pursued with undiminished energy.

On the Melawi most of the longhouses were intact and a generally traditional life was still being practised. We became used to staying in what I believe to be the most satisfactory housing arrangement ever devised. Each family has its own front door and private quarters, with storerooms, sleeping accommodation and a kitchen (often separated by a short bridge for security against fire) out at the back. The remaining half of the building, running straight and wide the whole length of the front, open on to the river below, is where all the social and communal activities take place. Women sit together and chat as they work; children play in

A Borneo longhouse, the ultimate in communal living. The
long gallery overlooks the river with kitchens and outhouses
hidden at the back.

safety under the watchful eyes of grandparents; men meet to talk and plan
fieldwork and hunts – to say nothing of dancing, drinking and flirting of
an evening.

We were always entertained with a party and it was very noticeable how
the quality of the music and dancing improved the further we moved up
river, away from the influence of missionaries and further from government pressure.

They were a very musical people, playing a wide variety of instruments
from small orchestras of gongs to wind instruments with four-foot-long
'organ pipes' emerging from a gourd, on which intricate tunes were
played; there were also guitars with two to six strings and drums of
various sizes. Some of the dancing was at first crude and clumsy, young
boys in dirty singlets giggling as they thumped inelegantly about. But
when they saw that we were serious and not disapproving, others put
their heart into it. The great gallery would become crowded with people of
all ages, their faces illuminated by a few oil lamps which threw shadows
into the dark corners of the rafters where paddles, fish traps and pots were
stored. Stripped to the waist, the sweat gleaming, they danced with
intensity and concentration wheeling and dipping to the complicated
beat, leaping and twisting over the uneven floor to put on performances

which showed that beneath a veneer of modernity the old passions burned as strongly as ever.

On this journey we had a particularly charming and intelligent policeman attached to us for security and presumably to keep an eye on us. At first we had viewed his presence with gloom, having had unfortunate experiences in the past with government spies, especially in South America. But Amri Bachtiar, born far up river to a Dayak father and a Chinese mother (surely a most unusual combination) but educated on the coast, proved to be an excellent travelling companion; understanding and sympathizing with our particular interests while at the same time taking great pains to make our travels as comfortable as possible. He had been converted to Islam on joining the police force and I assumed that with his relatively sophisticated urban background and the prestige of his uniform and official status he would tend to look down on tribal life, regarding it at best with tolerant condescension. Instead I learnt to my surprise that his mind was very open and that his own evident ambition to succeed as a civil servant was tempered with a genuine respect for the Dayaks and their traditions. This was one of the most encouraging and admirable features of many of the Indonesians we met throughout the country. Whereas in South America we had grown used to meeting the consistent disapprobation by petty officials of the native tribes with their 'dirty habits' and inferior life-style, we were to find in Indonesia that far more of those in positions of authority genuinely appeared not to regard the isolated tribes as inferior, although they seldom went so far as to question the benefits which instant civilization would bring them.

On our return to Nangapinoh, his base on the river, Amri excused himself as soon as we landed, saying that his wife had been due to have a baby some days before, a worry he had not burdened us with while we were away. He returned later to tell us that she had had a son whom he wanted to call Tenison Amri Bachtiar if I would give my permission. I was delighted to acquire a godson in Borneo and hope to return and visit him one day.

One anthropologist I talked with before leaving Kalimantan was pessimistic about the tribes' future. While he had seen no indications of real oppression through forced change, he felt sure that the culture was slowly dying. Many of the Dayak groups had been exploited for centuries as a source of slaves by the Arab sultanates which reduced their numbers and caused them to fragment and flee into the interior. Then, later, the Chinese had taken over the control of all commerce and trade, so that when most of the Chinese were removed in recent years, a vacuum was left behind which neither the Dayaks nor the coastal Malays were capable of filling, and, as a result, the people went hungry. Meanwhile, Western influences were creeping in, creating needs which could not be satisfied and causing discontent.

We agreed that the first priority was more research into both the peoples and their problems. Intense research into agricultural techniques should also be undertaken, both as regards the existing rice cultivation and as regards the development of alternative indigenous sources of food. Only when the local economy is on a firm footing, and some semblance of independence and security has been established, should roads, lumber camps and mineral exploitation be introduced. These priorities were being applied in reverse order, which could only have a catastrophic effect on the indigenous communities.

The next two islands, Sulawesi and Ceram, contrasted strongly with each other and left a much more cheerful impression than Kalimantan. In Sulawesi we visited first the Toraja, a strong people like the Bataks in Sumatra, with whom we had earlier spent some time. Their houses are among the most spectacular and beautiful to be seen anywhere in the world and their pride and culture was strong. The chief threat hanging over them came from the impending surge of tourism. An all-weather road was being built into their previously inaccessible and exquisitely beautiful country, where they had developed a highly efficient and productive system of terraced rice farming. Hotels were planned and group tours. Already there were signs of what was to come in one or two villages, where cash was demanded for taking photographs and the people's traditional hospitality had been undermined. But these were minor dangers with which I felt sure the dynamic Toraja would be able to cope.

Tourism has an insidious tendency to cheapen and in time even eliminate the very thing which brought visitors in the first place. On the other hand beauty, such as the Toraja have created in an idyllic setting supplied by nature, belongs to the whole world. It should be shared as well as protected.

More interesting for me were the rumours I heard of totally isolated peoples in the rarely visited eastern arm of Sulawesi. Helicopters from a mining company at Malili had landed in the remote interior and met tribes who appeared to have had virtually no contact with the outside world. There was no time to reach them then as the helicopter flights had ceased and it would be a very long journey overland, but I resolved to do so one day.

I also met the Rajah of another remote tribe to the north who happened to be in town. While he was telling me how many of his people still used bows, arrows and blowpipes to hunt and how many still tattooed them-selves, I showed him some photographs of Brazilian Indians. He became very excited, recognizing many of their practices, such as wearing large plugs in the earlobes, and artefacts like feather headdresses and flutes were apparently very similar to those previously made by his own tribe.

In southern Sulawesi we visited other strange and exciting peoples, coastal boatbuilders and fishermen as well as an extraordinary mystical sect who had never previously allowed Europeans into their territory to meet their sacred leader, the Ama Towa. Our session with him confirmed for me, as have a few other encounters with mystics, that there is more to life than what we see on the surface and that if we did but know the secrets and have the strength and patience to unravel them, we could discover powers undreamt of in our shallow plastic world.

Across Wallace's line in Ceram we were able to reach by diminutive coastal trading boat, outrigger canoe and a long, hard walk inland, the Hua Ulu, one of the last pure tribes who still remain true to their culture which, incidentally, included head-hunting. They had vowed to take the head of any missionary who tried to approach them, but had allowed an Italian anthropologist and his Swedish wife (Valerio and Renée Valeri) to live with them for the past year. We were the first other Europeans to visit them.

Their small village of attractive thatched houses on stilts, built along the lines of miniature longhouses, in which two or three families lived, was peaceful and beautiful. Once again we were struck by the contrast between the noisy crowd of staring, shouting children which nearly always followed us on the coasts and in the larger towns and villages of Indonesia and the quiet good manners of adults and children alike in the remoter parts of the interior. The Hua Ulu were shy but friendly. The men in bark loin-cloths and striking red turbans showed us their skill at carving bas-reliefs of animals on the uprights of the houses while the women in sarongs brought us interesting stews of rancid pork and fresh crayfish with wild vegetables cooked inside wide bamboo tubes, followed by coconut and bananas.

The thing which impressed me most about them, an often unrecognized feature of societies where all information is shared and passed on orally, was their outstanding memories. Valerio told me that in the course of his work he would sometimes ask a man to sing him one of the traditional myths, literally thousands of verses taking several hours to complete. Even more striking was their ability with languages, necessary because of the 35 separate dialects spoken on the island, but impressive when the same singer would be able to repeat his song verbatim six or seven times, each time in a new language. This is a talent our culture has largely lost, firstly through our practice of storing information in books or computer data banks. While our technology demands complex and extensive retrieval systems to hold vast quantities of information, who is to say that the quality of knowledge retained by human brains, unchanged in size and capacity from those of our fairly recent hunter-gatherer ancestors, is not superior or more satisfying to the human spirit?

The Hua Ulu wanted to remain where they were, on their ancestral land. Their isolation was not only physical but also a state of mind. They passionately wanted to remain true to their culture, worship their ancestors, follow their ritual and continue to be Hua Ulu and animist. This need not, we felt, necessarily conflict with the adoption of new techniques. In the medical field especially, unlike many other peoples in Indonesia, they saw a clear distinction between physical and psychological illness. They recognized the difference between practical steps such as chewing curative roots and applying plants to wounds, on the one hand, and placating spirits, calling back souls which had wandered off, and calming emotional disturbances, on the other. A sensitive doctor, willing to help rather than effect a complete change, would certainly have been a great asset to them, even if he could only visit them two or three times a year. The main problem facing the Hua Ulu, and one which they longed to solve but had no cure for, was a rapidly declining birth-rate which was reaching a stage where there was a real possibility of extinction. This might have been genetic or there might have been some quite simple physical or dietary explanation. Valerio was convinced that it was not psychological as with some of the Indian tribes in Brazil who wanted to die out because life had become unbearable. The Hua Ulu, on the contrary, were proud and confident about their future, and wanted more children so as to make themselves even stronger as a tribe. At that moment they were protected from most other threats by their isolation, the natural barrier of the hills and jungle between them and the coast and by the fear with which outsiders regarded them. It seemed unlikely that these defences could be upheld indefinitely.

A much more extreme case of isolation and oppression greeted us on the island of New Guinea, about half of which belongs to Indonesia. The huge indigenous population of Irian Jaya was being paternalistically administered by an Indonesian military and civil service with no sympathy, understanding or respect for the culture or values of a black race whom they regarded as totally inferior. Hardly a case of an ethnic minority being swamped, it was and remains closer to apartheid on the South African model; yet because the dominant minority is not white it is an issue which has hardly ever been raised in the United Nations. Ignored by the international community, the population resorted to intermittent guerrilla activity but they were overwhelmingly outgunned by the Indonesian Army and they achieved little or nothing. The few educated

Papuans left behind by the Dutch when they left in 1962 were killed or imprisoned and the vast majority of the population lived in the rugged interior, members of several hundred different tribes speaking different languages and with the barest of contact with their colonizers.

Dani women beside the military airport in the Baliem valley, Irian Jaya, Indonesia, in 1973.

We were able to spend some time with the Dani of the Baliem valley and the Asmatters of the south coast. The Dani, naked except for the imposing gourd penis sheaths of the men and the briefest of net mini-skirts of the women, were magnificent gardeners. Digging the rich, dark soil of the valley with stone implements, they grew fine crops of sweet potato, cabbages, bananas, and other vegetables and fruit. Their plots were skilfully irrigated and drained by a network of ditches. They were potentially prosperous with their herds of fat pigs, but as all communication with the outside world was by air, making exports prohibitively expensive, they had no way of raising the money to buy the recent influx of metal and plastic goods which were both attractive as novelties and useful in the case of axes and spades. As a result some discontent was apparent. Meanwhile the increasing numbers of military personnel arriving were putting a strain on the remaining forests of the valley sides, which were being cut down for timber, so that environmental problems were also looming.

Nonetheless we found the Dani delightfully friendly and welcoming. Most of the work in the fields was traditionally done by the women, leaving the men free to guard them and indulge in periodic ritual battles with their neighbours. Since these had been banned by the missionaries and the military they had more time on their hands and perhaps that added to the warmth of their greeting. As we walked between their villages of round, low, thatched houses reminiscent of African *kraals* we would meet them on the well-trodden earth paths, ambling along with their hands behind their backs and all the time in the world for a chat. We would exchange a crisp greeting *'narak'*, followed by a firm left-hand shake and a warm embrace. Since their glistening black bodies were usually daubed with rancid pig fat, as well as being painted on the arms and chest with red ochre, we soon felt, looked and smelt like Dani ourselves. The warmth and genuine affection of these greetings were most endearing. We felt as though our arrival had been expected and looked forward to for months. When we saw that the same joy was manifested when they met each other too, as much between men and women as between members of the same sex, we decided that whatever devils the persistent missionaries were attempting to exorcize from them could not be wholly evil ones.

Most welcome in Irian Jaya were the examples we met of caring pragmatism among some of the Catholic (but alas none of the Protestant) missionaries. Father Camps, who had lived with the Dani for over 20 years, had a robust approach which was a relief after so often having to steer a course between die-hard progressives and hopeless sentimentalists. 'The Baliem people are in danger,' he said. 'Outsiders will come and take their land from them unless they are careful. They don't understand money yet and are easily cheated. Recently a chief near here sold quite a large field for two spades. His relations were angry and came to me to ask me to sort it out, which I was able to do, but it is becoming harder. At the same time, they are great realists. Seeing the things for sale in the market they want them and know that they must change if they are to get them. Education is important.'

'Yes, but what sort of education?' I asked. 'All too often, children in remote areas are led to believe that if they pass their exams the world is at their feet and they will be able to get jobs in the big cities. They are not taught the things they need to know about their own history, culture and environment. Then they become dissatisfied with their own region, but they have nowhere to go.'

'I agree, and there is not a lot one can teach these people about farming here that they don't know already. But they must learn to handle money

The Dani always gave us a friendly greeting and wanted to stop for a chat when we met them walking through the valley.

and look after themselves. Given time they will make excellent traders. I don't know what the future holds for them, but it is too late to stop the clock. We can only try to help.'

Father Camps's awareness of the difficulties of helping the Dani, and his own humility with regard to what he believed he could himself achieve, impressed us. He fully accepted that in physical matters, apart from medical aid, change was initially likely to be for the worse, since if they lived according to their traditional patterns they were a rich people and excellent farmers. On the other hand, there was certainly room for an infusion of the milk of human kindness into their way of life since some of their traditional practices – such as cutting off fingers whenever anyone died, their methods of abortion, punishment and revenge – seemed unnecessarily crude and cruel. But kindness could only be taught by example and advice. The Dani were not people who could be easily forced to do or not to do anything. Their greatest strength lay in their independence and realism. They were masters at playing rival missionaries and the civil authorities off against each other; given time to absorb all the confusing and far-reaching influences which had descended on them during the last few years, they might well be able to channel their enthusiasm for life in such a way as to succeed and prosper in competition with the modern world. The valley, with its 60,000 inhabitants, had after all only been discovered by accident when a plane crashed there during World War II, while a post had only been established in the valley barely 17 years before.

The changing Catholic attitudes to their mission, and their readiness to sacrifice preconceptions in their search for how best to serve the people among whom they worked, were well illustrated by a quote from the Bishop of Asmat summing up one of the wide-ranging conferences they held from time to time in co-operation with anthropologists and government officials to discuss these problems: 'To insist that a people who are labouring under a delusion as to what Christianity is all about be obliged to follow its tenets is to negate freedom and respect for man's dignity and integrity – basic rights which we profess to uphold.' Unfortunately the representatives of the American fundamentalist churches, also working in the region, take a different view, and are all too often obsessed with the need to save souls at whatever cost to the body. Paradoxically, this attitude is highly reminiscent of the early Catholic Spanish conquerors of South America, who eliminated so many of the Indians in the early days of conquest.

When we had flown down to Asmat, the bishop, who was himself only just 40, invited us to stay and we talked at length about his hopes and fears for the Asmatters, an estimated 40,000 of whom lived on the vast tidal swamp which stretched inland for 150 km. Many had not yet been contacted and still practised cannibalism in the interior but most had been settled in villages nearer the rivers on the coast.

He spoke of his deep concern that if lumber companies moved into the region in a big way, as they were showing signs of doing, it would bring little of value to the people since the companies preferred to import their own labour force. Meanwhile the sole valuable asset which the Asmatters had, the hardwood trees growing in the jungle, would be removed and they would be left without a basis on which to found an economy. As with the Dani, the desire and need for imported commodities had been created in them and they needed to be given the opportunity to earn money to acquire them, without becoming dependent upon charity or open to exploitation. The mission had set up a chain of small co-operative saw-mills, which the Asmatters operated themselves and which were slowly beginning to fulfil the need, but they had to diversify if they were to prosper, and on the infertile saline swampland where they lived alternatives were not easy to find. Sago was their staple diet and grew wild, but already, with an increasing population, concentrated in a smaller area, they were having to go further in search of it. They themselves were still not fully aware of the difficulties they faced and believed that they could 'always go back to the way things were before' if the going became too rough. I wondered aloud if they might not be better off in some ways if they did, but had to agree that the taste for civilization which they had acquired, in particular their recent and passionate addiction to tobacco, would be hard to give up, and anyway where would they go if their forests were cut down and their land taken from them?

Longhouses, in which the Asmatters used to live, were abolished by the Dutch in accordance with the familiar desire to settle the peoples in 'modern' accommodation in 1954, and we were depressed by the regular rows of shacks, all built to the same pattern, which then comprised most of their villages. Unlike the Dani, the Asmatters had a history of intermittent contact, including a considerable amount of activity in their area during World War II, and some previous trading on the coast. However, for the most part, their territory was avoided and outsiders were, with good reason, afraid to penetrate the rivers. The majority of those contacted wore clothes, which were kept on until they literally rotted off their bodies. They were also suffering from many more diseases than the Dani and their health was generally less good; a recent epidemic of whooping cough had killed off a large number, 20, at the first village we visited. It was likely that the clothes and the prevalence of disease were linked, since in the tropics clothes can constitute a considerable health hazard unless they are washed regularly.

The Dani, rejecting clothes and continuing to cover themselves with pig fat and remain unwashed, had tended to stay in better health.

I asked another priest how he saw the future of the Asmatters. 'I really don't know what the next 15 or 20 years will bring,' he said. 'The population is growing, their way of life is changing and their needs are expanding. But it is outsiders who are deriving most of the benefits from the shops and the lumber business. Only the mission has kept the people going so far, and this is a real danger. They should not be dependent on us. So many changes of attitude have been forced on them by successive administrations. At first they were told to burn down their longhouses and destroy their carvings. Now, they are told to start making artefacts again, so as to encourage tourism. Social centres are being built, but most of the old longhouse activities are prohibited due to their association with head-hunting and the old days. It's like making people build a church and then not allowing them to worship in it.'

Consideration of the Asmatters' future in these terms seemed to me to approach the root of the problem, and the philosophical implications of such thinking, touching upon the very nature of man, takes us a step nearer to finding valid hypotheses on which to work. If one accepts that, allowing for certain relatively insignificant variations, all members of the human race are equal and capable of fulfilling a potential far greater than that which each of us usually does achieve, then the stimulus to create must to a great extent depend upon the cultural environment in which we grow up and live. Man's capacity to break out of his culture and conquer new worlds, whether physical or intellectual, is what truly makes him different from animals, but he must equally have a rich, strong culture out of which to break.

The missionary who cannot face his own religion as a complete idea within himself, but needs to assert and justify it by bringing it to others and making them conform to his model, is running away from himself. Just as a wise man can achieve serenity through concentrating his own mind, so the isolated tribe may achieve a higher satisfaction within its own culture. Outside influences will certainly impinge but we do not have the right to impose fundamental changes of attitude. The missionary who dedicates his life to helping others, without preconceptions and implied condemnation of beliefs and modes of life which differ from his own, is fulfilling a valuable and admirable function. If he has also taken vows of celibacy and poverty, he is relieved of the responsibilities of family and career which make it even harder to endure the loneliness and sacrifice of total commitment. Such men, however, are rare.

Thanks to the presence of the Asmat mission, I felt that the people stood a reasonable chance of success in the future, whatever it is that success in this context means. But then, trying to answer that question for tribal people is, I believe, what Survival International's work is all about. In three months we had seen only a small part of the problem in Indonesia, and we had only scratched the surface of possible answers; but that large numbers of tribes were in need of help and support if they were going to survive was no longer in any doubt.

In Indonesia change was happening so fast, and attitudes towards development were being formed at such a rate, that the main danger lay in the problems of tribal minorities being overlooked rather than in their being insoluble. While protection and preservation were undoubtedly needed in some cases, there was hope that in the long run respect for alternative cultures might find its place in the national ideal, alongside the current obsession with trying to copy the Western materialist dream.

Some projects did result from our Indonesian visit, notably that in Siberut which still continues, but it was hard to penetrate Far Eastern bureaucracy and inertia. I felt that I knew too little about the subject, and the time might well not be right to publish a report on the status of Indonesia's minority peoples. The authorities I spoke to were largely uninterested, preoccupied with what they regarded as more urgent short-term solutions to intractable long-term problems.

Scattered over three-quarters of a million square miles of islands were more than 300 ethnic groups administered from the small, overcrowded island of Java. Indonesia possesses the richest fund of cultural diversity of any nation. We left hoping that their government, whose national motto, after all, is 'Unity in Diversity', might one day come to recognize the value of all its different people.

---

on following pages

With Penan friends on the recce for the site of the Mulu expedition, 1976.

Looking over the Gunung Api massif in which the world's largest cave system was discovered by our expedition.

Some of the extraordinary limestone pinnacles up to 50 metres tall found on Gunung Api.

8

The Next on the List

Let us make no mistake: the awakening of public sensitivity to the tragic fate of 'primitive' peoples, the sympathy and even the revolt which the end of the last Indians of the Amazon have led to, are less the result of sudden clearsightedness or generosity, than that of a deeply selfish reaction. We identify ourselves with these people whom we have condemned at the very moment when discovering that we are the next on the list.

Claude Levi-Strauss, *Journal de Genève* (28 July 1973)

The journeys Marika and I made to Brazil and Indonesia were tremendous challenges and we derived great pleasure and satisfaction both from travelling together and from publishing the results. Though extremely exhausting, they were not very demanding physically. Strangely, a few months after each, I was able to satisfy my perverse desire to stretch myself physically back in each of the respective continents we had been visiting.

In 1972 I was able to travel alone again in South America while loosely attached to a large and mainly military British expedition. It was led by the ebullient Colonel John Blashford-Snell, a man for whom I have always felt the highest regard and friendship, although we appear to disagree on almost everything, from our approach to exploration to the objectives we wish to fulfil. He knew from the outset that I opposed the expedition's avowed purpose and I was grateful to him for inviting me to take part.

There is a fat red line on the map which runs from Alaska almost to Cape Horn. In the middle is a break of some 250 miles across the isthmus of Darien, known as the Darien Gap. How could the civilized world tolerate so small a break in a main road 32,000 km long? The purpose of the expedition was to prove it was possible to bridge the gap by taking two new Range Rovers the whole way, including spending three months pioneering a route across the isthmus. The bulldozers would follow. Scientists were attached to examine the flora and fauna before they were destroyed, as undoubtedly they would be, if not by the road itself then by the settlements which would follow it. My job was to assess the impact which the road would have on the Indians.

John Blashford-Snell described me generously in his book *Where the Trails Run Out* (London, 1974):

Robin, champion of primitive peoples, already knew more about the jungles of South America than any of us. His charm and eloquence, combined with an easy, self-assured attitude, had a settling effect on the tense nerves of some of our colleagues. With the minimum of fuss, he had gathered a few stores and set off into the forest to make contact with his beloved Indians. From time to time, this elusive and almost mythical figure, whom many of the expedition never saw, would emerge and quietly restock his rucksack with film and small gifts. Those who met him during these fleeting visits to civilization heard the case against the road skilfully put and realized that there was another side to the argument. But for most of us the jungle was a cruel enemy contesting every step. . .

Harmodio was a Choco Indian of the rain forest. He had never seen the sea before, although the Pacific was only 60 km from his home to the west and the Atlantic was no more than 100 km to the north and east. He shrank from the breakers crashing on to the golden sand, whiter and louder than any of the rapids on the shallow river where he swam and poled his narrow dugout canoe. When I dived into the water he called to me to be careful as he had heard that there were fish like *tigre* (jaguars) who would tear me apart. I persuaded him to join me but when a wave broke over him he fled to the land and stood shaking with fear. His pale skin was painted black with genipapo up to the level of his upper lip and his face was etched with delicate designs.

I caught a wave and body-surfed to land at his feet. Taking him by the hand, I led him in again, reassuring him that it was really fun. Soon he began to enjoy it. I told him that where I came from men sometimes carried flat boards out with them and rode in on the waves, standing. After a while he walked up the beach to where we had left our possessions, returning a few minutes later with his machete and a long, wide piece of driftwood. I made suggestions while he shaped and smoothed it. It was a bit heavy and had no fin but it would pass as a surfboard. Within an hour he actually stood up on a wave, arms outstretched and a beatific expression on his face.

Harmodio's people, the Embera Choco, lived as far as they could from the coast, far up the little hidden tributaries, where no settlers penetrated, where they could hunt and fish and grow a few crops without being put upon by black or white outsiders. They are a gentle people, the Choco, who have survived by never fighting back but instead choosing to melt into the jungle, friendly to them, unfriendly to those who do not understand it. Quite possibly the first mainland Indians seen by visitors from the old world, for Columbus sighted the Darien isthmus on his last voyage, they have resisted change for nearly 500 years. First came the Conquistadores, carrying the gold looted from Peru from one coast to the other through the swamps and over the mountains. Then the pirates who preyed on them, ambushing and fighting on land in the bays and open seas around the coast. Later black slaves from Africa were brought to dig for gold in the hills and work plantations of sugarcane and coffee. When they escaped and in time were freed to settle the river estuaries, the Choco moved back into the interior. Later still men came to dig the Panama Canal and great ships moved from ocean to ocean, cities grew and fishing fleets tapped the rich offshore shoals to feed them. Through the centuries, while slavers hunted their bodies and missionaries their souls, the Choco retreated a little further, protected by the inhospitable jungle and the malarial swamps. No one acknowledged their right to any land and no reservations were created for them but at the same time no one succeeded in settling them in towns or forcing any of the other trappings of civilization on them, for they posed no threat and made useless slaves, dying when captured or running away to places where no sane man would go.

I had two other Indians with me besides Harmodio – Manuelito, who was young with a wife and child at home, and Guillermo, who was old and whom I privately called Father William because, although he did not actually stand on his head, his strength and energy were such that I was constantly tempted to ask him whether he thought at his age it was right. Arriving at their village of Manene on the Balsas river, the only large Choco settlement, in the expedition's light Beaver aircraft which seemed able to land on a pocket handkerchief, I had slept in the hut of the wise old chief, Loro, talking for most of the night about the Choco and their problems. Loro was firmly opposed to the road, as was every Choco I spoke to subsequently, both in Panama and Colombia.

'If the road passes through or near our land it will be taken from us,' he said. 'We have gone up the rivers as far as we can and already it is harder to catch fish in the shallow water and find game in the high mountains than it used to be lower down. Now there is nowhere left for us to go. If they take our land from us we will be forced to move to Panama City where we will become beggars.' Several of the men had been to the coast and had worked on ships or in the towns. None had stayed and none wanted to go back.

Loro, the wise old Choco chief, with his daughters, with
whom I stayed in 1972.

'It is good to have money,' they said, 'to see the world and buy a few things to impress our friends. But when the money is gone, the batteries are flat in our radios and our shirts are torn, we prefer not to go there again. The price is too high and our life here is better.'

One of the great fallacies which has dogged our traditional relationship with primitive tribes has been our belief that once they have tasted the fruits of civilization they will never be satisfied until they have clawed their way up the economic ladder to the Great American Dream. This belief is ingrained into our Judaeo-Christian ethic from the moment we are taught about Adam and Eve being expelled from the Garden of Eden. Apart from the fact that almost no representatives of such societies have, by the very nature of the world we live in, ever achieved such dubious heights, usually failing to pass even the first rung on the ladder, I have time and again met and stayed with people who have tasted the fruits, examined them wisely and, adjusting themselves slightly to their new situation, have decided in their wisdom to go no further in that particular direction. Thus a Stone Age society, once they have encountered metal, will not revert to the laborious business of making stone axes, but will develop a trade with the outside world to satisfy their need for steel ones. The possibility of extending this trade to the extent that it involves total destruction of their whole life-style and cultural patterns is quite consciously rejected, although the pressure from outside is constant and unremitting. Instead, like the Choco, they ask those who bother to consult them about what they need and how their lives could be better, to please help them to secure their rights to the lands they have always occupied and remove the pressures on them to change whether these come in the form of government policy, missionaries, timber or mining concessions, or roads.

The Choco had had as long as any society in the world to consider these matters and it was a sad reflection on the presumption and hypocrisy of our world that I was apparently the first person to have consulted them.

I had arrived bearing a sack of gifts from the expedition store. Since I intended to spend my entire time with various groups of Indians and as little time as possible with the expedition itself I had been allowed to help myself to anything I might need from the Aladdin's cave presided over by the quartermaster. As a result I was able to present Loro with a considerable quantity of packaged and tinned foods, cooking utensils, fish-hooks and fishing line, razor blades and needles, .22 ammunition, rope and plastic bags, as well as a couple of knives and machetes. I kept for myself only the .22 rifle which had to be returned, a small amount of ammunition, a torch, blanket, mosquito net and hammock. Members of the expedition, which was superbly equipped and organized, had also been issued with a supply of high-quality coloured china and glass beads which were, as it turned out, much appreciated by the Choco.

Loro accepted my bounty with dignity and immediately gave most of it away. He asked me what he could do for me. I explained that it was my desire to ascend the Balsas river to its source, cross the watershed and descend to the Pacific coast by the Jurado river, visiting Choco settlements on the way. Later I hoped to make a similar journey further south to the headwaters of the Nauca river in Colombia. I understood that both these traverses were occasionally made by the Indians themselves and wondered if any young men of the village might feel like undertaking them in my company. Prolonged discussions resulted in the three men I have mentioned deciding to set out with me at dawn, Father William because he wanted to visit relations he had not seen for several years, Manuelito because he wanted to see something of the world and Harmodio because the time had come to look for a wife.

The Choco are superb canoeists and we began with me sitting amidships since I could contribute nothing at this stage, while the three Indians, standing up in the 12-metre by 50-cm dugout, poled us along at high speed. For a couple of days we travelled in this way, only stepping into water when we came to rapids or shallows and the canoe grounded under our weight. All too soon there was no more deep water and we walked, often cutting corners on foot as the river looped while Manuelito, who could pole the dugout on his own along a channel no more than 15 cm deep and 60 cm wide, went round the long way, sometimes reaching the next shallows before us. Once, while edging my way along a fallen tree trunk, I met a two-metre green snake as thick as my wrist coming the other way. It slithered sensibly down into the water but, unnerved, I lost my balance and fell on top of it. We spent some time struggling to disentangle ourselves but when I finally reached the bank I thought the Indians' mirth was in poor taste. Unlike me, they had known from the start that the snake was harmless. But on the whole our days were idyllic and tranquil. We slept on sandbanks where I slung my hammock from overhanging trees or from the roots of a forest giant swept down in a flood, while the Choco, who do not use hammocks, slept on the ground.

Our staple food was plantains, the vegetable banana, which we gathered on the way and boiled in a cooking pot. They make extremely dull, stodgy food and whereas the Indians could eat up to twelve at a sitting I could seldom force down more than one or two. The monotony of our carbohydrate diet was, however, amply compensated for by the variety of our protein supplement. As he poled along, Manuelito would sometimes continue his forward swing to reach for the unbarbed metal rod with sharpened point lying in the bilges. Without altering the rhythm of his movements he would stab over the side with this, bringing up a wriggling fish, the sheer momentum of his stroke preventing it falling off the end. We always camped by a pool in the evening and he and Harmodio never failed to add more fish to our larder, diving under the banks with home-made goggles. They also caught delicious crayfish which turned bright red when boiled, and once we feasted on iguana's eggs, yellow and crunchy, a cross between herring roe and an omelette. Several times I shot large turkeys with the .22 rifle – the first one from a sitting position in the moving canoe as it stood on a branch high over the river. Unsporting perhaps but not a feat I would guarantee to be able to pull off again. We were hungry for fresh meat and I was glad to be able to do something useful.

Mostly we travelled in silence, the Indians now and then making a soft, melodious whistle denoting minor exertion. As a result, the wildlife was not disturbed until the last moment. Parakeets, waterfowl and kingfishers accompanied us, an orange and black squirrel with bushy tail stood up to watch us pass, a long, black unidentified feline ran smoothly up a log and vanished. Small, yellow monkeys ('not good to eat') watched us from the trees and chattered; howler monkeys ('good to eat') howled in the mornings and evenings and one was, I regret to say, shot by Harmodio with the .22 and eaten by us all with relish.

The portage was when I came into my own. The Indians, though very strong, were small and light. At five foot nine and ten stone (63.6 kg) I represented bulk. They yoked me to the front of the canoe with sweet-scented lianas and for a long, hot day we sweated and heaved in unison over a steep, muddy ridge. We could move the heavy dugout for fifty metres or so at a stretch on level, soft ground but on the hills two or three metres at a time was all we could manage. The Indians' whistles changed to sad whimpers like a litter of puppies and they would stop and come to bend and rub my liana, sniffing the elusive scent with obvious pleasure as though it gave them strength.

That night we slept on the ground in an exhausted heap, too tired to sling my hammock or cook a hot meal. My back has never been the same since but we had made it to the Jurado and incidentally crossed the border from Panama into Colombia at the same time.

Harmodio now began to take an undue interest in his appearance, using up the batteries of my torch painting careful designs on his body to signify that he was still a bachelor in preparation for meeting marriageable cousins.

In the midst of a riverine dawn there is no more beautiful dwelling in the world than a single Choco hut tucked into a fold of the hills above a sandy bay. Smoke escapes through the conical thatched roof which sweeps down to a few feet above the circular open platform on stilts where the family sit and look down on the river. We arrived in silence and without a word mounted the notched pole and settled ourselves near the fire. For a while nothing was said. Then gradually conversation was opened, became animated when relationships were discovered, serious when I was introduced and began to ask questions, friendly as we shared a bowl of hot fish soup. We left again in silence without a backward glance, handshake or voices raised in salutation. That is the way.

Father William found an uncle, Tombini, younger than himself who had three daughters. The eldest was married and had children, the youngest was still a child, but the second, a shy, shapely teenager was, we all knew at once, destined for Harmodio. He was looking particularly handsome that day, groomed, polished and painted, fine red designs on his face and a spotlessly clean, new, red chola round his loins. He had spent an hour before we left our camp bathing in the river, combing and parting and oiling his long black hair, making up face and body with the help of a small mirror and finally tying on for the first time a silver and bead necklace.

The girl, Maria, who could not have known that we were coming but could deduce Harmodio's intentions at once from his make-up, was

Harmodio making himself beautiful before meeting his future bride.

Maria, who knew what she wanted – and got it.

dressed only in a short, flowered, wrap-around skirt. She was beautiful and demure, with plump, round breasts and a restrained air of knowing exactly what she, too, wanted. While I alternated between entertaining the children with my last two balloons and talking seriously with Tombini, the young flirted decorously and by the time we left I gathered that an understanding had been reached.

The Beaver aircraft flew along the coast looking for me. The pilot and I had made a plan that on a certain day he would pass that way and if I had arrived I was to fire a flare to attract his attention. If he was able to he would land and take me back to the expedition's base camp. It had seemed like a good plan when he had dropped me at Manene, but as I paced the beach at low tide after surfing, there seemed a lot that could go wrong. I had marked out a runway on the sand fit for a Boeing 707 and as the day wore on and the tide crept back in, it was gradually washed away and the beach became narrower until only five metres of hard sand remained. Then a speck low over the sea materialized into an aircraft; I fired my flare, the plane landed and, without stopping the engine, so that we were barely able to say goodbye, I was hauled aboard. With the waves lapping the wheels, we took off and I was able to spend one night at the base before being dropped the next day into a new area.

Tombini's family had presented us with three succulent pineapples, white-fleshed and juicy, which we had enjoyed on the last day down the river. He also pressed on me a leg of meat, the smoked ham of an agouti, which had been wrapped in my hammock for safekeeping so as to keep the flies off it. At the outset of the expedition the 65 members had been given a strict lecture on food and hygiene. 'No local food is to be eaten,' we were told. 'There will be ample compo rations consisting of tins and dehydrated food. Water must always be boiled and a sterilizing agent added to it.' Feeling that this diet might be beginning to pall, I produced the meat at the mess that night and offered it round, pointing out that the flesh was tender and pink like smoked salmon.

'What is it?' I was asked.

'Agouti,' I replied, 'a large rodent and a rare delicacy.'

'Rat!' they said, and no one would touch it. They eyed me askance as I gnawed on the bone at dinner and when I preferred untreated Jurado river water from my own water flask to the sterile taste of theirs, I could see that if I stayed longer than overnight I might undermine morale. Talk was all of what hell it was out there, how the jungle fought the Range Rovers every inch of the way, how half the members had had to be evacuated already with insect bites and upset stomachs. How could I say that with the Indians I had found it one of the most idyllic places I had ever been and that I was dead against the road and all it stood for.

It would be hard to find two more different Amerindian tribes than the Choco and the Cuna, the other indigenous residents of Darien. While the Choco are shy, wear next to no clothes and run away from trouble, the Cuna are proud and tough, wear elaborate and full dress, both men and women, and have fought determinedly over the centuries to preserve their rights and honour. Most of the tribe moved in the 19th century to the San Blas islands on the Atlantic coast where they grow coconuts, tolerate some tourists and have a certain amount of autonomy. They are now fairly acculturated and besieged by at least four different rival sects of missionaries, but their aggressively independent nature has helped them to retain their sense of identity and thus their dignity.

The rest of the tribe, about 1,200, remained in their ancestral homeland in the Bayano valley in the interior and were regarded by all the Cuna people as the guardians of tribal tradition and lore. Successive governments guaranteed them their lands in perpetuity and they strongly resisted any incursion into them. Now their future was being threatened, not only by the road, part of which was planned to run through their reservation, but also by the building of a huge dam which would, when filled, flood three-quarters of their land. In Panama City I was shown the plans by the construction company which gave the before-and-after picture as well as illustrating very clearly some of the problems the dam would create.

Seven Cuna villages, representing two-thirds of the inland population, would be flooded and have to be resettled.

Owing to the contours of the valley bottom, much of the resulting lake would be shallow. As the trees were not to be cut down many of them would still stand above the water's surface, creating a fetid swamp. Moreover, as the waters rose and fell, a wide muddy area, perfect as a breeding ground for disease, and useless as anything else, would be created.

The Bayano river constitutes the main outflow along that coast into the Pacific where the fishing fleets provide the basis of the local Panamanian economy. Interrupting the flow was likely to have a serious effect on the fishing.

The dam was needed to provide electricity for the Panama Zone. Apart from the fact that this area was leased to the USA so that the power was in a sense being exported, there were said to be several other suitable rivers for harnessing which would not involve any forced movement of population.

I asked the director of the dam project what he thought of it all. He told me that ecological considerations were not his concern, he was simply being paid to build the dam – but, if I wanted his opinion, the whole thing looked very doubtful as, with a 25-metre maximum rise and fall, large areas of land would become unusable and the disease and mud problems were certainly going to be a headache to someone some day.

I had been warned that the Cuna would not be friendly and for the first few days I and Jerry Pass, the young cameraman from the expedition who flew in with me, were regarded with some suspicion. Our first frustration was that they would not let us film, and the Bayano Cuna, especially the women, were highly photogenic. Dressed in brilliant colours, with bright red and gold predominating in the shawls which they wore over their heads, reminding me incongruously of Berbers in the Atlas Mountains, they wore green, blue, black and gold patterned skirts down to their ankles and superb embroidered blouses called *molas* bearing stylized designs which are reminiscent of – and said by some authorities to be – Mayan. Many had gold rings through their noses, again like the Berbers, as well as red and yellow anklets bound above and below the calf.

The men on the other hand seemed at first dowdy by comparison, in shirts, long trousers and hats. Their shirts, however, were most unusual, being modelled on the 16th-century tunics they had acquired from the Spanish and the marauding British pirates. With three-quarter-length sleeves, they ended above the navel, leaving the midriff bare and looking as though they had been issued for an Errol Flynn movie.

Ritual, too, played a major part in their lives so that, although one or two owned outboard motors and they seemed on the surface 'modern' by comparison with the Choco, in fact every action was dictated by traditional considerations rather than purely economic ones. This gave them rare strength and cohesion which had helped them to retain their independence and pride. Almost every evening at nightfall, heralds went through each village summoning the people to the congress. This role was played by two or three teenage boys wearing shirts and trousers but carrying ceremonial staves with a carved bird's head at the top after the fashion of the Roman eagles. On their heads were ordinary trilby hats, but with feathers round the rim, reminiscent of the great feather headdresses their people had once worn. From their hip pockets hung coloured handkerchiefs and as they walked they called like town criers. I was told that the question of our photography would be discussed at the congress and that I should attend.

From the outside the congress house looked much like any of the other palm-thatched and wooden-walled square huts of the village, but inside tiers of wooden benches mounted the walls round a central arena. I placed myself near to the chief or *sahila*, who was reclining in a hammock, and watched as most of the village arrived and settled themselves into groups. The women sat together stitching *molas* by the dim light of a few burning oil wicks, the young men argued noisily in the background, children played and romped without quite undermining the parliamentary dignity of the proceedings and the elders talked earnestly about the evening's agenda on the privileged front bench. The atmosphere was quite extraordinarily similar to that of a modern constitutional assembly, and yet this was no externally imposed democracy but the way in which tribal decisions had been arrived at throughout Cuna history since long before the Conquest.

Proceedings were always conducted in the Cuna language even though many of those present understood Spanish. In front of the *sahila* stood his Secretary who kept order and to whom all remarks were addressed. The meeting was called to order and various matters were discussed. A few impassioned speeches were made from the back benches, to which laconic replies were given by the chief or one of the elders. At one point I gained the distinct impression that an objection was being raised to the presence of a 'stranger in the house', and hostile stares were directed at me from one section. But it was apparently overruled and nothing was said to me direct.

As new arrivals came through the door one of the heralds ushered them to their places and it seemed that another of their roles was to act as 'whips', organizing group support or opposition on certain questions, but I may have been reading more into their activity than was really taking place. When an elder arrived late much ceremony was expended in finding him exactly the right place to fit the order of precedence. Several rose and offered him their places with great politeness before the matter was settled to everyone's satisfaction.

When at last I was called upon to speak, the Secretary said that the *sahila* wanted to know exactly why I had come to their territory and what it was I wanted. I took the floor and began in my far-from-fluent Spanish to explain how my organization, Survival International, tried to help Indians who were facing problems and that I had some experience of this work in Brazil and elsewhere. Phrase for phrase, what I said was translated into Cuna by the Secretary. Fortunately, I had spent some time with him the day before, so that he was able to give full rein to his eloquence, elaborating my fairly simple remarks. I said I understood that the Bayano Cuna faced two developments which would unquestionably affect their lives. One was the dam which was due to flood their lands within the next two years and the other was the projected road. I assured them that the expedition of which I was a member was there at the invitation of the Panamanian Government and that I was not trying to cause trouble but merely gather information about what they themselves felt on these matters, so that their views could be taken into account. On the other hand I was in no way connected with the government and was therefore quite free to oppose government policy if it did not appear to be in their best interests.

'Our land,' they answered, 'is good land and no one will take it from us. Men came from the government and showed us other land, far up river, saying we should move there, but it is bad land. There are no gardens there, no fish in the river. We said we would stay. When the flood comes we may have to move our village back from the river bank but we will not leave. Surely the flood will not move us. Even the worst floods our old men can remember only came up to the village.'

I asked if anyone there had ever visited their cousins in the San Blas islands off the Atlantic coast. Several said that they had.

'There are mountains between here and there, are there not?' I said. 'When the dam is finished, the water will reach right back to them. It will make a sea like you saw around the San Blas islands, only there will be few fish and coconuts will not grow.'

At this they became concerned and produced documents signed by successive presidents of Panama guaranteeing them their lands in perpetuity and saying they would never be moved off them.

'No one told us this before,' they said. 'What can we do?'

I replied that it was probably too late now to stop the dam, although there were many who believed that it was a mistake and I would try to fight it, but my organization was new and had little strength.

'You should send representatives to the President, asking him to save your land, but I am afraid you should also begin now to plant gardens in the new lands you have been given so that if you have to go there you will be able to feed yourselves, otherwise you will go hungry for the first few years until your crops grow.'

'But our gardens here are old. It takes many years for the fruit trees to bear and for the best land to be known. We will not leave our land. We will fight for it as we always have.

'Many years ago, when the settlers began to move up river, we lost much of our land and many moved to San Blas. But we resolved to stay and at last the government agreed that the settlers should come no further. Now there is no room on the islands and anyway we do not want to leave.'

The debate continued and I asked them what they felt about the road. Here opinion was divided. Some said that it would be an advantage to have rapid transport to Panama City, as it would help trade and they would become richer. Others feared the bulldozers which were already working at the edge of the reservation removing the timber and destroying the forest.

'They are taking away our best trees and paying us nothing for them. We have protested but they said that the land was to be flooded and so they would be destroyed anyway and were worth nothing. We thought that they were only saying that because they thought that as we were Indians we were stupid and could be robbed. Now we see that it is worse than we thought.'

This seemed like a good moment to raise the question of photography.

'Many people,' I said, 'believe that Indians are ignorant, naked savages who are not fit to manage their own affairs. If I can show what rich lives you lead, how wise and strong you are, it may help to teach people that Indians are not inferior and are worthy of respect. This would strengthen your case for opposing the dam and the road.'

The lamps had burned low and the women had stopped sewing to listen and smoke short, wooden pipes. They contributed to the discussion, arguing on equal terms with the men, shouting sometimes that the men were stupid and not fit to govern, urging them to fight and not be cowards. Some of the children slept now, curled up on the floor or on their mothers' laps. The *sahila*'s young son lay in his father's hammock, his eyes drooping.

The conclusion of the congress was that they did not object to our filming, but they could not give a final ruling on this question. That would have to come from the *sahila* of Icanti, a few kilometres along the Bayano river. He was the overall chief of the whole reserve. I should go there next day and if he agreed then I could return and all would be well.

The *sahila* of Icanti was busy preparing medicinal plants which he had just returned from gathering in the jungle when Jerry and I arrived next morning. He was not interested in our photographic problem and dismissed us tetchily, saying yes, yes, we could do what we liked; then more politely that we should come back in the evening to talk and attend his congress. We hurried down to the river just in time to jump into the last of half a dozen dugout canoes setting out on a fishing expedition with about 30 men on board. They had with them a huge black net which belonged communally to the whole village of Icanti and which they told us they only used a few times each year.

'Otherwise,' they said, as though it were the most obvious thing in the world, 'we would soon remove all the fish in the river and we would go hungry. Normally we fish with hooks and line, one by one. This is slow, and we usually catch enough to feed our families. If we are unlucky we help each other out.'

Using nets was a fairly new development for the Cuna. Their sensible attitude towards the conservation of fishing stocks – one from which the trawler fleets of the great nations could well learn – was yet another example of the way in which Indians are well able to handle the introduction of new technologies without either undermining their traditional patterns of behaviour or becoming greedily and dangerously dependent on externally provided materials which they are not able to replace.

In a wide stretch of the river where gravel banks shelved gently out into the water we came on two more canoes with men who had been throwing pieces of maize and boiled plantain on to the surface for some time to attract the fish. A large area was encircled and we all plunged in to drag the net to the shore, splashing to prevent the fish escaping and diving down to the bottom to make sure the net had not become snagged.

The result was far and away the greatest draught of fishes I have ever seen caught in this way. By the time the net was firmly held in the shallows and they began to throw the catch on to dry land there was a seething mass of fish, mostly of the same species – and ranging in size from one pound up to about six pounds (500g–3kg). I counted well over 400 which, taking a conservative average of $2\frac{1}{2}$ pounds (1.2kg), made nearly half a ton of fish in one cast of the net. They went on fishing for the rest of the morning, then the heavily laden canoes returned to the village, the catch was shared out equally and the fish dried and salted and hung in the rafters – enough basic meat and protein for all for several months. The net was also stored away, not to be used again until the congress decided that the river was ready to deliver up another harvest. It seemed especially ironic that a river which was so well managed should be the one chosen to be dammed, since once the waters began to flood the Cuna would never again be able to fish in this way and, even assuming the indigenous species of fish could adapt to the new conditions of a stagnant, shallow lake, they would be much harder to extract from it.

At the Icanti congress that evening I was again put through my paces and once more I was shocked to find how ill-prepared the Cuna were for the changes the dam would bring. It is not pleasant to be the bearer of bad tidings and it angered me that so little had been done officially to warn them about the apparently inevitable results of such an expensive and far-reaching government scheme. As with so many large-scale developments throughout the world it seemed that no one had thought to weigh the social and environmental costs against the immediate short-term benefits.

Well into the evening there was a commotion by the entrance to the house and an old man with a woven basket over his shoulder was escorted by the heralds to the centre of the congress house. While the debate continued he proceeded to remove all his wet clothes before dressing again in a dry shirt and trousers which he took from his basket. He was, I learned, the chief of Piria, a village far up river, who had just arrived in his canoe. A dark-skinned, wizened old man, he ignored the assembled company until dressed again, when he formally greeted the front bench and spent some time speaking to the *sahila*. With half a dozen others he was then led out again by the heralds and I was invited to go too. It is traditional with the Cuna that when a stranger arrives in a village he is entitled and indeed urged to eat in every house. We tramped in single file in the bright moonlight, over a small hill, through some plantations to the first house of the village, one of the heralds leading the way with his staff of office held up for us to follow. Seated in a circle inside, bowls of boiled rice, plantains, soup, stew, were handed to each of us and we ate. When we had finished, gourds of water were passed round for us to drink from and a larger calabash in which we washed our hands. No sooner was this done than we all trooped off to another house where we ate and drank again – and again, and again. I have a small appetite at the best of times and I had already eaten earlier in the evening, but it was simply not done to leave anything in one's bowl and if I tried to do so I was urged by all present to eat up quickly so that we could move on to the next place. My stomach felt like a dangerously over-inflated tyre and I became drunk on food and water alone, something I had heard of but not believed possible. At last, in confusion, I drank down the bowl of hand-washing water which the others had all used and in the ensuing hilarity I was reprieved and allowed to return to the congress house. But no sooner had I sat down than I was summoned urgently away again and, thinking that some crisis had occurred, dutifully followed the herald only to find that yet another feast had been prepared for my special benefit and this one I was expected and made to eat alone.

By now I was being treated with a, for me, familiar mixture of guarded respect for my knowledge of matters concerning the world outside and tolerant scorn for my ignorance of tribal ways, a happy compromise which is, I believe, the best one can hope for on short acquaintance with a completely different culture from one's own. As long as one is able to strike a balance between a superior attitude and total buffoonery, a basis of genuine cross-cultural friendship and mutual respect can quite easily be achieved.

They asked me where I was going to sleep and I said that I proposed returning to the other village about an hour away where Jerry, suffering from an upset stomach, had decided to have an early night and where my hammock was slung. It was now past midnight and they begged me to stay in Icanti, offering me a hammock there and saying that the jungle was dangerous and that I would be eaten by a jaguar. Fearing that I might be made to eat yet more and asserting with rather more bravado than I felt that jaguars did not eat Englishmen, I set off with my dim little torch alone down the narrow jungle path. Halfway I began to regret my decision and believed that I was being followed in the darkness. I lost the path and panic was near. Then to my horror I felt something large and scrabbly crawling up the inside of my trouser leg just above the knee. For a stricken moment I shone the torch on the slowly moving bulge, before taking a deep breath, closing my eyes and striking down hard with the palm of my hand. Whatever it was bit me before it died but I ground it to a pulp against my leg and limped on hurriedly without investigating. I arrived without further trouble, washed off the sticky black mess in the river, slept and awoke next morning with only a slight swelling.

The dam workings, when we passed them on our way down river a few days later, were a frightening sight. A cleft between two low ranges of hills was being inexorably filled by a fleet of bulldozers and dump trucks. The scars reached far back on either side. But even more disturbing was what we saw as we passed the limits of the Cuna reservation. A straight line marked the legally defined boundary. On one side virgin jungle, vibrant with life, the tall canopy of trees protecting a lush vegetation and dark brown soil which, carefully rested for years at a time, would produce valuable crops. On the other side, land outside the reservation which had been 'developed'. Bare red earth stretched as far as the eye could see, rivers of erosion scarring the surface to leave bare rock and laterite soils below. A few dead trees accentuated the desolation, while a handful of starving cattle wandered hopelessly in search of blades of dried-up grass.

There are two approaches to the question of how to handle the fragile planet we inhabit, two attitudes towards life and the survival of our species. One derives from the assumption that the fast return based on conquering nature is all that matters, since there will always be new lands to rape. The other is based on the superstitious dread of offending the spirits of the forest by taking from them more than tradition dictates or, put another way, recommends the sound use of the environment and the limited resources available to us because it is aware of the inter-relationship of all life. Can anyone doubt which is the wiser policy?

Those who have been privileged to live for a time in the company of primitive societies are never quite the same again. Whether they have spent years studying them, learning their languages, analysing their customs and kinship patterns or whether through accident or design they have simply shared their lives for a period, the basic tenets of our civilized world are seen in a different light, and assumptions about life which had previously gone unquestioned are now a little suspect. We return to our worlds and re-enter the battle for power, prestige and wealth, seeking whatever security they can give. But we no longer believe that it is the only way to live, the only destiny, the only happiness. We have tasted something of the other route man might have taken on this earth, living as a sapient part of his environment, recognizing the unity and harmony of life, instead of fighting constantly to overcome and dominate all other species, a process which can only lead eventually to man's own annihilation. It is far too late for us to return to what we were before, but by observing and respecting our environment we may learn to temper our arrogance enough to be allowed to survive a little longer ourselves.

And the road? The Indians and I were not alone in opposing it. Three years later, in 1975, a test case was fought in the District Court in Washington between the Sierra Club, the Audubon Society, the Friends of the Earth and the International Association of Game, Fish and Conservation Commissioners as plaintiffs and the US Secretary of Transportation and the US Federal Highway Administration as defendants, claiming that the US government, which was putting up most of the money for the road, was breaking its own environmental code in doing so. I had written a report after the expedition as well as several newspaper articles (including one in *The Times*) on the effect the road would have on the Indians, and these were used in evidence. The judge ruled that the defendants were 'enjoined from entering into any contracts, obligating any funds, or taking any other action whatsoever in furtherance of construction of the Darien Gap Highway'. It has still not been built.

The dam, however, went ahead and the Cuna were moved. Films were made of the efforts of conservationists to save from drowning the large numbers of wild animals marooned on shrinking islands as the huge lake grew, but I saw no references to the effect it was all having on the Cuna. And I have not been able to go back and visit them. Funds are not available to Survival International for such purposes and we have to rely on occasional reports from anthropologists and travellers. So far none has reached me.

There are a few successes and many failures, but as long as people believe that lines on a map are more important than environmental and social destruction – and many still do, although they might not put it quite like that – the Darien Gap, one of the most fragile ecological regions of the world, as well as those who dwell in it, man, beast or plant, are threatened.

Before publishing my book on Indonesia which, being critical in parts, might have brought me to the attention of the authorities, I decided to slip back to see whether the rumours I had heard of little-known people in Sulawesi were true.

I had intended to go alone since there is a special dimension to solitary travel which heightens awareness as well as sometimes making it easier to establish rapport with strangers from different cultures. However, there is no doubt that it can be more fun travelling with a friend. While staying with my brother Patrick at his beautiful farm in Jamaica in 1974, I met again

Hugh Dunphy with whom I had happily hitch-hiked around Japan 17 years before. After a decade living in Jamaica, I felt he would be soft and ill-equipped for the discomfort and rigours of life in the jungle. But he insisted that he was coming with me and would go into training for the two or three months before our departure.

Our starting point was in eastern Sulawesi where a chain of small fishing villages, mostly inhabited by seafaring Bugis people, hugged the southern coast. From there we planned to walk across the peninsula, a 300-km stretch of country where it seemed no European, and possibly no other outsider, had ever travelled before. Even reaching there had involved a series of minor deceptions as we persuaded successive authorities that we were tourists, mountaineers or naturalists, depending on which seemed the most plausible and potentially acceptable explanation of our desire to reach such an inhospitable region.

'Don't go into that terrible country!' the coastal Bugis said. 'The people there are wild and dangerous. They wear no clothes and have no religion. We would be afraid to go there.'

No one can doubt the courage of the Bugis on the sea. They are a great maritime people who have sailed the eastern seas for centuries in beautiful small craft and often with no more navigational aids than a white cockerel in the bows to warn of approaching reefs. But they and the other Arab and Malay people who have settled around the coasts of Indonesia have always feared the wild interiors of the islands. As Muslims they cannot eat the wild or domesticated pigs which make up most of the meat away from the sea, and as sailors they find the jungles and the mountains confining. Consequently, in many places the earlier inhabitants of the islands who retreated into the hills in the face of successive waves of settlers, have remained unknown and unconverted to Islam or Christianity.

The To Wana of the region ahead of us were said to be still largely nomadic. It was late evening only two days after we left the coast when we first made contact with them. We had been walking inland up the Sinkoyo river. The river was not navigable, but wide and muddy near the mouth, so that we went at first parallel to it across the flat, cultivated coastal plain. Later there were sandbanks and shallows, and by then the land was rising, virgin jungle, green, thick and impenetrable along the foothills. We were able to walk along the river itself, the only open route through the forest, skirting one shore as long as possible before being forced by a high bank dropping into deep water to wade across and try the far side. Slow progress, forcing waist-deep against the current, trying not to slip and fall on the uneven bottom, anxious to keep at least our cameras dry.

Sometimes it rained and the leeches were bad. Every half hour or so we had to stop and scrape them off our legs. If we missed any, they were able to gain a proper hold before the next time and although they still came away easily the wound they left would not coagulate and the blood flowed thick and dark like blackcurrant jelly.

Perversely I was irritated when, as a result of his strict training, Hugh proved the tougher of the two of us. He also walked faster, partly through being taller and longer of leg, and partly because I was having trouble with my feet. For years they had tended to let me down under pressure. Crooked toes developed blisters, toe-nails would fall off during or after long walks and occasionally a broken toe would spew out a sliver of bone through a suppurating sore. During the summer I had resolved to cure all that and, submitting myself to the tender mercies of the finest specialist in Harley Street, I had had two of my worst toes shortened and straightened by the insertion – and retention for an agonizing six weeks – of steel pins. Now they were being put to the test, and failing. The first few days along the coast and on the river had opened impressive blisters and I shuffled through the gravel and sand, both inside and outside my boots, muttering bad-temperedly about 'bloody doctors' and 'bloody feet' and 'bloody people who walked too fast'.

Gradually the river narrowed and became more rocky as we climbed into the mountains. The going became easier as we were able to step from rock to rock and avoid long stretches of wading. As we rounded a bend, looking about us now for a camp site, we stopped dead. Ahead were two boys diving for fish in a pool and we had come upon them without them hearing us. They looked up, startled and afraid, but it was too late to run away and so instead they stood their ground as we approached – the first white men they had seen, as they later told us. At first their fishing equipment was disappointingly modern for members of a tribe which was supposed to be virtually uncontacted and unknown. They had goggles of wood with inset pieces of glass and crude spear guns with metal tips and thick rubber elastics. Hardly the gear of Stone Age man. Moreover, instead of bark loin-cloths, they wore brief, tattered bathing suits. But nonetheless they were the first representatives of the people we had come to meet, the wild, nomadic, independent To Wana (or Wana people). They had caught some good fish and these they showed to us. Their camp was to be on an open stretch of gravel and while we waited for our three guides to catch us up – Wana-speaking but Islamized boys from Sinkoyo – we bathed in the deep, clear, cool water of the pool where they had been fishing. Later, more To Wana arrived until there were about fifteen in the group including three or four children and a pure white new-born baby. In no time at all, they built lean-to shelters from branches and palm leaves while we decided to risk the rain and sleep out in the open on the gravel.

The two women in the party were both young and vivacious, full of

The nomadic To Wana of Eastern Sulawesi building a
waterproof shelter in what seemed like no time at all.

energy and humour, ready to laugh or shout at the least excuse. This we
found to be a familiar trait among To Wano women who were much
bossier and less embarrassed by our presence than the men, delighted to
be photographed at work or when breast-feeding babies and always
bringing us presents of food. At this magical first meeting we did
especially well, receiving delicacies to compare with the finest and most
expensive food anywhere in the world. A whole fish, cooked in its skin,
the flesh white and succulent; freshwater crayfish, boiled until pink and
wrapped steaming in stiff green leaves; finally the largest hunk of heart of
palm I have ever seen, casually brought in on the shoulder of one of the
late arrivals like a long log for the fire, before being hacked up and shared
out amongst us all.

Nomadic people give a deceptive impression of taking life easy, of
having all the time in the world, of doing each thing they do simply
because it seems like a good idea. Settled man, no matter how he may love
the wilderness and even though he will have rare moments of real peace in
it, spends most of his time consciously working to control his surroundings or make his life comfortable. Whether we like it or not, remote places
are alien to us and frightening. We cannot help trying to change and tame
them.

In the morning the To Wana lay and watched us get up. We went and washed in the river, streaking the clear water with brief scars of soap and toothpaste. We packed our knapsacks, then unpacked them again, remembering we needed fresh reels of film from the dry plastic bag at the bottom. We hung dew-damp clothes to dry in the first rays of sunlight, we brewed tea and went down to the river to wash out our mugs. At last we were ready to set off. Within seconds two To Wana men were ready to accompany us and show us the way. Without them we might get lost and, besides, they could help carry our things. Payment was not discussed. During the time we adjusted the straps on our packs and looked around to see we had left nothing behind, one of the men made a knapsack from a palm leaf and strips of liana. It was the dryest container we had and when the rain fell later in the day, that was where my camera case went.

They walked fast and we hurried to keep up with them, leaving the boys from the coast trailing behind out of sight. We were rewarded. We came to a wider stretch of river with gravel beaches pushing back the under-growth. For once we could see several yards ahead as though down a long dark canyon between the trees. The leading Wana stopped and pointed. At the edge of the water, not far away from us, stood an anoa, disturbed from drinking, its head raised in fright. As we saw it, it lowered its head, stretching it out in front so that the short, pointed horns lay back over its shoulders, and then it bounded off through the water, across the river and up the far bank. I had been to see the pair of anoas in the Jakarta zoo. They had been small, the male aggressively charging the retaining fence as I approached. They are the smallest species of wild buffalo in the world, only found on Sulawesi, and were thought to be almost extinct. This one was much bigger and darker than the ones in the zoo and although the To Wana were excited to have seen it, they assured us that they were exceedingly common. Indeed, as I told the World Wildlife Fund, who had just added anoas to the Red Book of threatened mammals, and with only a small degree of exaggeration, much of our time thereafter as we walked up the river was spent in avoiding stepping in anoa pats along the banks. Later we were to stay with a family which ate anoa at least once a month, although they had none for us, and everywhere we went the To Wana said they were common, especially the Highland variety which is small and red while what we had seen was the larger, blacker Lowland. The local Indonesian name for them is *sapi hutan*, meaning 'jungle cow', a rather inelegant description of a beautiful animal which few outsiders have been lucky enough to see.

We spent one night near the top of the pass over the mountains. It was cold at over 1,000 metres and the rain was chill on our backs. Huddled on the ground under the collapsing remains of a long-abandoned temporary shelter, we were too tired and wet to strip and search for leeches. Hugh produced his secret emergency luxury, a single bar of Kendall mint cake which we shared. It must have been invented for such moments, and we slept.

Beyond the mountains fever or relief at being alive made the scenery wilder and more romantic. Waterfalls and deep, dark pools. Sudden red flowers sparkling among the endless shades of green. Deep gorges and high Renaissance outcrops of rock. It was a friendly jungle, the prickles less prickly than in other jungles, the ants less aggressive and the insects, flies and mosquitoes more discreet. We stayed with an old shaman, a healer and a man of knowledge. He cured our headaches, sucking the pain from our foreheads and throwing back into the air the stings which the spirits had thrown at us on our journey through the mountains. He killed a chicken and divined in the entrails that we were not evil and would live. He told his family not to be afraid of us and when we admitted to having a little *obat* of our own, some few pills and ointments in a sponge bag, he brought his sickest grandchildren to us, confessing without shame that he could not cure them of the 'new disease'. Sweet children, happy and unafraid with big round eyes, they would suddenly double over and cough until the blood came and then lie exhausted. Almost all appeared to have TB.

Their settled cousins near the coast, with whom they traded rice, rattan and Damar gum for metal tips to spears, for glass for goggles, salt and trinkets, laughed at them because they wore no clothes, only a loin-cloth or sarong made of bark cloth. Throughout all the ages they and the ancestors of those they traded with had worn no other clothes and had survived to populate the land. Now they were told it was savage to go naked, that people with a real religion would not walk around thus, and they were given rags and cast-offs to dress in. These became wet in the rain and the rivers but they went on wearing them for the illusion of warmth and because of the shame of nakedness. They developed colds and when the children, too, started to shiver, they dressed them in other rags. Their clothes became dirty but they had no soap to wash them in or others to change into. TB, already prevalent on the coast, moved into the interior. It was hard to have to tell the old man that there was no easy answer and that a proper cure would take months of professional treatment.

The old man was called Daye. He was sad when we had to leave, blessing us elaborately so that we should have a safe journey. He lived at the junction of two rivers, a place called Bulang, open to the sky and alive with bird song in the valley; remote and secret under the mountain, yet visited by To Wana from all directions along hidden paths. Fewer than before live in the jungle now. Most had been persuaded to move nearer

the coast and become 'civilized'. Those that remained in the interior had
plenty of land and the land was good, though nearly always steep. Their
clearings were as nothing in the vast expanses of greenery and none went
there to trouble them. But all this could change overnight. The mature
hardwood trees were valuable and the rest could be destroyed in the
process of removing them. Exploitable minerals certainly awaited prospectors underneath their mountains and to extract them would require
roads. More settlers would come and take their land away in the name of
progress. Then the To Wana would move to the coast, the anoas would be
killed off as they have over most of the rest of Sulawesi, the rivers would be
polluted and the Batui mountains would become like so many others –
perhaps unchanged from a distance, from the air, but dead underneath,
because the people, the animals and the forest giants would have gone.

Are we strong enough to replace what we take away, to create new life-
support systems once we have destroyed old ones? Possibly, but the greed
of self-interest and short-term gain usually get in the way. Not a hundred
miles from Bulang, out among the reefs of the Molucca Sea, a hundred
Japanese trawlers were fishing for shrimps – and only shrimps. Each ship
made about eight trawls a day. Each trawl landed two or three tons of fish.
Only about ten per cent of the catch was shrimps so that the rest went back
overboard to die and sink to the bottom. Two thousand tons of fish
destroyed and thrown away each day because it is the most economic way.
When catching other fish, it is easier to use dynamite, when ten per cent
will float and can be gathered off the surface. The rest sink. A diver who
had gone to the bottom after the fishing fleet had passed described to me
acres upon acres of dead fish carpeting the sea bed. At Ujung Pandang
(once called Makassar), the capital of Sulawesi, 800 km to the south, a
barium sulphate factory had recently been completed. Without the strict-
est pollution control, which was not planned in this case, such factories are
among the most lethal of man's inventions, the cooling water killing all
marine life and the smoke bearing deadly fumes wherever the wind
blows. No other country in the Far East would allow such a factory to be
built anywhere near them and the American engineers, sent out to
approve the site, had said that a worse one could hardly have been found,
lying next to a bakery and beside a harbour from which a fishing fleet of
small boats set out daily. But the government was said to be delighted at
this manifestation of progress and at the revenue which it was beginning
to bring in, even though at a vast cost of human and marine life.

Is it any wonder some say we are no longer fit as a species to dominate
the world? Most primitive societies, like the To Wana, respect life. Not
sentimentally but in a spiritual way which is often the same as a practical
one. A man who is about to go hunting tells no one. He may make an

offering to the spirit of the animal he will kill to placate it. He feels bad about the necessity of killing and apologizes to the spirits for having to do so. While hunting he will not swear or use bad language as this would bring bad luck and even sickness. Instead he becomes as one with his prey and as well as being more successful he is also being respectful to nature and his environment in a way which we are increasingly forgetting how to be. The modern hunter on his own is not so far removed from this awareness as we think. Alone and absorbed in the hunt, he soon reverts to the pure hunter, like his ancestors who painted their prey on the walls of caves a few thousand years ago and his cousins who live by hunting today. D. H. Lawrence describes this eloquently in a passage in his short novel *The Fox*.

It's no good walking out into the forest and saying to the deer: 'Please fall to my gun.' No, it is a slow, subtle battle. When you really go out to get a deer, you gather yourself together, you coil yourself inside yourself, and you advance secretly, before dawn, into the mountains. It is not so much what you do, when you go out hunting, as how you feel. You have to be subtle and cunning and absolutely fatally ready. It becomes like a fate. Your own fate overtakes and determines the fate of the deer you are hunting. First of all, even before you come in sight of your quarry, there is a strange battle, like mesmerism. Your own soul, as a hunter, has gone out to fasten on the soul of the deer, even before you see any deer. And the soul of the deer fights to escape. Even before the deer has any wind of you, it is so. It is a subtle profound battle of wills which takes place in the invisible. And it is a battle never finished till your bullet goes home. When you are *really* worked up to the true pitch, and you come at last into range, you don't then aim as you do when you are firing at a bottle. It is your own *will* which carries the bullet into the heart of your quarry. The bullet's flight home is a sheer projection of your own fate into the fate of the deer. It happens like a supreme wish, a supreme act of volition, not as a dodge of cleverness.

It is a difficult concept to understand if you are not and never have been a hunter. But without it the pursuit of animals, birds or fish for food is in danger of becoming selfish slaughter and indeed by extension the very harvesting of the earth's resources becomes the rape of what is not ours by right.

We have the power to destroy all other life on earth and we know it. So we ritualize our hunting, using weapons which are not the most advanced our technology could produce and fishing line lighter than the weight of the fish we wish to catch. We talk of the skill required and the sportsmanship involved. But I believe there is more to it than this. There is man's need to establish the relationship with other species which only the face-to-face struggle for survival brings into focus. The illusion that failure in the hunt means death; a brush with the reality of our first few hundred thousand years when it was the only truth. Vegetarians, and many others, would deny the need for this and they may be right. It may be that an age is dawning when killing dies out and men learn to leave all other species in peace. But this thinking is not evident in the society entering the preserves of the world's remaining true hunters. Those who would usurp their land will destroy everything in their way and, except in a few places where sufficiently fertile soil exists for settled permanent agriculture, they will leave a wasteland behind them.

The existence of the To Wana and other peoples like them is strangely reassuring. Their life is not idyllic, but it is a lot better than that enjoyed by many of the civilized peoples of the coastal towns and cities. They have chosen to live it and wish to continue to do so. I need to know that such people still exist; in addition to being moved by their plight, impressed by their specialized knowledge, gladdened by their art and artefacts, angered by injustices perpetrated against them and saddened to see them sick and dying, the help I feel impelled to try and secure for them is intended as much to assert their right to choose their own way as to alleviate their suffering. But then I am suspicious of much of the activity that goes by the name of charity today, both as to its motives and to its benefits to the recipients. Too often the very help we give only prolongs the suffering while salving our consciences. How can we help without destroying?

Thanks to Hugh's energy and determination, we covered the ground fast, visited several groups of To Wana and became saddened by the TB from which many were dying. Well across the central mountain range and within only a few days' walk of the north coast and relative civilization, we kept hearing of another tribe, the Kahumamahon, traditional enemies of the To Wana, who spoke a language called Saluan, and were said to be relations of the To Loinang far to the east. On the frontier between the two tribes we heard stories of clashes still taking place and of how the Kahumamahon used very powerful poison on their arrows.

I was tired and my feet hurt. On my own I might have given up and hurried to the coast, but Hugh was adamant that having come so far we should go on and so we cut across country to the upper reaches of the Balingara river. For days we had been in jungle, friendly jungle it is true with little but leeches to bother us and fairly easy going along stream beds where we walked up a series of waterfalls with clear pools between and ferns growing on the banks; over steep ridges where the undergrowth was sparse. But jungle nonetheless with the confining curtain of trees and greenery all around and only seldom a glimpse as through a window of a hilltop or the range ahead.

Now we entered a completely different and unexpected stretch of country. The Balingara river was wide, shallow and fast-flowing. It curved between high bluffs and over wide shingle beaches, giving views upstream of distant mountains and with casuarina pines in groves. A stag with a fine head of antlers, like a Landseer painting, stood grazing unaware of our presence on the shore. Tall and powerfully built, it fitted the romantic landscape. Back in the jungle it would have been out of proportion. When we moved, it bounded off over the rocks in great leaps. Tracks of anoa, too, were plentiful and of wild pig. This was a place to settle but there were no people until we reached the Kahumamahon at Koloko.

High on a cliff-top at the head of the river, where the water swirled in a deep pool below at the base of the outcrop, were two houses. From their strategic position they could see far along the river in both directions and the only access was along a ledge in the cliff and up an almost vertical path. We had been observed and our climb was watched in silence, but we were welcomed with shy friendship by the leader of the small clan. We had no common language as he spoke almost no Indonesian but we developed an amiable relationship through smiles and mutual expressions of pleasure and gratitude.

Since our journey was nearly at an end we could afford to be generous with our remaining store of presents and he was overwhelmed with a heap of fish-hooks, darning needles, fishing line and tobacco which I set before him. In our turn we enthused over the boiled wild rice and little mud fish on which he and his family fed us. I asked what other meat they ate and understood that most of this came from hunting with the pack of dogs which shared the house with us, lying in the ashes of the central hearth and watching sharply for any bones or scraps which might be dropped. Deer, wild pig, *babirusa*, a strange long-legged creature with tusks which curve upwards like horns and are the reason for its confusing name meaning pig-deer, and both the Highland and Lowland anoa were hunted with spears and dogs. They killed almost one anoa a month, they said, indicating that they were very common, but when I tried to find out which meat they preferred they failed to understand what I was driving at, insisting simply that all meat was good.

The Kahumamahon people at Koloko were small and sharp-featured, intense but friendly and deeply interested in us. They and their children all seemed healthy and they were quieter and even shyer than the To Wana. All the men wore loin-cloths and I saw no shirts or trousers, while the women were bare-breasted with simple sarongs. When asked if they preferred living where they did to moving down to the civilized comforts of the coast they made it very clear that only force would make them leave their homes, and certainly I can imagine no more idyllic setting. We sat up late by the light and sweet smell of burning Damar gum. Unlike the To Wana who burned the aromatic gum in solid rock-like lumps, the

The gentle Kahumamahon secure in their inaccessible clifftop
house. Eastern Sulawesi, 1974.

Kahumamahon had prepared long torches of leaves and gum bound together which could be stuck in the walls like tapers in a mediaeval baronial hall, illuminating everything. In the rafters hung rows of dried jaw-bones of wild pigs, shades of the old head-hunting days when human skulls would have been similarly displayed. In a rack over the fire, preserved by the smoke, and protected from the cockroaches, was some dried meat and baskets of grain and herbs and home-grown tobacco. One of the women played a few warbling notes from time to time on a little flute which she was whittling from a small piece of bamboo, while the older children brought us water from the river far below in hollow pieces of bamboo three or four feet long. A diminutive tame parrot with vividly coloured neck feathers flew from shoulder to shoulder to peer at us inquisitively from all angles. A space was cleared for us and with a great feeling of security in our impregnable cliff-edge fortress we slept soundly on the hard floor.

The cold woke us every now and then to hear the multitude of noises always present in the tropics when it is dark. There can be more silence in the heat of the day when only the intermittent grating of crickets disturbs the background hum of insect life. At night sounds carry further so that each distant cry and hoot was heard sharply over the steady plashing of the river far below. A cock crowed loudly out of turn at the moon and a dog yelped as it touched a hot ember in the ashes of the fire.

I lay awake thinking about what I was doing there and what could be done for the gentle, quiet people whose hospitality we were enjoying. They asked for nothing and, being healthy, needed nothing. Yet they were so vulnerable and it would be so easy to undermine their lives in critical ways.

I had heard nothing but a few little rustles, as though the chickens perched under the house were adjusting their feathers against the dawn mist rising from the river. I opened my eyes to see that it was almost light and that Hugh and I were alone. Without a sound men, women and children had slipped out without waking us to bathe in the river, to fetch water and firewood. A few minutes later I poked my nose out of the warmth of my sleeping bag and the fire was blazing while the family huddled round it for warmth, and some rice was cooking in a bamboo tube. It was a scene from the Stone Age and it was time to get up.

They built us a raft to go down the river. It would have taken three days of hard walking on foot. Instead we travelled in comfort and style, sitting on a raised bamboo platform where our baggage was kept dry while our feet rested on the partially submerged logs. There is no finer way to travel on a river, poled skilfully and at speed over rapids and through narrows by the wise old man Yali Udi who came with us, drifting leisurely on wide stretches. When it was too deep to pole and the current was sluggish we swam behind, pushing. When the current was faster we drifted along, floating on our backs at the same speed as the raft. Once we saw a boa constrictor swimming urgently across the surface to the bank where it slithered into the undergrowth and disappeared. Later we heard a pig squealing pitifully in the distance and Yali Udi said it had been caught by a snake and was being squeezed to death. We stopped on a sandbank to dig for the eggs of the Maleo bird. They bury their eggs three or four feet underground, leaving the chicks to hatch on their own and struggle up to the surface. The nests are betrayed by mounds in the sand and by the birds themselves which flock in the bushes and trees around, clucking like chickens and about the same size. They are black on top, pale pink underneath with longish blue legs and a blue wattle on the head. But the most remarkable thing about them is the size of the eggs which are seven times as large as a chicken's egg and excellent to eat. It seemed inconceivable that such a small bird could lay such a big egg but they do and the eggs are regarded as a great delicacy in that region. The nesting sites are much sought after and we even saw one place on the coast where a site had been fenced off and the flock of some 200 Maleo birds semi-domesticated.

We rafted right down the beautiful and almost deserted Balingara river to the open sea where we were once more among the maritime people whose horizons stretched away to cities from which giant aircraft linked the continents. A gentle day's travel was all that separated two worlds as different as the whole span of man's recorded history.

9

A Year in the Rain Forest

'Through the Jungle very softly flits a shadow and a sigh –'

Rudyard Kipling, *The Song of the Little Hunter*

So many of my travels have been through tropical rain forests and so many of the people with whom I have been concerned live there that it was only natural that I should develop an interest in that particular type of environment. In a much more spectacular way than occurred at the time of the founding of Survival International, when the fate of primitive peoples was world news for a short while, there was a coincidental surge of interest worldwide in the subject of forest destruction in the late 1970s. This concern has lasted and grown, perhaps because the results are visible to the naked eye from space, and the effects forecast are laden with doom. Many more people are directly involved.

The two environments I have loved have been deserts and rain forests and I have often been asked which I prefer. It is a fairly silly question as they are so different, but if I must answer I would say that while deserts are more spiritually satisfying, allowing a bright harsh light to illuminate the soul while hardening the body, rain forests are more interesting and, on balance, I feel more at home in them. The more I learn about them the more fascinating they become, thus providing another of my laws of travel: 'The more you try to understand an environment and the less you try to fight it the kinder it will be to you.' This, of course, is precisely the approach of its indigenous inhabitants. But even those who do not live in or even near tropical rain forests should recognize their significance.

In Brazil we had flown over seemingly endless and indestructible vistas of forest, where the greenery stretched from horizon to horizon. I was

once lost in such a jungle and it taught me always to treat it with respect. I had wandered a few yards off a path in pursuit of a wild turkey and I had lost my bearings. Under a cloudy sky and the dense canopy of the trees it was impossible to tell where the sun was; everything looked familiar yet slightly different in all directions and the constant insect hum made concentration difficult. Was that tree with its massive trunk supported by elegant buttresses the one I had just passed or was that one already behind me and out of sight? Had I already pushed my way past that curtain of lianas or had I been about to do so? If I made the wrong decision and hurried on there might be several thousand miles of trackless forest ahead and I would soon die. In one direction only lay safety. Luckily I stopped in time before panic set in, sat down and waited before carefully retracing my steps, shouting and firing shots until my companion replied. Since then I have always been careful to mark my route at all times with broken twigs and slashed leaves.

But we also flew over man-made deserts in the north-east. Once some of the richest land in Brazil, now good only for cactus thanks entirely to man's stupidity and greed. In western Kalimantan we had been surprised how little virgin forest there was left. The island of Borneo is usually described as having most of its surface covered with dense, impenetrable vegetation. This was certainly not true of the country we flew over for mile after mile inland from the west coast. Almost all the level ground has been cleared and appeared abandoned, uninhabited and clothed in scrub. Only a few scattered areas were under cultivation. Extensive logging followed by agriculture over a long period had brought about the familiar end product: a barren waste for the sake of a few years' crops. Meanwhile, other factors had caused the population to increase, thereby accelerating the process and creating an irreversible vicious circle.

Already in Indonesia I was becoming aware that destruction of the forests was a dangerous step which would not only change the ecology and perhaps the climate, but would bring poverty in its wake. The headman of one of the riverine villages had summed it up: 'For two years the rice crops have been poor, owing to the failure of the rains. We are near to famine. In the old days we used to be able to gather sago and hunt in the forest if we were hungry, but now all the forests and the game are gone.

---

on preceding pages

The Deer Cave, Mulu: half a mile inside the largest cave passage in the world.

The longhouse Base Camp of the Mulu expedition.

A Penan family in the Gunung Mulu National Park.

Even the rivers are hard to fish now, as they flood easily and are full of logs which destroy our nets.'

The forests themselves are demonstrably productive: trees, plants and wildlife abound. How much more significant it would be for the well-being of mankind, I thought at the end of our Indonesian expedition, if as much effort could be put into finding ways of harnessing that potential as was being expended in cutting it all down. It never occurred to me then that I would in time be invited to play my part in just such an effort.

Marika and I had planned to make a journey in Malaysia similar to our Brazilian and Indonesian journeys. Shortly before we set off in 1976 John Hemming told me that the Royal Geographical Society was considering mounting an expedition to Borneo but that no location had yet been chosen. Our journey became a search for a suitable site and, after seeking widely in Sabah, Brunei and Sarawak, I learned of a large, newly created national park in one of the wildest and most beautiful parts of Sarawak. The Sarawak Government invited the Royal Geographical Society to produce a management plan and I was asked by the Expeditions Committee of the Society to lead the expedition.

It developed into a new sort of undertaking for the Royal Geographical Society and also the largest British scientific expedition ever. In order to

In 1976 I explored much of Borneo in search of a suitable site
for a major Royal Geographical Society expedition.

produce a worthwhile management plan – the first ever of a tropical rain forest national park – it was necessary to understand the environment as fully as possible. To do that meant bringing in scientists who were specialists in every field: botany, zoology, geomorphology, the standard trio of scientific research and, perhaps most importantly in the context, forest ecology, the study of how the whole complex system worked.

It was one of the most exciting and stimulating times of my life. For a start, to be asked to lead a major Royal Geographical Society Expedition in the tradition of the great names of exploration was a great honour and I had no idea if I had any talent as a leader. Secondly, it was a massive and challenging logistical undertaking since we ended up taking 140 scientists into the field and spending 15 months there.

Thanks to finding a highly competent and enthusiastic team to help run things and being guided by a wise and sensible committee, I found the burden of responsibility extraordinarily easy to bear. Of course I was more used than I had realized to taking decisions alone on my own farm, in my earlier travels and especially during the formative and often lonely days when Survival International was having its early growing pains. On the Mulu expedition it was Nigel Winser, my immediate deputy, who really made my life easy.

With Nigel Winser, the organizing genius behind the Mulu expedition (1977–8), and some of the stores with which we sent scientists into the field.

The Mulu Expedition Base Camp seen from the air. Built on
the pattern of a Borneo longhouse, it housed up to 100
scientists and local helpers at a time.

During the heavy and almost daily rains, the Mulu Base
Camp was a safe refuge for work and relaxation for the tired
expedition members.

With constant energy he shouldered every problem without ever under-mining my authority, which is not an easy balance to strike.

During 1977 and 1978 the scientists came and went, spending anything from three weeks to three months with us in the field. Only six of us were there for the whole time welcoming new arrivals, looking after them during their stay and seeing them off again at the end. We provided their food, camping equipment, and travel arrangements. Most work was done in small sub-camps which took us a day or two to reach from our comfortable Base Camp. This was built on the model of a longhouse and here, after two or three weeks in the field, the scientists were able to relax and refresh themselves before setting off again. As a result, a very great deal of work was achieved under conditions which would have proved very difficult for scientists working on their own. We met people with totally different interests and learned things we might never otherwise have suspected through working and living together. Botanists and entomologists, for example, were always discovering during dinner that their respective, obsessively studied plants and insects depended upon each other for pollination and as food, thus forging lifelong scientific links. Meanwhile scientists from quite foreign disciplines and countries were developing friendships which have continued long after the expedition. We all had a lot of fun and at the end the whole exercise was regarded as having been an outstanding success scientifically, logistically and as a model of multi-disciplinary work and international co-operation. Literally thousands of new species were identified, a whole ecosystem was much better understood and our management plan was a model for other tropical rain forest national parks.

Collecting was important in order to establish base lines for further research. Samples and specimens were dried, packed and sent off in a constant stream to the Sarawak Museum in Kuching, where first examples were deposited, and to the British Museum (Natural History) and a dozen other museums and universities around the world from which scientists had joined us. But the object of the whole exercise was much more complex than a simple collecting trip. The multi-disciplinary studies planned and carried out over the period into nutrient recycling, the weight and rate of fall of leaves, the effects of different insects and lesser forms of life on decomposition, the many fascinating examples of symbiosis between plants and animals all constituted significant research.

However, my heart being ever preoccupied with Survival International, the most important aspect for me was that we were living with and being helped by local people who understood their environment better than we could ever hope to. Throughout, the majority of these were Berawans from the nearest longhouse some 30 miles downstream. Mulu was

A longboat loaded with scientists and local people setting off
from Base Camp.

Diverse groups of experts from ten nations came together at
the Mulu Base Camp dining-table to compare notes on their
work.

regarded as part of their traditional hunting area and some of them had small farms near the edge of the national park. They were delightful, tough, self-confident people, quite rich in the sense that their land provided a surplus for sale, but glad of the chance to earn the good wages the expedition provided. Cheerful and hardworking, our welfare and comfort were their constant concern; independent and proud, they made it clear that they were working with us rather than for us and I always appreciated that. Most of the younger men spoke English which they had learnt in school and which was then still the second official language of Sarawak. This made them good companions for those who had not learnt Malay, while some of the older men were famous hunters who had penetrated far into the hinterland of the park in pursuit of game.

The Gunung Mulu National Park had only been gazetted the year before and it was very little explored. Scientifically the attraction lay in the fact that within its boundaries almost every tropical forest type could be found growing on a wide variety of soils. The result was an incredibly rich diversity of species of plants and animals living quite close together. There were all sorts of other treats in store for us. The great limestone cliffs and pinnacles were staggeringly beautiful and contained a network of gigantic caves, one of which we were able to prove was the largest of its kind in the world. Part of our team, who went back a year later, discovered another one four times as big and easily the largest cavern in the world. Wembley Stadium would fit into one end.

Marika and our children – Lucy, who was 17 and had left school, and Rupert who had his seventh birthday at Base Camp – joined me for eight weeks near the start of the expedition. Lucy, who had thought that she would be bored without rock music and boys of her own age, took to the jungle like a natural. She was bitten by no insects (presumably she has inherited my immunity). Moreover, some of the young bearded scientists coming in from long stints in their solitary sub-camps were stimulating company and she had a good time. She even climbed the 2,400-metre mountain after which the park was named, becoming the first woman to do so, although she had never been known to take exercise voluntarily before.

Rupert suffered badly from bites and was really too young to benefit fully from life on an expedition, but he was very brave and had a lot of fun playing with Berawan contemporaries around the longhouse. Marika and I hardly saw each other; my time was taken up by the other members with their endless problems concerning work and arrangements. Marika was busy organizing the Base Camp kitchen and devising clever menus to help the cooks who followed her to make the most of the peculiar ingredients available to us, ranging from fresh snake to freeze-dried

A rare moment alone with Marika, Lucy and Rupert in the jet
boat, which could speed with ease over the many rapids
separating us from the outside world.

processed soya bean meat substitute; and we both resented the fact that
we had so little time alone together. Being apart, as we were for the rest of
the year, except for two brief trips home, was almost easier to cope with.

We heard that there were members of the shy forest nomads, the Penan,
living in the park, although I had been told before leaving that none of
them still lived traditional lives in Sarawak. My informant had been Tom
Harrisson, who had parachuted into the interior of Borneo to raise a very
successful local force against the Japanese during World War II and who
had subsequently been Curator of the Sarawak Museum for many years.
Sadly he was killed in a car accident just before the expedition.

For the first couple of months we saw no Penan, although we saw
abandoned *sulaps*, their simple lean-to shelters, and the Berawans, who
regarded them as inferior, said they thought they were watching us from
the cover of the forest. Then one day a muscular man carrying a blowpipe,
a bamboo quiver stuck in his bark loin-cloth and wearing nothing else,
walked straight across the clearing between the river and our longhouse
and shook my hand. He had a strikingly different face from the Berawans
who looked to me much more European than either the Chinese or the
coastal Malays. His eyes had the epicanthic fold and his earlobes had holes
through them. There was an instant chemistry between us such as I have

seldom experienced on meeting someone for the first time. There was a sense of mutual trust and respect which never left us for the next year, much of which we spent in each other's company.

His name was Nyapun and he was the headman of a small group of Penan. Telling only Nigel Winser and Marika where I was going, I slipped out of camp with Nyapun early the next morning. We were going to visit his family and I did not want either to alarm them by taking anyone else or offend anyone by refusing to take him. I also had no idea of how far away they were.

We trotted fast and silently for five hours with one brief ten-minute stop. At first I found it difficult to adjust to Nyapun's pace. While I was concentrating on slogging along steadily with my eyes on the path to avoid tripping, he was alert to every sound and movement in the forest around us so that he kept pausing, turning aside, looking and listening. He seemed to glide along, invisible and silent, making me feel gross and awkward, though by then I rather prided myself on my ability to move quickly and quietly through the forest.

Of all my many meetings with forest peoples, my encounter with Nyapun's family was the most pure and magical. None of the women and children had seen a European before and there was a stillness about them like startled deer. We walked the last few yards up a wide shallow stream-bed towards three thatched *sulaps* on the high bank ahead. We had seen no sign of life, neither path nor clearing on our way, yet here suddenly were human beings at home. Nyapun had two wives and ten children. The oldest boy was about 16, almost an adult, and able to help his father hunt and gather. They greeted me calmly, and with great dignity accepted the presents I had brought of sugar, salt and tobacco. The little children came to take my hand then stayed holding it, gazing at me with big, dark eyes. Then, while the women prepared food, we went to wash and play in the river, the children splashing and shouting as they caught small fish with their bare hands.

I slung my jungle hammock between two trees next to the hearth and watched as they settled down for the evening. The women and little girls wore simple, rather old and faded sarongs; the boys tattered shorts or loin-cloths. The only metal objects they had were two cooking pots, two *parangs* (the eastern equivalent of a machete) and the spear-like blades bound to the end of each blowpipe. Otherwise everything they needed was woven or carved from what grew around them. Their basic diet was wild sago, which they gathered and prepared for eating from a new site every three weeks or so, and meat from the herds of wild pigs which were the commonest of game there. They never stayed in one place for long and so their camps rarely became fouled and smelly, as tended to happen for

Nyapun with his family beside their *sulaps* deep in the forest.

The Penan family greeting me calmly, gazing at me with big
dark eyes.

example around a longhouse where domesticated pigs acted as excellent scavengers but made their own mess.

They fed me on smoked mouse deer, river prawns and heart of palm followed by brown sago mixed with some of the sugar I had brought, clearly a great treat for the children. A more delicious meal would be hard to find in the world's finest restaurants. Then by the light of the fire the women played music on a simple bamboo guitar, perhaps the oldest instrument in the world, and danced on the bare forest floor. Nyapun and the elder boys danced too, a curving warrior's display with hands bent back, knees flexed and stamping feet similar to that practised almost nightly in the longhouses. But the women did a dainty, skipping twist, quite different from anything I had seen elsewhere.

Next day when I set off to return to the Base Camp, they quietly gathered their very few possessions and with no fuss at all came with me, abandoning their temporary home without a backward glance. They settled near us and from then on more and more Penan appeared until we were able to calculate that some 300 of them lived in and around the park although officially there had been thought to be none.

My policy was to attach a Berawan or a Penan to each arriving scientist, trying to match their characters and needs. Soil scientists, much of whose work involved digging deep pits and carrying heavy loads of earth back to camp for analysis, clearly needed a team of tough young Berawans, used to working their rice crops. Some of the botanists, on the other hand, greatly appreciated the intimate knowledge of the Penan of certain types of plants. Our palm specialist, a leading world expert, was deeply impressed by the Penan allocated to him. Without of course knowing their Latin names, or anything about our scientific methods of classification, he was able to identify not just the different species of palm and rattan but he could put a use to each. Some were good for making baskets or mats, others bore good fruit, could be made into sago, or had medicinal uses. With this help our expert was able to increase the list of known species in the region from ten to over 120 in a few weeks.

While the Berawans made delightful energetic companions who we felt would somehow survive in the modern world whatever was done to their environment by the approaching loggers, the problem of the Penan was sadder and more frustrating. Here were people whom some of the world's best scientists regarded as masters. The mutual respect with which they worked together gathering samples, observing animal behaviour and preparing the collections was the single element of the Mulu Expedition of which I was most proud. Yet the Penan were regarded by their Berawan neighbours and by the government as somehow inferior because they did not employ the trappings of civilization, nor did they cultivate rice. Efforts were constantly being made to encourage them to settle in villages by the larger rivers where they were promised schools, medical facilities and agricultural advice. Many had done so but the services had usually failed to materialize, largely because few coastal or city people wanted to work in the interior, and the Penan found the labour of clearing, planting and harvesting rice too much for them so that the crops failed and they starved.

I talked at length with various Penan about their problems, ashamed that I had no easy answer to their trusting questions. Most recognized the inevitability of change although they were mostly not aware that their territory had been declared a national park, and many wanted their children to be educated if only so that they could resist exploitation. But they saw how much worse off were their relations who had settled, and hesitated to join them. The only answer I could give was that change was never easy and it would be as hard for them to adapt to village life as it would be for me to live for ever in a *sulap* and survive on hunting.

Because there was strong feeling in Malaysia both about interference from representatives of their previous colonial power and about the whole subject of isolated peoples, raising the issue of the Penans' future formally through Survival International would probably have done more harm than good. Efforts in some quarters to remove this supposed blot on the social landscape might well have been speeded up. Fortunately there were others in a better position to speak out who did so quite strongly. Teams from the Sarawak Museum and the Sarawak Medical Service undertook ethnological and nutritional surveys of the Penan. They found that many of the Penan only used the park intermittently for hunting and gathering produce; some, living closer, spent up to half their time inside it, while only a few lived there all or most of the time. They arrived at a figure of one Penan to every 3.8 sq. km of territory. In their subsequent Report, one of the several submitted by the teams as part of the expedition's published work, they stated: 'This cannot indeed be considered to be too restricting for the Penan, nor would it cause undue imbalance of the park's ecosystem.'

Nonetheless, the question of their impact on the fauna and flora and the problem of their own future remained, and certain decisions needed to be taken urgently. There was no evidence that man had any serious impact on the smaller mammals of the park. The larger mammals, on the other hand, were being hunted energetically by the Penans and Berawans, as well as by other longhouse people entering from the north and east. These people used shotguns exclusively while, with only a few exceptions, the Penan used blowpipes. The Report suggested that wildlife was probably in far more danger from shotgun users than from the Penan and that: 'It may well be proper to ban the use of firearms completely in the park.' Even so, a day would come when a replacement source of protein was needed for the Penan as hunting activities were reduced and certain species barred to them.

As I have mentioned, the chief food of all the Penan was wild sago. Even settled Penans, who had been cultivating hill paddy rice for some ten years, collected sago from far away in order to supplement their poor rice crop. For rice is a difficult crop for beginners and the Penan do not share the overwhelming predilection for it shown by nearly all other Sarawak and Malay peoples. The scope for teaching them to grow other crops such as maize, tapioca, bananas, beans, sweet potatoes and pumpkin was enormous and opened up an interesting and potentially valuable agricultural future. They also had a wide knowledge of edible and medicinal plants, and it might be possible to bring some of these into cultivation before the knowledge about the plants is lost or forgotten.

The Government Report on the Penan spoke of the urgent need for land to be set aside for those Penan who wished to settle, and pointed out how valuable these areas would be as buffer zones to protect the park. The area which had been made into the Gunung Mulu National Park comprised a large part of the traditional hunting grounds of the Penan. In many conversations they stated fervently that it was their land and without it they would starve. If this happened they would become a burden on the government, adding further to the great number of malnourished shifting agriculturalists in the country. The first priority, therefore, seemed to be to establish their rights to land and to continue hunting, albeit with certain restrictions to accord with the Game and National Park laws. Change was coming inevitably to them. The park existed and would continue to be used, bringing visitors who would influence the Penan in the process of bringing employment. A road was planned to run through the park and this would expose them still further to modernization as well as increasing vastly the dangers of shifting cultivators moving in and complicating the management of the park. In time their cultural heritage, their gentle, retiring characters and their ability to live in total harmony with their environment would be affected. It was good to see these qualities defended so eloquently in the Sarawak Museum Report which stated: 'If they are lost due to rapid cultural change and the complete disorientation of the Penan people, it will not only be a loss to Malaysia but also to mankind.'

The problems arising from the transition of a people to a fundamentally different way of life, especially where it has concerned the settlement of a previously nomadic society, have seldom, if ever, been satisfactorily resolved anywhere in the world. The enlightened approach of the Sarawak Government, as revealed in these Reports, led me to hope that the Penan might be an exception. The solution they proposed to the difficulties made it seem that they were not insuperable. While asserting the absolute right of those Penan who did not wish to settle to continue a nomadic way of life, they pointed out that their numbers were relatively small and might well not exceed what the park could sustain without serious damage to the wildlife. Moreover, if hunting by the other neighbouring peoples was reduced and a buffer zone for the exclusive use of the Penan established around the park that territory would be secured.

Those who chose to take the first steps on the road to becoming settled would need the most help and understanding. Everyone hoped that the development of the park would bring economic benefits to the region from the employment of local people as guides, as well as through the provision of river transport and accommodation. Although the Berawans and other longhouse communities were ready and well able to take advantage of these opportunities, I hoped that the incomparable knowledge and skills of the Penan would not be neglected. No one knew the park better than they did and no one was better qualified to assess what hunting might be taking place and what effects visitors were having on the fauna. They worked willingly and tirelessly for the expedition and, though some members preferred to have Berawans with them in view of their knowledge of English and their cheerful companionship, properly trained and supervised Penan could form the nucleus of an expert corps of park wardens. This would begin to compensate them for the loss of meat denied them through certain species being protected.

It was most important that educational plans for both Penan adults and children should take their special needs into account. Experience elsewhere, for example in the USA with Amerindians, has shown that children from a radically different culture, however bright they may be, suffer academically when introduced to schools dominated by others. Schooling is also a danger since too much enforced absence from parents means that a child fails to learn the traditional skills necessary for survival in the forest. If this schooling is then unsuccessful the child will end up with the worst of both worlds. No one who met the attractive and intelligent Penan children who invaded our camp from time to time, cheerfully interested in everything that was going on, but always behaving impeccably, could doubt that dedicated teachers in a special school on the spot would be able to release much hidden talent.

For the parents, too, there were things it would be necessary to learn. Apart from the whole range of possible agricultural futures, their transition from a nomadic to a settled life would involve an entirely new approach to hygiene. If clothes were to be worn in order to conform, then they would need to be washed and soap would have to be bought. For

A Penan girl in her *sulap* has all she needs for a healthy,
happy life, but change is coming and sadly it is likely to be
for the worse.

trade and understanding of money, basic arithmetic and perhaps some
reading and writing would be necessary.

It was in health and medicine that all the Penan, whether settled or still
nomadic, most needed and sought help. As a result of increased contact
with the surrounding population and, indeed, if tourism were to develop,
with people coming from all over the world, a whole spectrum of new
health risks and diseases would be introduced. Changing diets and life-
styles would bring deficiencies and stresses with which their existing
remedies would not be able to cope. If their nutritional level were to
improve – and it was by no means likely that it would, at least in the short
term – then the Penan population could begin to increase rapidly,
imposing further stresses, unless contraception was provided. Already
this was a subject of great concern to Penan and Berawan women alike,
which they regularly discussed with our expedition doctors.

Our successive doctors and nurses were with us primarily to take care of
our own members' health problems, but these were surprisingly few: half
a dozen cases of dengue fever and minor skin and stomach ailments were

all they had to worry about, and so they were able to devote a lot of time to holding clinics for the locals. This probably did more for our popularity than anything else, as well as providing some fascinating opportunities for the doctors themselves to do research and gain experience in fresh fields. One of the most outstanding doctors, who has since been on several other expeditions with the Royal Geographical Society, was a local general practitioner I recruited in Cornwall.

When we left, the Penan problem, though fraught with moral, social and practical difficulties, seemed far from insoluble to us. The main need was a realistic and sensitive approach. All were agreed that the Penan, at the receiving end of pressures which they did not fully understand, deserved special consideration and attention from people appointed to look after their affairs and protect their legal rights.

Sadly, reports that have filtered back since the expedition indicate that all is not well with the Penan. They are said to be hungry, ragged and abused by everyone. I long to do something but feel helpless, since anything I do is likely to make matters worse for them. I tried to go back in 1982 but was told officially that I would not be allowed into the park. One day I will return there, tell Nyapun that I am still his friend, laugh with his children and show that I still respect and admire them even if no one else does. Sometimes it seems that is all one can do to help people oppressed by prejudice and bigotry.

What we were able to do, which may in the long run be just as important as Survival International's work for the Penan and people like them, was to pursue the whole question of the destruction of tropical rain forests in a practical and thoughtful way. Until the scale of the problem, the alternative policies available and above all the actual function of that unique ecosystem is better understood, the people who live in it will still be subjected to disturbance and harassment from those destroying it.

The sadness of my final parting from the gentle Penan, who, I felt, were probably doomed and for whom there was so frustratingly little I could do, depressed me and I began to wonder if anyone was capable of defending their own values against the rolling force of plastic modernity. Soon after my return I was invited to spend a couple of months living with just such a people, the Yanomami of Brazil.

---

on following pages

Dr Conrad Gorinsky towering above a Yanomami Indian in 1968.

A Yanomami *yano* – the ideal human habitation for the tropical rain forest.

A Yanomami family hearth.

Yanomami boys practising with miniature bows and arrows.

10

The Last Great Indian Nation

The Yanomami Indians are one of the last great Indian nations in Brazil which still preserves its original way of life. But this does not protect them from the threat of disintegration which looms over them with the approach of our society.

Claudio Villas Boas

The first group of Indians I had met with Conrad Gorinsky on the Hovercraft expedition in 1968, the ones who chased us away, were Yanomami. Later, at the end of my 1971 tour of Brazilian Indians, I had dropped in briefly on a couple of Yanomami groups. Even then I had recommended in my Report the need for urgent action in demarcating the area which should be protected for them. I had also found it quite extraordinary that FUNAI were doing nothing for, and appeared to be unaware of the existence of, what was already being recognized by anthropologists as Brazil's largest single tribe of Indians. No FUNAI man had ever visited them. Yet I and the subsequent Aborigines' Protection Society mission both did so, which made a nonsense of FUNAI's claims, as expressed by the disastrous General Bandeiro de Mello, that 'Everything necessary was now known about all the Indians in Brazil so that anthropologists were no longer needed.' The General was subsequently dismissed but, in spite of perhaps naive hopes each time successive presidents of FUNAI were appointed that they would prove both willing and able to do something for the Indians, things became progressively worse. Only unremitting vigilance by the press, both worldwide and Brazil's own, prevented unconstitutional changes to the law and other repressive measures designed to eliminate the Indians altogether. Survival International's lone voice was joined by a few others, and especially significant were signs of growing concern within Brazil itself which made it easier to monitor the situation. This was both timely and very necessary as the threats to the Yanomami were now accelerating.

The reason for their survival in such numbers and the lack of outside interference in their lives lay in the remoteness and inaccessibility of their territory. Almost alone among American Indians they appeared never to have been forced to migrate, either by the mass movements of other Indians such as the Aruaks and Caribs or by successive penetrations of the interior by colonists in search of slaves, souls, gold or rubber. As a result it was thought that they might be descendants of some of the very first people to cross the Bering Straits perhaps 30,000 years ago and to have lived on their present lands for as much as half that time without being conquered or forced to migrate. I know of no other people in the world of whom this could be said.

Numbering about 20,000, they live on and around the watershed between the Orinoco and the Amazon, which at that point happens to mark the border between Brazil and Venezuela, so that they are arbitrarily made citizens of two different nations. Their country is dense tropical rain forest in which they hunt, gather and farm superbly well but which has until recently been regarded as inhospitable by everyone else. But in the early 1970s they began to face invasion of their territory on a number of fronts.

One of the least justified threads of the trans-Amazonian web reached out towards them. Cynical Brazilians referred to the original highway from the parched north-east to the dense forests on the borders of Peru as 'a road leading from where one dies of thirst to where one dies of hunger'. This northern tentacle, the Perimetral Norte, was described as 'a road leading from nowhere to nowhere'. If completed it would have cut straight across 600 km of Yanomami territory. As soon as the first road gangs reached the first groups of Indians disaster followed. Within a year most of the Indians near the road had died from epidemics of influenza and measles. The disorientated survivors were reduced to begging and prostitution.

Then came the prospectors. Following the discovery of tin and rumours of uranium deep in the heart of the Yanomami homeland, more than 500 miners began operating illegally. Contact again sparked off epidemics among the Indians.

Next, millions of hectares of Yanomami land were designated as part of a vast cattle ranching scheme which would mean clearing and burning all the forest.

Something had to be done before it was once again too late for the Indians. The Yanomami became Survival International's number one priority. Pressure was also growing in Brazil to defend the Yanomami. Thanks to the superhuman and extremely courageous efforts of a few qualified individuals some progress was made. The road stopped, mainly it must be said from lack of funds, but the pressure undoubtedly helped. The miners were all forcibly removed by the authorities when the presence of large numbers of Indians was proved beyond question and the law about invasion of Indian land cited. Other development plans were shelved.

FUNAI at last produced a plan for legalizing the Indians' occupation of their land. Twenty-one small disconnected areas were declared as being occupied by Yanomami, a recipe for disaster, guaranteed to expose the Indians to the maximum contact with outsiders. Outraged, the Indians' defenders formed a committee for the creation of the Yanomami Park. An excellent counter-proposal was prepared by the leading anthropologists with knowledge of the Brazilian Yanomami. It was published by Survival International and the campaign began. Our embryonic branches in Washington and Paris took on a lease of life as the campaign gathered support and momentum. In Brazil it became a serious issue and suddenly the Yanomami had friends everywhere. Still the wrangling went on and in spite of all the promises nothing was done.

In 1981 I was sent by Time-Life Books with a photographer and an anthropologist to live with a group of Brazilian Yanomami Indians for two months and to write a book (*Aborigines of the Amazon Rain Forest*) about them. One of the few positive actions of FUNAI had been to prevent anyone visiting Indians anywhere in Brazil without formal permission. This did have the effect of protecting some of the Indians from being exploited but caused difficulties for serious researchers, especially those from outside Brazil. No permits were being granted. Meanwhile those who wished to get to Indian villages illegally for whatever purpose were often able to do so.

While waiting in Manaus for our permission to come through, I heard of an agency running tours for foreigners to a Yanomami group. They advertised wildlife safaris and there was no mention of Indians in the literature. But when, pretending to be a sensation-seeking tourist, I called there I was surreptitiously shown photographs of 'real wild Indians' and spun an unlikely yarn about how they were a lost tribe who had been saved by the illegitimate son of an Indian chief and a German nun, who had led them like a Messiah to their present home. Some of the pictures showed German and Scandinavian tourists with them and I was told I could go at once if I wished. They were unmistakably Yanomami. I reported the incident to the local FUNAI delegate but without material evidence there was little he could do.

Thanks to some very hard bureaucratic work over three months in Brazilia by our anthropologist Bruce Albert, we were the first researchers to be granted permission to stay with a group of Brazilian Indians for nearly a year. Even on the very last day of his vigil when the new President of FUNAI (a colonel now) was to sign the final document for Bruce we would probably have failed but for a small miracle. As he was waiting to be summoned into the Colonel's presence there was a commotion on the stairs and a group of 20 angry Xavante warriors burst into the ante-room demanding to see the President of FUNAI, their supposed defender, who had yet again failed to prevent the seizure of some of their traditional land by rich settlers. They were dressed in shorts and little else but red and black war paint; they carried clubs and they were not about to be stopped by anyone. A frightened policeman held them off for a moment during which the President escaped by a side door and the Indians, after searching for him in his office, set off again in pursuit. As a result it was a rather frightened and hurried colonel who greeted Bruce a few hours later across his wide desk. On one side, waiting to be dealt with, lay a pile of correspondence and Bruce saw that the top letter was an angry protest from Survival International requesting the reinstatement of some Indian students whose grants and permissions to study in Brazilia had been arbitrarily withdrawn by FUNAI. The letter was under my name as Chairman of Survival International but thanks to the fortuitous diversion by the Indians the President had not noticed and so my permit was duly stamped.

In spite of all I had read about the Yanomami, all the campaigning we had been doing on their behalf and all my happy experiences with other isolated peoples, I was not expecting to like them very much. A great deal has been written about their savagery in recent years since anthropologists began to study them and I believe this has done them a grave disservice. In particular they have been accused of being excessively warlike, and of practising infanticide as well as cannibalism. These are such taboo subjects according to our Judaeo-Christian system of ethics that the very mention of them tends to condemn practitioners without the implications being considered. It also tends to justify abuses against them since even distinguished academics who should know better have been known to comment that certain peoples, including the Yanomami, have such vile habits that they should be allowed to die out.

In fact not only was I deeply impressed by the superb skill of the Yanomami at organizing both the harvesting of the rain forest in which they lived and their own social life, but I also found them gentle and loving people, warm friends and a joy to live with. A whole new anthropological perspective has been brought to bear on them which does not prejudge them but instead recognizes the extraordinary sophistication of their lives.

Bruce Albert has played an active part in all this as one of the most energetic and concerned anthropologists to have worked with them. During the weeks we lived together in the *yano* at Toototobi Bruce was not only an excellent and considerate companion but came to represent for me the ideal standard against which I now set anthropological behaviour in the field.

For once there was ample time to talk subjects through as we lay in our hammocks and I questioned him on every aspect of Yanomami life I could think of. Around us the normal activities of the group continued; by day there were the constant comings and goings of the women as they fetched firewood and water from the river; noisy interruptions from the children as they played their games, all imitative of adult behaviour, hunting small creatures, cooking tiny feasts. In the evening the men returned to talk and eat, bringing the spoils of their hunting with them and giving it all to others. No Yanomami will eat his own catch. Generosity is the supreme virtue of their society. As we watched, Bruce interpreted for me both what

Victor Englebert, the photographer, and Bruce Albert, the anthropologist, who accompanied me during our stay with the Yanomami Indians of northern Brazil in 1981. The small boys have pet marsupial rats on their heads!

was said and the meaning of what we saw. Thanks to him I was able to feel
involved in and part of what was happening and I also began to understand the huge gulfs between superficial appearances and the hidden
meanings behind cultural behaviour.

Bruce himself recognized clearly the fundamental dichotomy of anthropological field work, especially perhaps in relation to the Yanomami who
were so confident that theirs was the only true way of life to follow. In
order to understand and study them properly he had to become fluent in
their language and this in turn demanded an almost total immersion in
their culture while living with them, since they recognized no other
possible motive for the arrival of strangers professing friendship than a
desire to be incorporated into the group. As a result it was necessary for
him to think and react with part of his mind and body as a Yanomami so as
not to appear different and alien, to accept uncritically their food, medicine and standards; and, as these became more familiar and automatic, to
view other ways of behaving with the same distaste as did the Yanomami
themselves.

Yet at the same time he was collecting copious notes on their myths for
his dissertation; studying their genealogies for the record; analysing their
kinship patterns and their linguistic practices for comparison with colleagues working with other groups; collecting, identifying and recording
the Yanomami names and uses of botanical specimens for ethnobotanists
back in Europe; all this quite apart from the daily chores necessary if one is
to remain healthy in the rain forest. In addition there were not only my
constant questions to answer and notes to check, but there were the
equally demanding claims on his time of our superb photographer Victor
Englebert. Although blessed with a jolly temperament and the power of
absolute concentration which gave him the ability to capture every human
activity and emotion on film, Victor too needed to have everything
explained and sometimes rearranged so that his photographs would
become intelligible to those at home. We competed amicably for Bruce's
time, vying with each other as to the relative importance of the visual or
the verbal image.

Bruce remained calm and clear-headed in all circumstances, never
lowering his impeccable academic standards in the clarity and complete-
ness of his analyses but, much more difficult and important, I felt, never
faltering in his utter loyalty to the Yanomami point of view. Not only did
he express their attitudes from an unbiased Yanomami perspective but he
absolutely refused to allow us to bend the truth of what we were observing
by making them behave uncharacteristically. He teased our European
sensibilities by translating stories and myths, most of which included
explicit references to bodily or sexual functions, exactly as the Yanomami,

free of our sort of inhibitions in these matters, told them. When, frustrated by the likelihood that we were going to miss observing part of the funerary feast, through having to catch the only light aircraft in the region for another month or two, I thoughtlessly suggested that they might care to fake it, he looked at me as though I were mad, making me suddenly deeply ashamed of the phoney standards of my own culture. To suggest that the taking of the sacrament by actors should be filmed for a television documentary about the Christian Church would probably not seem blasphemous to most Christians today. But to the Yanomami the undertaking of any important ceremony without due reason and reverence would be unthinkable.

When not living with them in the field, Bruce has campaigned tirelessly on behalf of the Yanomami. He was one of the authors of the proposal for a single national park for them which Survival International published and which has now largely been adopted by the Brazilian Government. His writings have contributed significantly to a better and more sympathetic understanding of them and his sensible and practical attitude towards their problems has helped to remove much of the undeserved stain from their reputation. For me he was an invaluable guide and mentor as well as a charming and entertaining companion during our time together among the Yanomami.

Even during a brief stay I was able to see what nonsense it had been to misinterpret their differences as somehow making them sub-human. Instead of being warlike as a result of some innate savagery, they recognized and deeply regretted the inevitability of conflict in human affairs. Most of their social and political activities are designed to control, channel and relieve aggression so that when hostilities do break out between different groups, injuries are kept to a minimum and deaths are rare. Compare this with our self-deluding pretence at peace while we secretly prepare to annihilate our enemies.

When a Yanomami woman feels her baby is ready to be born, she goes alone into the forest and delivers it herself. She then decides whether or not to keep it and on the basis of several criteria may choose not to do so. These include deformity, inability to look after it properly because she still has a child at the breast or has no way of supporting another, or the fact that she already has two or three children of the same sex, since it is important for a Yanomami to have a balanced family; daughters are just as valuable as sons since they bring sons-in-law, the most desired of all Yanomami relationships. If she returns to the *yano*, the circular communal dwelling of the Yanomami, with no child no one will comment or criticize. If, on the other hand, she returns with a baby that child immediately becomes the total responsibility and concern of every member of the clan.

In a sense it is not born until it enters the *yano*. More important, and perhaps difficult for us to grasp, is the total lack of any sense of guilt or shame on the part of the mother. For her, too, the child never had an existence. We have a confused and often totally illogical set of values regarding contraception and abortion. Who are we to condemn the Yanomami who have a system which they believe absolutely to be the right one and which works excellently for them?

Cannibalism is the most ridiculous accusation of all. After death a Yanomami is cremated. Some of the ashes are kept in a small calabash for about a year and then disposed of finally at a special funerary feast. At some of these the ashes are simply buried in the ground, at others they are added to a communal plantain soup and consumed. Is that what is meant by cannibalism with all the overtones the word has for us of killing for greed and the lust for human flesh? On the contrary, it is a very solemn sacrament.

Living in a *yano* with the Yanomami confirmed my belief that we have not begun to understand how to manage tropical rain forests. For the Yanomami who have lived there since before the dawn of history, it provides everything and from time to time great surpluses which are used for feasting and forging bonds with neighbours. We were there at a season of plenty and spent much of our time at such feasts. Huge quantities of the traditional fruit or vegetable soups were prepared on these occasions as well as mountains of smoked meat and manioc.

Nothing is preserved by the Yanomami. It is against their philosophy to hoard or acquire personal possessions and, besides, the forest supplies all the year round; the only use for surpluses is to give them away and so make better friends.

The major harvest of their gardens comes at the end of the dry season in the spring, when we were there, but the large game like tapir and pig are fattest during the rains, even though it is difficult to travel and hunt them. There are also trees and shrubs which fruit at different times, fungi, tubers, insects, reptiles, shellfish, frogs and many other plants and creatures to be gathered in their season. It has been calculated that the Yanomami gather at least 500 different animal and vegetable products from the forest, knowing exactly which are edible and when. With such largesse at their doorstep they have no need of the inconvenience, insecurity and immobility of an economy dependent on stored supplies. The pleasure they derived from food came far more, I noticed, from its variety than from its preparation.

What a contrast with the consciously poor settlers around the fringes of their land! Dependent on a dreary, unimaginative diet of beans and rice, they struggled to rear scrawny cattle in totally unsuitable terrain. The resultant meat, sold to buy the food they cannot grow themselves, is too poor for city-bred Brazilian tastes and mostly ends up as hamburgers in the USA and Europe. What a waste of food for a starving world such profligate and ignorant destruction of a rich land represents! The Yanomami system of farming, hunting and gathering supports in contented affluence an approximately similar population density to that which can be achieved by unhappy but land-hungry immigrants who do not understand and who indeed detest the terrain. But modern technology and science could learn from the Yanomami how to live richly in the rain forest and perhaps in time improve discreetly on their wisdom.

Scientists like Conrad and my friends from Mulu are full of ideas about how this could be done. An almost endless supply of species of plants await cultivation trials to see how they would compare with the dangerously few crops upon which the world's food supply currently depends. The same goes for animals which could be domesticated or harvested, while the cultivation of the rain forest itself in such a way as to retain its fertility while tapping its richness is still as little understood as the way in which it functions when undisturbed. But this is not an area where research funds go.

One example which particularly appeals to me of the many ideas waiting to be tested concerns termites. I ate the grubs of these several times with the Yanomami and found them perfectly palatable made into a sort of paté, once their origin was forgotten. Since insects are so prolific and such efficient converters of food there are those who believe that one of man's major evolutionary mistakes was in domesticating mammals instead of insects when, a few thousand years ago, he needed a regular source of food to support living in cities (becoming civilized). Termites have at least as much protein as prime beef and three times as many calories, weight for weight, but the resistance by most people to eating them would take a long time to overcome. Nonetheless they do occur in quite staggering quantities in the rain forest – about ten times as much *weight* of termites per hectare as could ever be achieved with, for example, cattle – and a way of exploiting them has been suggested. If the settlers penetrating the fringe of the undisturbed forest were to be encouraged to keep pigs and chickens instead of inefficient cattle, then these could be fed on termites. Thus the repugnance most people would feel for eating termites direct would be avoided as would the need to supply the animals with other food. The technical problem of extracting such surplus as the termite community could afford (and insects are notoriously prolific, especially if some of their predators are removed) should not be too difficult to overcome. Almost insuperable, however, would be the difficulty of weaning the Brazilian male from the macho image associated with cattle-ranching as opposed to chicken- or pig-farming.

Instead, as long as the Indians survive, we are likely to be left with a situation where two quite different peoples confront each other across an apparently insuperable divide. Both the Indians and the settlers are officially classified, according to United Nations criteria, as among the poorest people in the world. Each regards the other as inferior, dangerous, degenerate, even sub-human. Their values are so totally different that they appear irreconcilable so that in time one system must succumb to the other and be destroyed or assimilated. We know which system nearly always wins but I wonder whether mankind, evolution, culture, the sum of human happiness and especially nature and life on earth are served in the process.

One system is represented by hungry people born in the image of Western materialism who want at first simply to survive. But if they do they will always want more and, exploiting the environment in the way they do, they will inevitably get less. For me, their struggle on the very fringe of the known world, these modern pioneers of the remaining wild west, illustrates in microcosm all the ills which the human race has brought upon itself by its profligate misuse of the planet.

The other system, the Yanomami's, but it could as well be that of many others of the peoples Survival International represents, consists of men and women who know that they are rich and that their environment will never let them down if they respect it. They have a strong cultural base which gives them confidence in their lives, a certainty that there is only one correct way to behave and act in any given set of circumstances; they believe in generosity as the sole valid human virtue and this is the clue to their real affluence.

Buddha said that all misery is brought about by wanting what you cannot have and that once you stop wanting you may achieve contentment. There is no way that the aspiration for material wealth and prosperity of the 4,000 million people on earth can be achieved by technical or any other means. But the Yanomami know what is available to them, grasp it with both hands and savour it, respect it and give it away to each other, thereby achieving the affluence which eludes us.

This is why I believe that they and people like them matter more than those who would displace them on their land. Not because any one human life is more valuable than any other, but because some societies, through their viability and the hope they can give to a desperate world which sees its own extinction as dangerously imminent, deserve to survive so that the species may survive.

In March 1982 the Brazilian Government took the first step in the

A Yanomami woman rich and serene in the security of her
yano.

creation of a real Yanomami Park. 7.7 million hectares were interdicted for
the protection of the Yanomami Indians, one continuous area along the
border with Venezuela and including 90 per cent of the Yanomami living
in Brazil. This represents a surface area larger than that of seven of Brazil's
states, a vast territory but land indubitably occupied throughout history
by the Yanomami and absolutely essential to them if they are to survive. It
was a marvellous first step, a really tangible result after all our efforts, but
the campaigning had to continue since interdicted Indian lands have often
melted away in the past and a final definitive decree establishing the park
was still needed. Even then the threats to the Indians would not evapor-
ate. Illegal incursions would continue, epidemics would break out and
conflicting pressures would still be brought to bear on the Indians from all
sides as government officials, Catholic and Protestant missionaries,
anthropologists, tourists and doctors all ground their respective axes.

The Yanomami represent one of Survival International's more important successes since our efforts have undoubtedly contributed to the
creation of a proper area which will with luck and constant vigilance be
safeguarded for one major group of Indians. It is an irony that in order to
protect a people against disastrous incursions from the surrounding
population it is necessary to make them better known, but it is the only

way. The alternative would be to regard them in the same way as we do wildlife – species to be conserved and kept breeding for the general welfare of nature and the planet. It is a double irony that the Yanomami know with an absolute certainty that they are superior to all other men, the inheritors of the only true 'Way', and I for one would assert that they have as much right to that claim as any people on earth.

I enjoyed my time among the Yanomami immensely and I hope one day to be able to revisit them. They will change, their culture will modify as it has in the past and they will adapt to new circumstances and relationships if they are given the chance to do so. They are strong in their beliefs and that is the most important factor in survival and the one which must not be undermined. Provided that they are insulated from and inoculated against the fatal impact of disease they will survive and I am proud of Survival International's role in one of the few potential success stories in the world's dismal record in such matters. A much more important indication that success may be within our grasp, however, is in the fact that our cause, while still not popular or well-funded, is now widely known and our purposes are much better understood. Ten years ago people used to say to me: 'Inferior species always succumb to superior ones and so the Indians will be replaced by modern man. Why try to fight evolution? Anyway they can't be permitted to continue living such nasty, brutish lives.' Today the same people tend to say: 'Why can't you just leave them alone? After all they are outside our mad world and do no one any harm.' It is a step in the right direction but they still do not understand the significance of what we are trying to do.

It is not we who fail to leave them alone. The process is happening inevitably as greedy and desperate people scour the world for its diminishing resources. Even if the concept of creating 'human zoos' were morally tenable (which it is not since all societies are dynamic and the freedom to interact with others is a basic human right), it would not be practical to try and isolate people from each other. Insulation and protection from disease and exploitation is, however, quite a different matter. We help them when others attack them. We defend their rights when bureaucrats and property developers in far-away cities they have never heard of try to steal their land from them. We alert the world to their existence and their problems, but we try never to pre-empt their solutions. These they must find for themselves, drawing on their own unequalled knowledge of their circumstances and needs, making their own mistakes perhaps, but masters of their own destiny.

11

The Quality of Life

All peoples have the right of self-determination. By virtue of that right they fully determine their political status and fully pursue their economic, social and cultural development.

Article 1(1) of the United Nations Civil and Political Rights Convention

At first our most important task as we turned Survival International from an idea into an effective organization was to work out our philosophy, so that our purpose and our message were clear. This was a time of agonizing over semantics while being viewed with very understandable suspicion by some anthropologists. The dialogue continues today but with so much to do and so few of us to do it, there is less time to indulge ourselves in intellectual exercises. We know at least some of the answers and try to concentrate our efforts where there is a chance of achieving results. There are more and more campaigns which are initiated and run by the people themselves under threat rather than by outsiders working on their behalf. This is absolutely as it should be, our role being then to represent the issues to the world, transforming what may seem unimportant local issues into matters of international concern.

From the very beginning I found that the concept of Survival International's work neatly fulfilled my view of the world as a practical idealist. For me there have always been two complementary aims to pursue, two equally important driving forces to which to respond.

In the first place we are humanitarians; we are concerned with a particular section of the world community, one which we have found to be far larger than we suspected when we began worrying about the plight of a few thousand Brazilian Indians. We now calculate that nearly 200 million people or about five per cent of the world's population are still isolated from the mainstream of modern life. Ranging from Australian Aborigines to South-East Asian hill tribes, from Kalahari Bushmen to the Polar Inuit they find their way of life, their cultures and their very existence threatened. Together they constitute the largest minority in the world.

We are disturbed by the suffering, exploitation, degeneration and extinction they so often face when confronted by people who want to change them. We believe that they have a right to the lands that they have occupied, often for thousands of years and often the first members of the human race to do so, and that they have a right to the ways of life which have evolved to suit their particular needs. Above all, we believe that they have a right to survive and prosper as equal citizens of whatever nation has grown up around them.

But there is also an intensely practical side to our work. I am convinced that, just as a concern for conservation has led to a greatly improved understanding of how to manage the environment more efficiently, so too respect for and study of the ways in which indigenous societies live and exploit nature could be of the greatest possible value to us all. Surely no one can deny any longer that all is not well with our planet and with mankind. Viewed from satellites and from the moon, the earth is seen to be small and fragile. Diminishing resources, combined with an exploding population and vastly increased material aspirations, have caused a rapid widening of the gap between the 'haves' and 'have-nots'. Productivity and economic growth cannot expand indefinitely and as we rape the planet to try and maintain progress we begin to lose more than we gain. The promises of the Industrial Revolution have not been fulfilled. For the vast majority of people the quality of life is not improving. The horrors of global wars, famines and epidemics are as near as ever. Perhaps we have developed too quickly over the last few centuries and the cause of our confusion and fear today lies in the strangeness of the selves we know. Losing the security of a strong cultural base in the confusion of rapid change makes societies vulnerable to breakdown and anarchy from which no one gains.

We may overcome these difficulties through our own abilities and resources. Technological innovations may provide the bases for new support systems. But solutions will not spring from thin air and we should look for examples and clues wherever we can. A logical first step in the search for where we went wrong and what we can do about it is to listen to and learn from those societies which have not yet fallen into the same chain of errors.

Just as in nature, when one system begins to break down and degenerate another, arising from the rich diversity of life forms, takes its place, so within the human race lies the capacity born of experience to adapt. There are experts all around us and yet every effort is still being made to discredit and destroy them. This is a subject we are barely able to speak about with assurance, heirs as we are to a culture and ideology which have imbued us with a conviction of our own superiority to nature. In spite of all the sudden awareness and concern for what we are doing in the world, all the enthusiasm for conservation, all the fear of famine, pestilence or war, we find it difficult to strike the right note between a blind rejection of our system and a pathetic faith in our technology. Only the heirs to millennia of seeing the world differently can do so with real authority. One of the most beautiful and profound environmental statements ever made was delivered in 1851 by Seattle, Chief of the Suquamish and other Indian tribes around Washington's Puget Sound. The city of Seattle is named for the Chief, whose speech was in response to a proposed treaty under which the Indians were persuaded to sell two million acres of land for $150,000. The threats and prejudice those Indians faced then were identical to those confronting Brazilian and other South American Indians today, as well as millions of other peoples around the word represented by Survival International. I do not believe the issues can be much better expressed than in Seattle's own words.

How can you buy or sell the sky, the warmth of the land? The idea is strange to us. If we do not own the freshness of the air and the sparkle of the water, how can you buy them?

Every part of this earth is sacred to my people. Every shining pine needle, every sandy shore, every mist in the dark woods, every clearing and humming insect is holy in the memory and experience of my people. The sap which courses through the trees carries the memories of the red man.

The white man's dead forget the country of their birth when they go to walk among the stars. Our dead never forget this beautiful earth, for it is part of us. The perfumed flowers are our sisters; the deer, the horse, the great eagle, these are our brothers. The rocky crests, the juices in the meadows, the body heat of the pony, and man – all belong to the same family.

So, when the Great Chief in Washington sends word that he wishes to buy our land, he asks much of us. The Great Chief sends word he will reserve us a place so that we can live comfortably to ourselves. He will be our father and we will be his children.

So we will consider your offer to buy our land. But it will not be easy. For this land is sacred to us. This shining water that moves in the streams and rivers is not just water but the blood of our ancestors. If we sell you land, you must remember that it is sacred, and you must teach your children that it is sacred and that each ghostly reflection in the clear water of the lakes tells of events and memories in the life of my people. The water's murmur is the voice of my father's father.

The rivers are our brothers, they quench our thirst. The rivers carry our canoes, and feed our children. If we sell you our land, you must remember, and teach your children, that the rivers are our brothers and yours, and you must henceforth give the rivers the kindness you would give any brother.

We know that the white man does not understand our ways. One portion of land is the same to him as the next, for he is a stranger who comes in the night and takes from the land whatever he needs. The earth is not his brother, but his enemy and when he has conquered it, he moves on. He leaves his father's grave behind, and he does not care. He kidnaps the earth from his children, and he does not care. His father's grave, and his children's birthright are forgotten. He treats his mother, the earth, and his brother, the sky, as things to be bought, plundered, sold like sheep or bright beads. His appetite will devour the earth and leave behind only a desert.

I do not know. Our ways are different from your ways. The sight of your cities pains the eyes of the red man. There is no quiet place in the white man's cities. No place to hear the unfurling of leaves in spring or the rustle of the insect's wings. The clatter only seems to insult the ears. And what is there to life if a man cannot hear the lonely cry of the whippoorwill or the arguments of the frogs around the pond at night? I am a red man and do not understand. The Indian prefers the soft sound of the wind darting over the face of a pond and the smell of the wind itself, cleansed by a midday rain, or scented with pinion pine.

The air is precious to the red man for all things share the same breath, the beast, the tree, the man, they all share the same breath. The white man does not seem to notice the air he breathes. Like a man dying for many days he is numb to the stench. But if we sell you our land, you must remember that the air is precious to us, that the air shares its spirit with the life it supports.

The wind that gave our grandfather his first breath also receives his last sigh. And if we sell you our land, you must keep it apart and sacred as a place where even the white man can go to taste the wind that is sweetened by the meadow's flowers.

You must teach your children that the ground beneath their feet is the ashes of our grandfathers. So that they will respect the land, tell your children that the earth is rich with the lives of our kin. Teach your children that we have taught our children that the earth is our mother. Whatever befalls the earth befalls the sons of the earth. If men spit upon the ground, they spit upon themselves.

This we know: the earth does not belong to man; man belongs to the earth. All things are connected. We may be brothers after all. We shall see. One thing we know which the white man may one day discover; our God is the same God.

You may think now that you own Him as you wish to own our land; but you cannot. He is the God of man, and His compassion is equal for the red man and the white. This earth is precious to Him and to harm the earth is to heap contempt on its creator. The whites too shall pass; perhaps sooner than all other tribes. Contaminate your bed and you will one night suffocate in your own waste.

But in your perishing you will shine brightly fired by the strength of the God who brought you to this land and for some special purpose gave you dominion over this land and over the red man.

The destiny is a mystery for us, for we do not understand when the buffalo are all slaughtered, the wild horses are tame, the secret corners of the forest heavy with scent of many men and the view of the ripe hills blotted by talking wires.

Where is the thicket? Gone. Where is the eagle? Gone.

The end of living and the beginning of survival.

As an accredited Non-Government Organization to both the United Nations (UN) and the European Economic Community (EEC) we are able to raise these issues internationally. The threat of embarrassment to a country from being criticized for its actions against its minorities may encourage action, but it must be said that the United Nations has not shown itself willing or able to be effective in this area so far. The Human Rights Division, in spite of some good intentions and courageous employees, has been prevented from exercising power. There have been some useful debates but the whole UN machinery is weighted in favour of governments and it remains slow to react and inflexible.

It would be nice to think that Survival International had saved numerous peoples from despair and extinction over the years, that we could list our successes and demonstrate how our small organization had changed the world for the better. But our achievements are harder to quantify than, for example, those of Amnesty International or the World Wildlife Fund, where numbers of political prisoners released or species saved can be counted. Our very existence is what matters, giving information, support and hope to those who might otherwise despair.

Survival International exists today to help them. Whether it will survive itself or not, whether it will change its character, thrive as a world force or fade away I do not know. The spirit is there to keep it going, but it will take more than the enthusiasm and dedication of the few who have so far recognized what we are trying to do.

Certainly it is already and will remain a very different organization from that which Conrad and I dreamt up in a dugout on the Orinoco, or Francis Huxley and Nicholas Guppy pleaded for in their letter to the *Sunday Times.* We were all naive enough then to believe that the crying need for an international body was enough to bring one into existence. Now we know better that this is a hard, cynical world where charity is a business, pounds of flesh are demanded and that it is usually the ambitious and tough operators, who would succeed as well in business as in welfare work, who get results. And yet there must be more to it than this. Understanding, love, humanity must come into the equation, for without them the whole exercise is merely commerce or sentiment.

We who have been privileged to live among and know the people of other worlds will always be the conscience of the movement, however it develops. And if it collapses through lack of funds and interest from those with power and influence to change our world then we, like those we would save, will have our memories.

The Yanomami may have a future if the pressure is kept up and their land is finally made over to them. The Choco and Cuna Indians may be spared the disastrous effects of a road through the Darien isthmus if the

American Courts are persuaded not to reverse their decision. The Guaymi Indians of Panama have one of the world's biggest reserves of copper in the heart of their homeland, but they do not own the mineral rights. The British mining giant Rio Tinto-Zinc and their partners in the Panamanian Government announced an enormous project which they claimed would bring many benefits to the Indians in terms of jobs and increased income. The Guaymi leaders disagreed, fearing that their land would be destroyed and that they would be left destitute. As one of the only three surviving Indian tribes out of the sixty living in what is now Panama when the Spaniards arrived, they have every reason to doubt the promises of their colonizers. Survival International mounted an intensive campaign to have the views of the Indians considered before any final decision was taken. Gordon Bennett, the dedicated international lawyer on our executive and the author of *Aboriginal Rights in International Law*, which was published as virtually the *only* source of information in that field, visited the Guaymi and represented their interests voluntarily. Meanwhile the world price of copper dropped dramatically and the project is at present dormant. How much our efforts have affected the issue is impossible to tell. I know they irritate RTZ as, at a moment of stress, a senior member of their board has threatened to 'squash Survival International like a fly' if we did not get off their back. It would be all too easy for such a Goliath to annihilate our little David but it has not happened yet and so we struggle on.

One of our very first projects in 1974 was to enable a small Indian tribe in Colombia to buy itself out of debt bondage. They were totally beholden to a white 'patron' who paid a low price for the rubber they collected from their own forests for him and charged exorbitantly for the goods with which he supplied them. Thanks to the presence of a French anthropologist and our own Projects Director, Stephen Corry, in that part of Colombia at the time, it was possible to persuade the 'patron' to agree that the sum total of the Indians' indebtedness was only US $1,000 and that if this were paid over to him they would then be free to trade direct with the outside world. Although we ourselves were living on an overdraft, as we have been for our entire existence, we sent the money and the deal was seen through. Since then several of the hundred or so Andoke have reverted to working for the 'patron' while others have struggled against great odds to retain their independence. The co-operative they set up has collapsed and they have been subjected to harassment from other settlers in the area but the idea has caught on with other groups of Indians, several of whom have also managed to escape from the iniquitous 'patron' system. Before he left the area in 1974 Stephen Corry overheard the Andoke 'patron' say that he would like to kill whoever was responsible for taking 'his' Indians away from him, and doubtless there are others in that part of Colombia who feel the same way about Survival International. But the Indians all know what has been happening, they talk about it and are a little less afraid.

Over 40 projects of varying kinds have been initiated by Survival International supporting medical programmes, indigenous organizations, newspapers and educational services, aboriginal schools and land rights battles. Some have faded away as the progenitors lost interest or were posted elsewhere. Others were overtaken by events, becoming redundant or receiving funds from other agencies, while others are still continuing as groups of people struggle to defend their rights and their cultures.

Through chronic lack of funds we have had to rely on time, faith and the small hope we can provide that someone outside their country or tribe cares about their problem. Unfortunately we don't have the means for the swift application of cash which, through being able to employ a local lawyer or pay for a school or printing press, might bring about a solution or instant relief.

The issues with which we are concerned are too complex to have much general popular appeal so that, although people are touched when they see films on television or read articles about disappearing cultures, they are not often inspired to part with money. Instead we have been funded largely by a few and irregular grants from foundations, from occasional fund-raising events which themselves demand the almost total abandonment of all other work by our staff, and by the loyal backing of our small band of supporters. Since these sources together have never yet put our bank account in credit, I have provided the essential safety net by setting my farm in Cornwall against the overdraft.

As a result we have survived successive financial crises by the skin of our teeth and the work goes on. Our network of contacts, informants and supporters around the world has grown and we have initiated a system of Urgent Action Bulletins which we have found to be the most effective method of alerting the world quickly to a problem when it arises and bringing pressure to bear on those in authority to do something about it. Often they are themselves hardly aware that a problem exists. So far we have produced some 40 bulletins on such disparate subjects as mining rights on aboriginal land in Australia, the problems facing various tribes in Brazil, including five on the Yanomami campaign, the setting up of bogus farming co-operatives on Indian lands in Peru and the disastrous potential effect of a huge dam proposed on tribal land in the Philippines.

The Urgent Action Bulletins are first sent to the Press in every country in which we have an outlet or willing volunteers. Then, following our own correspondence from the office, supporters, especially those with any direct knowledge or experience of the issue, are urged to write to a few key individuals who have the power to influence events, either by removing the threat to the tribe which the bulletin outlines, or by making sure that the indigenous people's rights are respected. It is surprising and gratifying how successful such campaigns have been. While it would be surprising if a government or multi-national company admitted that its policies had been altered as a result of such pressure, there is no doubt that in Australia, Brazil and at least two other South American countries our intervention has had some effect.

A recent bulletin concerns two tribes I visited briefly in 1980. The Waimiri and Atroari, two politically united Carib-speaking peoples, live in the forests north of the Amazonian capital of Manaus. For 300 years they have been attacked and massacred first by slavers and later by those wanting to exploit the rich crops of Brazil nuts, rubber and rosewood growing wild on their land. In recent years the attacks have intensified as a main highway was driven through the centre of their territory. Plans have been drawn up for a mining project, a hydroelectric scheme and the sale of land for farming – all on land which has always been recognized as being Indian, which they have defended fiercely and which in 1971 was decreed as a reserve. The Waimiri and Atroari resistance to invasion over the years has made them legendary among Brazil's Indians, since they have never capitulated or compromised, whether the approach was aggressive and heavily armed or pacific, bearing lavish gifts. Instead they have fought back and while this undoubtedly accounts for their continued existence today, the retribution taken on them has been savage, reducing their numbers from an estimated 6,000 in 1905 to about 600 today.

While the road was being built during the early 1970s, FUNAI, which had had little or no success with its approaches, was subordinated to the Military Command of Amazonia who appear to have treated the whole exercise as a private war, bombing, machine-gunning and burning any Indian villages they could locate from the air. Their strategy for dealing with the Waimiri and Atroari was spelled out in a document which included among other measures 'that the army, in the event of an approach by the Indians, give a demonstration of force, to show them the effects of a volley of machine-gun fire, or grenades and the destructive power of dynamite'. I heard many stories of these measures being used and the FUNAI posts I visited in 1981 were heavily armed and devoid of Indians, except for two nervous young boys who looked ready to run off at any moment. That same year the government decreed the reduction of the Indian land by a third and changed its status from reserved to merely interdicted land. Just as the Yanomami success story is only as effective as the government's will to honour its promises to give full reserve status, so the existing supposed security of the Waimiri and Atroari as well as other

Brazilian Indians whose lands have full reserve status can be removed at a stroke.

FUNAI is incompetent and unwilling to combat such commercial and governmental pressures, being itself merely a minor department of the Ministry of the Interior which is committed to the development of Amazonas at virtually any cost. With the exception of a few outstanding employees, it has no interest in defending Indian rights, but more often appears to exist to protect settlers and prospectors from Indians until such time as the 'problem' has finally disappeared.

The Waimiri and Atroari have friends in Brazil who do campaign on their behalf. But however vehemently and cogently they argue their case they will always be a tiny minority against the powerful forces which oppose them. Moreover, they face very real dangers themselves in a country where opposition of any sort to government policies is readily seen as subversion, and the concept of even a small amount of self-determination and control over their own affairs by Indians can be interpreted as a Communist-inspired plot. What a nonsensical world we live in when anyone who pauses for a moment would realize that precisely the same accusation (except that the epithet applied would be 'Capitalist'-inspired) would be levied against anyone trying to assert the rights of any of the many cultural minorities in Russia or China. Unfortunately it is much harder to gather information, let alone do field research there, so that we are seldom able to raise issues concerning those countries and so achieve the balance which would pre-empt accusations of political bias. I treasure the memory of a delightfully dotty article about me in a Brazilian newspaper following publication of my first Report, which 'exposed' me as a Bulgarian-trained agent, a member of the 'Paris clique' committed to overthrowing the legitimate Brazilian regime!

To be scrupulously non-political and non-denominational, as Survival International is, does not mean that we are prevented from attacking the actions of governments or religious sects, simply that our sole motivation is the best interest of those we represent.

This is not always as easy as it sounds. Much of our financial support comes from some of the major international charities and these in turn are often funded by religious organizations. When we attack the activities of fundamentalist missionaries in South America we are sometimes regarded as Communists, and pressure is brought to bear on the charities to stop supporting us. Interestingly the case of Nicaragua has recently resulted in our being accused of being 'lackeys of the American Government', with the threat of similar financial sanctions. Until now all the Latin American governments we have criticized for their treatment of Indians have been military dictatorships or at least right-wing regimes. The Miskito Indians, like so many tribes, live partly in Honduras, where they have been trained by the CIA as 'contras' to infiltrate across the border; and partly in Nicaragua where, under the left-wing Sandanistas, they have been forcibly removed from the border area, now a war zone, and put in camps where disturbing conditions have been described. Because so much hope has been placed by some aid workers in the fragile spark of democracy seen by them to have been lit by the Sandanistas, we have been warned that we should ignore ill treatment of Indians in this case for the greater good. If we dare to criticize the Sandanistas in any way, even though they themselves admit to having made mistakes over the Miskitos, we need expect no further funding. Unfortunately, the deprivation of the Indians' basic human rights and the prejudicial attitude of most South American people towards Indians is not something which is instantly affected by political change. Meanwhile we must say what we believe to be true, without fear or favour.

It is too soon to know what effect our campaign on behalf of the Waimiri and Atroari is having. But the facts are now available to all, the issue has been raised and sometimes surprising allies appear from within the ranks of development agencies, government departments and mining companies; people who have seen for themselves at first hand and may have begun to question the wisdom of what they are doing.

Even if we fail totally, in a case like the Waimiri and Atroari, to save a single Indian from the annihilation which now confronts them, at least their passing will not have gone unrecorded and unprotested. The movement for the defence of them and people like them has grown immeasurably in the last decade and their example will add fuel to the fire. What we stand for, what we are trying to achieve is now generally accepted as being right and sensible on both humanitarian and practical grounds. Without the simple belief that justice and sense will eventually prevail against all the odds, most of the better works of man in the world would cease overnight.

It would be giving a greatly distorted picture of Survival International to suggest that ours is a powerful organization, effective and active globally. Most of our overseas branches are run by volunteers, while the international office in London has a staff of three underpaid and overworked people, two of whom have been with Survival International for more than ten years.

Barbara Bentley, the Director, has held the organization together, running the office, editing the Review, masterminding campaigns to change government policies and to raise money, dealing with an endless flood of correspondence, keeping the accounts as well as paying the bills, calling meetings, attending conferences and always being there when she is needed. She is one of those rare and remarkable people whom everyone trusts and therefore leaves everything to, knowing she will do it.*

Stephen Corry, Director of Projects, has made several long field trips to South America on our behalf. These, combined with his unique ability to relate to Amerindians and anthropologists alike, have made him the definitive expert on the real status of the Indians of Colombia, Peru and Ecuador. He started work in 1972 with the wildly ambitious intention of compiling a World Red Book of Threatened Peoples, an idea I put to him while discussing his then still-to-be-created role in Survival International. There are probably too many different people in the world and their problems change too rapidly for any such book ever to be a valid proposition, but Stephen has himself become over the years the nearest thing to a living version of the book.

Luke Holland's background as a child in Paraguay led him to return and make a photographic record of missionary activity among the Indians there. His exhibition of photographs with commentary on this subject has been the most telling and effective piece of publicity material we have produced, alerting public and government here and in the USA to the appalling bigotry and genocide being perpetrated against Paraguay's Indians by fundamentalist missionaries with the full connivance of the government. He has doubled for Stephen as Director of Projects and represented Survival International at many meetings.

What we have been able to achieve from such a precarious base has been remarkable, and the way in which so many people with quite different backgrounds and political aims have worked together for our movement has been heartwarming. Volunteers have given their time to help catalogue our unique library of books, reports, cuttings and correspondence, often confidential and potentially dangerous to those who trust us. Many anthropologists have been unstinting with their time and expert knowledge, alerting us to situations that they have encountered, providing background material and writing articles. They are the professionals in our field and should lead the fight but regrettably many seem less ready to leap to the defence of the subjects of their research than, for example, botanists and zoologists when species are threatened with extinction or archaeologists when buildings or historic sites or works of art are destroyed. Some have justified their lack of involvement by saying that they can be of more use to the people they study by demonstrating through their presence among them and interest that their lives are valid and worthy of respect. This is particularly necessary where all around believe them stupid and inferior.

* Barbara Bentley retired due to ill health in 1984.

I have heard this point of view expressed by many anthropologists in the field but I do not feel that it goes far enough. The argument can too easily be turned around so that the researcher ends up accused of exploiting the people himself, using them as guinea pigs for his own academic ends. Researchers of all disciplines working in developing countries today often have to endure such criticisms, but I do not believe they can salve their consciences by remaining aloof from the real problems, even if it makes their lives easier. An intellectually courageous anthropologist should be able to study his subject in depth while at the same time involving himself in their future, becoming their ambassador and advocate in a hostile world. A growing number of young anthropologists subscribe to this view supported, as is so often the case in human affairs, by those elder statesmen whose reputations and authority are unchallenged. Naturally, tact is required, as well as understanding of the practical difficulties of the national government. Often hardly aware of the existence of some insignificant minority within its boundaries, and always beset by far more pressing affairs of state, governments may be surprised and even offended that concern should be expressed for people who may represent the opposite of all their progressive national ideals. But change can only be brought about by the government and it is surprising how a little pressure applied in the right way can sometimes produce vehement protestations of a willingness to improve matters.

I have seen a world movement grow from the ideas of a few individuals, from the passionate conversations of a handful of concerned people who wish to change the world. It is an immense privilege to have been part of it all and to have seen the dedication and energy with which some have grasped the idea and even devoted their lives to it. But the frustration at being unable to break through the barrier of indifference displayed by governments, international agencies and, it must be said, the general public is sometimes almost unbearable. We have created the basis from which so much could be achieved. We know how to alleviate many of the ills which beset the remaining cultural minorities of the world and could with minimal support and goodwill secure their futures. Far from costing their neighbours and governments anything I am convinced that in a short time their survival would soon produce tangible benefits in the form of better environmental management, food production and even an improved quality of life for those prepared to acknowledge alternatives to the banal model currently being propagated worldwide.

The will is there and so are the experts, but without proper funding our hands are tied and our effectiveness is minimized. Our people should be able to travel and confront problems when they arise, representing the oppressed in the field and in state capitals where influence can be brought to bear direct and quickly by those with a knowledge of the law and the courage to state it. Instead they can only write letters of support and send out Urgent Action Bulletins in an attempt to raise interest in a problem which would otherwise be ignored. Even then they have to be careful about the cost of postage.

I have always imagined that somewhere there is a philanthropist who will recognize that while it is pleasing and admirable to donate a new wing to a museum, save the tiger or endow a school, to save whole cultures of mankind from extinction must represent the greatest charity of all. My failure to tap such philanthropy so far has been my greatest disappointment; my association with the movement has been the single thing of which I have been most proud.

Peoples which are called primitive, simple, backward, unacculturated, savage, tribal, native, isolated or whatever, are not essentially different from us. The evolutionary separation from other men is as nothing when set against the aeons of time during which we were all hunters, the few thousand years since the earliest beginnings of agriculture and the domestication of animals, let alone the mere flicker of history since industrialization commenced. But they seem strange – and, to some, inferior – because they express themselves differently; their vision of the world is not the same as ours and, while possessing a rich and harmonious concept of life, they lack the narrow blinkers of a scientific, materialistic ideology which assumes the ability to control and understand all things but has in truth barely scratched the surface of life's diversity. If the arrogance of the last century is replaced by an inquiring humility in the face of the problems which beset us, then our attitude towards those remaining societies which have not yet accepted the dubious tenets of our own, may change. Then, instead of having to search in the dark for new philosophies, there will still be working models to learn from; not to copy slavishly, for it is no less impractical to suggest that we can survive without technology as it is to believe that universal happiness can be achieved through uncontrolled growth, but by combining the knowledge and approach of both. As lessons are learned about the dangers of rapid change and ill-conceived tampering with fragile ecosystems, as the energy crisis grows and the raw materials necessary for an expanding industrial society shrink, it may be that we will even go cap in hand to seek the remaining 'primitive' societies and ask their advice. It will be ironic if, when we do so, we find that they no longer exist, for they are the yeast in the bread of humanity.

Survival International

Part of the royalties from the sale of this book will be donated to Survival International, a London-based charity that aims to deflect the destructive influence of 'civilized' society. It aims to achieve this by providing tribal people with the means to defend themselves, to protect their rights. It is still relatively small and unbureaucratic. It is *not* paternalistic, political, or denominational. Its members include anthropologists, lawyers, doctors and concerned members of the general public.

Any reader wishing to know more about Survival International's work should contact the headquarters:

Survival International
29 Craven Street
London WC2 5NT

Telephone: 01–839 3267

Index

NB: For names of individual tribes see under Tribal Peoples